Passage Through
EL DORADO

Passage Through ELDORADO

❈ TRAVELING THE WORLD'S LAST GREAT WILDERNESS ❈

---

by Jonathan Kandell

William Morrow and Company, Inc.
New York / 1984

Library of Congress Catalog Card Number: 83-63237

ISBN: 0-688-02664-8

Printed in the United States of America

2 3 4 5 6 7 8 9 10

BOOK DESIGN BY VICTORIA HARTMAN

To Nicole

To Nicole

Acknowledgments

I owe a great deal to the Council on Foreign Relations in New York for the financial assistance, office space and moral support provided me there as an Edward R. Murrow Fellow between September 1981 and June 1982. The Carnegie Endowment for International Peace was kind enough to make me a resident associate and offer me their splendid offices in New York from August to December 1982. I was able to finish this book in 1983 thanks to the New York Public Library, which allowed me to enjoy all the writing and research facilities of the Frederick Lewis Allen Memorial Room.

There are many individuals who aided and encouraged me throughout the conception and writing of this book. I owe most to the following three: my editor, Bruce Lee, for innumerable suggestions, detailed editing and generous allotment of his time; my agent, Wendy Lipkind, for helping me crystallize a jumble of notions into a viable book proposal; and Nicole Bourgois, who patiently read over many times the several drafts of this book and always offered encouragement and insights.

Finally, I would like to thank Andrew Sabbatini, manager of the Map and Chart Section of *The New York Times,* for the invaluable maps that he drew to accompany the text.

LIST OF MAPS

1

How well I remember my first disastrous attempt to journey into the South American wilderness.

I had been working, back in 1973, for *The New York Times* as a roving twenty-six-year-old correspondent based in Buenos Aires. Perón was returning to Argentina after a long exile, and Allende was tottering in Chile. Most of my reporting was confined to the political turmoil in Buenos Aires and Santiago, two capitals as cosmopolitan as many European cities.

But I was eager for a different sort of story, something that would take me to the jungle frontiers of South America, the vast heart of the continent which almost nobody was writing about. So when the first sketchy reports of a potential oil boom in Peru's Amazon rain forest filtered out, I quickly booked a flight from Buenos Aires to Lima.

On a brilliant, warm afternoon in April, a few days later, I boarded another commercial jet from Lima, on the Peruvian coast, to Iquitos, an Amazon River port 650 miles northeast that served as headquarters for the new oil exploration in the jungles. The plane swept out over the blue-gray Pacific Ocean. After gaining altitude, it banked sharply inland over the coastline, rimmed by a band of desert several miles wide, and covered with a powdery sand so startlingly white that I mistook it for snow. This narrow, littoral strip quickly dissolved into dun-brown foothills, corrugated and barren as if their vegetation had been scraped away with a dull knife. Minutes later, the terrain vaulted steeply upward to the majestic green and purple Andes. With dozens of jagged peaks rising fifteen thousand feet and higher, the mountains stretch north and south as far as the eye can see. They traverse the entire length of South America from northern Colombia to the southern tip of Chile and Argentina, giving the western edge of the continent a thick, four-thousand-mile backbone more than three times as long as the American Rockies.

Below my plane, the Peruvian Andes were laced with squibbly roads and tightly clustered Indian villages, many of them dating back hundreds of years before the arrival of the Spanish conquistadores in the sixteenth century. The Incas had ruled over several million subjects in these small, fertile valleys and highland terraces nestled in cold, forbidding mountains. Even today, close to half of Peru's population still clings to the slopes of the Andean range.

Barely thirty minutes into my flight, the mountains slid down into primeval jungle, an emerald-and-blue carpet webbed with sluggish, tan, serpentine rivers, devoid of any sign of human presence as it unfolded over the eastern two thirds of Peru. The terrain inclined so gently that it was impossible to tell exactly where highland jungle turned into lowland rain forest. But gradually, the green mat below me became soggier, with huge puddles and ink-black veins where rivers burst their beds.

An hour later, I was unmistakably over lowland jungle. Iquitos, partially concealed by a cloud layer, looked like an island. Even in the dry season—a misnomer, really, because the rains never cease for more than a few days at a time—the city is almost enveloped by a broad bend of the Amazon River and by two of its smaller tributaries. Now, the torrential downpours of the rainy season had inundated the single wedge of rain forest jutting southwest from Iquitos.

The two Amazon tributaries flanking the city are called the Nanay and Itaya. Born from other rivers and streams in the highland jungles to the west, the Nanay and Itaya are at their fullest volume as they plunge past Iquitos and into the Amazon River. But compared to the giant Amazon waterway, they are tiny capillaries. If they suddenly dried up there would be no visible impact on the world's greatest river. For the Amazon has almost a thousand tributaries that surrender their waters along its 3,912-mile course from the slopes of the Andes to the Atlantic Ocean off the northern coast of Brazil. Only the Nile is longer—by a few score miles—but it carries less than two percent of the Amazon's volume. Every day, the Amazon spills enough water into the Atlantic to supply two hundred times the municipal needs of the entire United States. At its broadest, as it nears the ocean, the Amazon is forty miles wide, so that from a boat in midstream it becomes impossible to make out either bank, and the illusion of a boundless river-sea is complete.

The River Sea is what the first Iberian explorers called the Amazon when they discovered its mouth on the Atlantic at the beginning of the sixteenth century. The river, with its invisible banks, disgorged itself with such force that ships were able to fill their casks with fresh water several miles out in the ocean.

The river got its present name from the first European adventurers to travel its length from the Andean slopes east to the Atlantic. That expedition was led by Francisco de Orellana, a Spanish conquistador, in 1541. He had joined forces with Gonzalo Pizarro, brother of the conqueror of the Incas, in search of El Dorado, a mythical Indian ruler who allegedly owned so much gold that he covered himself daily with the yellow dust. Depending on the various versions that have come down through history, Orellana either drifted too far downriver from Pizarro and was unable to sail back against the strong current, or else he willfully struck out on his own to find riches and fame.

Father Gaspar de Carvajal, the friar who accompanied Orellana and chronicled the expedition, claimed to have seen women warriors—like the fierce Amazons of ancient Greek mythology—leading an Indian attack against Orellana's boats as they neared a village on the river.

"We ourselves saw these women who were there fighting in front of all the Indian men as women captains, and these latter fought so courageously that the Indian men did not dare to turn their backs, and anyone who did turn his back they killed with clubs right there before us, and this is the reason why the Indians kept up their defense for so long," wrote Carvajal. "These women are very white and tall, and have hair very long and braided and wound about the head, and they are very robust and go about naked, but with their privy parts covered, with their bows and arrows in their hands, doing as much fighting as ten Indian men, and indeed there was one woman among them who shot an arrow a span deep into one of the brigantines, and others less deep, so that our brigantines looked like porcupines."

Other expeditions failed to locate any of these women warriors, and undermined the credibility of Father Carvajal's account. But the name, River of the Amazons, stuck.

In later centuries, the words *Amazon* and *Amazonia* became synonymous with the vast tropical rain forest and savannas that are drained by the river and its tributaries. This territory, nearly forty percent of South America, includes most of Brazil and Peru, and large parts of Bolivia, Ecuador, Colombia, Venezuela, Guyana, Suriname and French Guiana. Thus, Amazonia, is almost equal in size to the contiguous United States.

The Amazon River has been called a highway through the heart of South America. But the image is too tame. In stormy weather, it bucks and heaves even sturdy ships. Hardly a year goes by without the capsizing of a major vessel with the loss of numerous lives. At the climax of the rainy epoch, the river's waters rise thirty feet and more, dragging trees, wildlife, livestock, huts, piers and island-size chunks of land and depositing them, battered and misshapen, hundreds of miles downstream. Even in the dry season, the Amazon's waves can pound its banks like ocean surf.

The bed of the river, which sometimes reaches down three hundred feet, never seems deep enough to hold its waters. All along its course, the Amazon splays out or bulges into hundreds of oxbow lakes, whose contours change with the rise and fall of the flow. The river broadens and constricts, curves and loops. And it is dotted throughout its course with hundreds of islands, some of them big enough to harbor villages.

By the time it reaches Iquitos, the Amazon has already traveled sixteen hundred miles from its source in the Peruvian Andes. At Iquitos, the river is five miles wide, although this span is obstructed by several islands. Still, the waters are broad and deep enough so that Iquitos is the last port for ocean-going vessels plying the Amazon from the Atlantic coast, twenty-three hundred miles to the east.

The Amazon's dominance over the terrain it drains extends to the atmosphere above it. In temperate zones, like the United States, thunderstorms seem to arrive from the far, high horizon and sweep over the land before breaking up or moving away. But here, one can actually see the tempests brewing at ground level.

As my plane circled Iquitos, clouds mushroomed up like silent explosions from the Amazon and its tributaries and the rain forest. They merged into a thick, low-lying, cottony layer of turbulence that swelled yellow and gray and black until it burst and poured sheets of water back into the rivers and jungle. One moment the plane was floating in tranquil, blue, glittery skies, and a minute later, it plunged into the low blanket of clouds, buffeted by winds and rain as it searched out the city that bobbed in the jungle and water.

With or without the seasonal inundations, Iquitos has always been an island city in the jungles. No roads ever connected it to the rest of Peru. Before the advent of airplanes, the distance traveled from Iquitos to Lima was as long as from Peru to Australia. To get to Lima, all cargo and passengers from Iquitos had to set out in the opposite direction—making the tortuous journey east by ship along the Amazon River to the Atlantic. Then the course shifted north to the Caribbean, west to the Panama Canal and, once through that waterway, south along the Pacific coast of South America. It was a seven-thousand-mile odyssey that took a month and more.

Rarely could this passage be made on a single ship. The simple reason being that there was not enough commerce between Iquitos and Lima to justify a regular boat line between the two Peruvian cities. A traveler usually had to count on taking one vessel to Manaus, the Brazilian port halfway down the Amazon, then boarding another boat there to Belém, near the river's mouth on the Atlantic. From Belém, the passenger transferred to a third ship headed for a Venezuelan, Colombian, or Panamanian port in the Caribbean. The final leg of the journey, through the Panama Canal and along the Pacific coast to Callao, Lima's port, might require yet a fourth ship.

Nowadays, people travel between Lima and Iquitos by commercial jet, a trip that takes no longer than a flight between Washington, D.C., and Chicago. Except for heavy construction material and machinery that are still transported by boat, the jungle city depends on airfreight for its essential supplies.

With the constant flooding, there is not enough land available on which food can be grown for the city's 175,000 inhabitants. So meat, vegetables and grains are flown into Iquitos every day from agricultural centers in the Andean highlands. Processed foods arrive from Lima and Brazilian cities. Even nonperishable items like clothes, stereo and television sets are flown in. Not surprisingly, this heavy reliance on air cargo makes Iquitos one of the more expensive Peruvian cities. Many of the passengers on my plane were returning home loaded down with mundane goods like cooking oils, rice and canned food that they bought more cheaply in Lima, the way tourists elsewhere purchase luxury items at bargain prices in duty-free stores.

Because of the overcast skies, the city became fully visible only during the final thousand feet of our descent. There was so little terra firma around Iquitos that the airport had been built well within the city limits. The plane pierced through the cloud layer, skimmed over a grove of palm trees and roared down the runway past rows of thatched-roof huts.

The squall had wrung itself out by the time we walked down the plane's ramp. But there was none of the cool relief that normally follows a heavy rain. Instead, a hot humidity lingered in the late-afternoon air. The temperature, in the eighties, was not much higher than it had been back in Lima only ninety minutes before. But the moisture was oppressive, like a Turkish bath, and I was perspiring profusely by the time I retrieved my luggage and found a taxi.

As the rusty car accelerated, hot air whipped in through the windows like a hair drier blowing in my face. There were hardly any trees along the way. It was almost as if they had been systematically stripped away to wipe out any reminder of the surrounding rain forest. For the first two miles, the road seemed too impressively wide and well maintained for the shabby wooden huts and the few decaying factories that lined its shoulders. But as we neared the downtown district, it was the road that turned shabby and pockmarked while the buildings pulled together and looked more solid. We were slowed by lumbering diesel trucks, overloaded buses and scores of motorcycles, each carrying two or three people who leaned synchronously left and right as their bikes wove through the heavy traffic.

The bustle of the vehicles contrasted with the languid pace of the pedestrians. Merchants stood with folded arms beside their wares, stacked high on sidewalk stands outside the stores. Small knots of young people chattered away, girls linking arms while boys leaned on each other's shoulders. Nobody seemed to be walking resolutely in any direction. People turned their heads from side to side as if hoping to locate a friendly face, an interesting store display or any excuse to while away a bit more time. In this heat and informality, nobody wore ties or suits, fashionable dresses or high heels; just denims and jeans, short-sleeved shirts and open-necked blouses, sandals and sneakers.

The faces were more varied than the Indian, Spanish and mestizo, or mixed-blood, types I had seen in the Andean highlands. Here, there were also Oriental, Middle Eastern, black and a few northern European faces as well—descendants of the adventurers who flocked to Iquitos seeking their fortunes in the rubber era at the turn of the century.

Iquitos was first settled in the mid-nineteenth century. But it remained for several decades no more than a small, impoverished frontier outpost in territory disputed by Peru, Ecuador, Colombia and Brazil. In 1863, it had only about four hundred inhabitants.

It was rubber that finally put Iquitos on the map. The combination of rubber latex from the surrounding jungles and deep-water port facilities in the village's harbor ignited an economic boom. The population mushroomed to ten thousand in 1905, and doubled a decade later as Peruvians, Brazilians, Spaniards, Portuguese, Germans, Arabs, Greeks, Turks, Americans and Chinese descended on the city to buy rubber and sell merchandise and services. Freighters from across the Atlantic unloaded textiles, machinery, construction materials and luxury goods in exchange for the black, smoked latex from the wild rubber trees. Iquitos became Peru's second port after Callao, Lima's harbor on the Pacific. Fully ten percent of Peru's export revenues were earned on its docks. Iquitos built Peru's first movie theater. It laid a short railway line between the harbor and the city center. It installed electricity. And it supported three newspapers at a time.

The rubber wealth produced some extravagant architectural flourishes as well. Portuguese and Jewish merchants constructed lavish mansions and stores with wrought-iron balconies and glazed blue-and-white tile facades imported from Lisbon. A local rubber baron was so impressed by the new Eiffel Tower in Paris that he bought a small, cast-iron building also designed by Eiffel and had it transported in pieces from Europe across the Atlantic and up the Amazon, and then reassembled it off Iquitos's central plaza. Just across that square, rubber money built a tall, single-towered, yellow-pastel cathedral, which the local newspapers hailed as a unique architectural style—"tropical Gothic." And then the civic-spirited rubber aristocrats turned to the waterfront. On the palisades above the Amazon River, they helped the municipality finance a wide promenade with an alabaster balustrade.

The boom lasted only a short-time. By 1913, cheaper rubber from Asian plantations was cornering the world market. By the 1920's, Iquitos and the rest of Amazonia were in a deep and prolonged economic depression. The tiny railway ceased functioning. The movie houses closed because there was no money to purchase or rent films. The arrival of ocean liners became rare enough to draw curious onlookers to the docks. Those merchants who were not bankrupt sailed away. Ambitious young professionals moved to Lima. Most people, jobless or underemployed, tightened their belts, waited and then despaired.

It was only fifty years later that Iquitos dared to dream of another economic surge, this time based on petroleum. Traces of oil had been discovered in the jungles, and wells were being sunk to the north and west. More than a dozen foreign oil firms had turned the city into the headquarters for their engineers, surveyors and drillers. Local youths were being hired as labor crews in the rain forest.

The new cars and trucks and motorcycles swirling around my taxi on the narrow streets were an early weathervane of shifting fortunes. But the city itself still had a dilapidated, lackluster appearance. Most of the buildings were one or two stories high, with thick walls of mud and brick, whitewashed and then dabbed with thin, peeling coats of yellow, green or blue paint.

My driver, the grandson of a Chinese seaman who had jumped ship here sixty years before, pointed out the monuments of the rubber era. Only a few of the tiled Portuguese mansions had survived intact. One was now a hardware store, another an ice-cream parlor, and the largest was the police headquarters. The massive "tropical Gothic" church loomed over the central plaza. And a block away, the strange, cast-iron box designed by Eiffel housed the town's social club—but only at night, because it was as hot as an oven during the day. Along the Amazon River, the promenade was in an advanced state of disrepair, its once-elegant white balustrades now chipped and crumbling.

My hotel, a hulking three-story concrete building that crowded all but a couple of shops off the block, was on the avenue overlooking the river. In the lobby, I recognized a cluster of oilmen. They were brawny, sunburned Americans with booming voices, dressed mostly in khaki safari suits. I sent my luggage up to my room and joined them in the bar.

Two of the men were engineers from Occidental Petroleum, and three others worked for Sun and Union Oil. Their companies were exploring huge tracts of rain forest that in some cases were almost two hundred miles away. But because Iquitos is the only sizable community in this part of the Peruvian Amazon, they had taken up residence here until enough oil was discovered to justify setting up base camps in the jungles.

They liked Iquitos. Some of them even loved it. Compared to the

frozen Arctic wastes of Alaska or the remote islands of the Indonesian archipelago where they had worked before, this was a real town, with comfortable homes, bars, restaurants and even a few discotheques. Planes chartered by the petroleum companies regularly flew in liquor and beef from Miami, a five-hour journey by jet. And the Americans were enjoying a honeymoon period with the locals, who saw the oilmen and their money as the foundation of a prosperous renaissance in Iquitos.

We were soon joined by other oilmen, a few young businessmen and their girl friends. A tall, husky, bearded Argentine named Claudio sat next to me. He had been living in Iquitos for three years. His family was Russian Jewish and had emigrated to Argentina decades ago. They were in the fur business, and Claudio supplied them with animal pelts he bought from the Indians in the Amazon jungles. Only twenty-four years old, he had made a sizable fortune and thought he could multiply it several times if an oil boom really occurred. He had recently become the city's sole distributor of Suzukis and Hondas, the motorcycles that were roaring down every muddy street.

Next to him was his best friend, Armando, twenty-three years old, an up-and-coming businessman from Lima. He was lean and square-jawed, and dressed in jeans and a shirt open to his waist. He had arrived in Iquitos a year before and set himself up as the city's only supplier of printing, copying and office equipment. The hot, dripping atmosphere drove him out of his office for all but a few hours a day. But in the hotel bar and nearby cafés, where overhead fans wafted a semblance of a breeze, he would hold court for his clients—the American and European oil prospectors, local government officials and Amazon tour organizers.

"I sell the machines cheaply," said Armando with a smile. Then, slamming his right fist into his left palm, "And I get them on the paper and afterservice."

As empty beer bottles piled up on the several tables that had been joined together, the talk grew more ebullient and blustery.

"It's fixing to be a hell of a town," said Henry ("Just call me Enrique") Molte, a short, skinny, T-shirted Texas surveyor under contract to Sun Oil. "We just made a couple of good strikes about a hundred fifty miles northwest of here."

Molte was thirty-four years old, with blue eyes and a broad smile that seemed to part his wispy beard into individual strands. He had spent a dozen years on oil expeditions that took him to Nigeria, Indonesia, Colombia and Ecuador. He said his dream was to retire to a beach house near Galveston, Texas, his hometown, with a wife "and a herd of kids." The house he had already bought. But his two marriages had ended in divorce. "Didn't blame them a bit. I was never around. An oilman's worse than a sailor."

Like the other oil company employees, Molte spent fourteen days out in the jungle and then a week on R and R. Sitting beside him in the hotel bar was his girl friend, Teresa, a voluptuous, copper-toned young native of Iquitos. He had helped bankroll her club, where the town's new elite gathered at night for drinks and T-bone steaks from Miami. Teresa said she had just installed strobe lights, a dance floor and stereo equipment in her club, and was hoping to make enough money in a few years to open a discotheque in Miami. "Ah, Miami," she swooned. "Real action in Miami."

Molte evidently fantasied a quieter life with her at his Texas beach house. "Teresa, you gonna love Galveston," he drawled, swaying his head from side to side and spilling his seventh or eighth beer on her lap.

By the time the drinking session ended, I had made arrangements with Molte to accompany him the following morning back to the exploration site where he was working. It was located on an Amazon tributary, and it would take us an hour to fly there in a twin-propellered plane chartered by his company and especially equipped to land on water.

I got up from the table and looked out the window. The setting sun had turned the river into a collage of pastels. I hurried up to my room on the second floor, certain that the view from there would be even more spectacular.

I remember thinking it had been a wonderful day. Gathering facts for an article could be difficult enough in a strange place. But to enjoy congenial company and get a feel for the pulse and atmosphere of a new town—all in a matter of a few hours after arriving there—was a real stroke of luck. And now I could look forward to a few days in virgin jungle, an adventure I had never experienced before.

My room was huge, at least twenty paces long. As I gazed out the wide window, an invisible sun sank behind me, casting lengthy red shadows on the dark, turbulent river flecked with whitecaps. Motorized dugout canoes puttered back to the harbor, passing branches, driftwood and whole tree trunks that were pushed swiftly in the opposite direction by the powerful current. A skein of white herons soared away from the city toward an island in the middle of the river.

Still staring at the water, I absentmindedly began to unbuckle my folded suitcase on the bed. My fingers brushed against a prickly, furry object, and suddenly I felt an excruciating pain on the ridge of my right palm. I yanked my hand away, and a hairy, brown-black tarantula the size of my fist fell wriggling to the carpeted floor. I cried out and stomped on the beast, but only managed to cripple a few of its legs. Its mandibles, almost as stout as its front legs, quivered, and its eyes, like a half dozen glassy beads, seemed to bulge out. I felt two waves of shock simultaneously in that fraction of a second: the pain, like an electric jab, and worse, much worse, the uncontrollable sense of panic and horror at the sight of that nightmarish creature. Could this actually have happened to me? Was that voice bellowing through the room really mine? I froze in place. My legs wouldn't budge.

A hotel attendant burst into the room. *"Qué pasa, señor?"* he shouted, his arms half-extended in a gesture of bewilderment and supplication. I couldn't answer him. I may still have been screaming. Then, spying the writhing spider near the bed a foot away from me, his jaw dropped and he gasped. He swiftly picked up a chair and crushed it down on the tarantula.

My hand felt numb and hot and throbbing, all at the same time. I collapsed on the bed in a cold sweat, dripping as if a bucket of water had been poured over me. The perspiration trickled into my eyes. I made no effort to wipe it away. I doubt that I could have moved anyway.

There were now sounds of other people shouting and scurrying about the room. I only vaguely remember two or three hotel attendants bantering nervously as they hoisted my arms around their shoulders. My legs buckled under me. I was being half-carried, half-dragged into the corridor, down the stairs, through the lobby past the dismayed faces of guests, and then into a car.

I regained consciousness the next morning in a room of a nearby clinic. A syringe from a serum bottle was attached to my right arm. A well-scrubbed, gray-haired doctor with a white robe was at my side. At first I could only make out snatches of what he was saying because I was still woozy. I said I was feeling better, but disoriented.

The tarantula, he explained, was normally not a deadly creature for human beings. I had suffered from anaphylactic shock, a hypersensitive body reaction to a foreign antigen, such as the spider's weak poison. It easily could have been brought on by a bee sting, even the bite of a large ant, and it could have been fatal. I told the doctor I had often been stung or bitten by insects and had never suffered from anaphylactic shock.

"Well, now you know you're allergic to tarantulas," he said with a shrug. And he told me that when I was carried into the clinic in a dead faint the night before, I was pale and breathing with difficulty and my blood pressure had dropped precipitously. He had given me an injection of adrenaline to alleviate the worst symptoms, but I would have to take antibiotics the rest of the week. The serum still flowing into my arm was mostly a saline solution.

The doctor warned me that I would feel weak and dehydrated for a few days, possibly with an uncomfortable bout of diarrhea and recurring headaches. He suggested I drink plenty of fluids, though preferably not any of the town's water. "Try Inca Cola," he offered helpfully.

"My God," I remember thinking, "what if this had happened in the middle of the jungle with no doctor or clinic nearby?" I was glad that I had missed my flight with Molte to the oil-drilling sites.

I checked out of the clinic two days later still feeling shaky. I found a small, adequate hotel with no view of the river but so coldly air-conditioned that any spider would have frozen to death. On the streets and at sidewalk cafés, I ran across some of the oilmen and their friends. My unfortunate experience had become celebrated, and I was asked to recount it again and again, provoking a mixture of gasps and guffaws. After a while, even I thought it was more grotesque than tragic. By the time my five-day stay in Iquitos ended, I felt more disappointed than relieved. I had traveled across the continent and failed to set foot in the wilderness. Even middle-aged American and German tourists in Bermuda shorts and immaculately pressed safari suits had ventured on overnight expeditions up the Amazon and into the rain forest. As my jet took off toward Lima, I was already planning to return someday.

2

I can trace my fascination with South America's frontier lands back to early childhood. As a son of American expatriates, I grew up in Mexico absorbing the myths of the Iberian Conquest and often wondering why, with so much popular interest in the American westward expansion, there was so little excitement over the South American wilderness. Like my Mexican childhood friends, I was addicted to the Hollywood westerns depicting wagon trains drawn in circles against Indian attacks, homesteaders fighting off cattle barons, prospectors scrambling after gold. But the same movie houses never screened films of Spaniards and Portuguese plunging forward into the frontiers.

Had I been less naive, I could have looked around the theater at the many Indian and mestizo faces and realized that this was not the kind of audience that would relish films about white Europeans overcoming savage Latin American natives.

Because so many Indians and mestizos survived the European onslaught in Latin America, history is taught in a more subtle and confusing way than in the United States. The tendency is to extol precolonial Indian civilization and to disparage the three centuries of European rule. Since Spaniards and Portuguese were not viewed as heroes there was nothing exalted about their conquest of new frontier lands.

In elementary school in Mexico City, we spent long days memorizing Indian names that were hardly pronounceable and even more difficult to spell. Huitzilopochli, Nezahualcóyotl, Cuitlahuac, Cuauhtémoc—the words still twist my tongue. We learned far more about these gods and chieftains than North American children were ever taught about Sitting Bull, Crazy Horse and Geronimo.

From the Hollywood films, we could see for ourselves that the Indians of the North American plains were half-naked nomads who dragged their tepees behind them as they trekked after deer and buffalo. But "our" Indians were founders of great civilizations that left little to be envied of the European societies that vanquished them. A teacher once herded us into a room of the Anthropology Museum to show us a plaster model of Mexico City before the Spaniards arrived in the New World. The Aztec capital, she pointed out, was constructed on a partially landfilled lake. With its network of canals, it looked like Renaissance Venice, only larger and more beautiful. Then, to back her claim, she made us copy a passage from Bernal Díaz del Castillo, who chronicled the conquest of Mexico by Hernán Cortés in 1519–21:

> When we saw so many cities and villages built in the waters of the lake and other large towns on dry land, and that straight level causeway leading into Mexico City, we were amazed ... because of the huge towers, temples and buildings rising from the water, and all the masonry. And some of the soldiers even asked whether things we saw were not a dream.

Besides the Aztec capital, our teachers told us, there were other wondrous Indian sites, like Cuzco and Machu Picchu in Peru, and perhaps, still hidden deep in the South American jungles, lost cities waiting to be discovered.

These were civilizations that achieved astounding feats of engineering even though they used few beasts of burden and no wheeled carts. They reclaimed land from water; erected temples and pyramids with perfectly balanced slabs of rock that needed no cement; designed long aqueducts to irrigate farmland and supply fresh drinking water; laid stone roads that connected mountain and jungle and coast; and domesticated fowl and wild plants in quantities that could feed scores of thousands of urban residents.

These societies were rigidly stratified theocracies. At the top were the richly bejeweled and robed monarchs and priests who communed directly with their gods and sometimes claimed them as ancestors. Below the ruling families were castes of warriors and then artisans and merchants. The toilers in the fields were near the bottom rungs of the social ladder, and further beneath them were vassal tribes who paid heavy tribute.

Our teachers portrayed the conquistadores as cruel, rapacious

igners, who crushed these remarkable civilizations by trickery
 1 superior firepower, plundering the Indian cities and then aban-
 ning the vast continental interior when no treasure was found.
)idn't the conquistadores misrepresent themselves to the Aztecs
 and Incas as emissaries of Quetzalcóatl and Viracocha, the white,
 bearded gods who according to Indian legend would someday return from afar to reclaim their rights over Indian lands? And even
after they realized that the Spaniards were mortals, what could the
Indians do against cannons and armor and horses?

Our teachers glossed over the failings of these native empires. The
vivid descriptions of widespread cannibalism, human sacrifice and
savage tribute exacted upon vassal tribes were dismissed as the ram-
blings of Spanish conquistadores anxious to morally justify their
own exploits. But the conquest was only possible because the Spaniards were able to rally to their side huge numbers of Indians who
loathed the rule of the Aztecs and Incas. Hernán Cortés arrived in
Mexico with only four hundred Spaniards, a few cannons and sixteen horses; yet by the time he laid siege to the Aztec capital, his
Spaniards counted on the support of twenty thousand Indian warriors who had once been vassals of the Aztecs. Francisco Pizarro had
only six hundred conquistadores when he disembarked on the Peruvian coast. They quickly subjugated the Incas by treacherously kid-
napping their monarch during what was supposed to be a peaceful
conference. Then Pizarro's small band was able to prevail because
the Inca empire had been weakened by a costly civil war.

Ambiguity continued to mark our history lessons as we waded
through the three hundred years of colonial rule in Latin America.
Mixed with the anger over the European invasion was a contradictory surge of pride that the Spaniards and Portuguese arrived in the
New World a century before the *Mayflower* Pilgrims and burst
across the Americas with a speed unrivaled in history.

While the first English colonists were establishing tenuous foot-
holds in Massachusetts and Virginia, the Spanish Crown already
had claimed the Caribbean, Florida, much of the land west of the
Mississippi River, all of Mexico and Central America, and the entire
South American continent. (Between 1580 and 1640, Spain ruled
over Portugal, and thus over Portuguese Brazil as well.) Before the
first English town was chartered in North America, the Spaniards
had established more than a hundred cities and towns in their Latin
American realms. While today physical traces of the English pres-

ence in the United States are confined to the eastern seaboard, the architectural legacy of the Spaniards and Portuguese is in evidence throughout the New World. The plazas and cathedrals and municipal council buildings they constructed are often still the focal points of Latin American cities. And their churches remain the most imposing structures in hundreds of smaller provincial towns.

While the Pilgrims were shivering through their first winter on the New England coast, the Iberians already had explored plains and mountains and jungles. They had carved huge ranches and plantations out of Indian lands and stocked them with cattle, sheep, pigs and crops brought over from Spain and Portugal. They had successfully transplanted vegetables, fruits and vines from the Old World, and introduced potatoes, maize, cacao, natural fibers and fowl to Europe from the Indies.

Before the English colonists had produced their first tobacco exports, the Spaniards had for decades been sending boatloads of silver to the home country from their bottomless mines in northern Mexico and the South American Andes. The treasure proved irresistible to pirates from the other European countries. Most of the bullion that entered Elizabethan England was booty recovered from Spanish galleons by bucaneers like Francis Drake, Walter Raleigh and John Hawkins, whose operations were often financed by British merchants and backed by the English court. But not even widespread piracy could stem the flow of New World riches into Spanish ports. In fact, so much silver was funneled into Spain that it stoked an inflation that priced Spanish goods out of world markets, stunted the country's industrial growth and eventually undermined the economic foundations of the empire.

These galleons of silver bullion became our metaphor of the Iberian plunder of Latin America, a plunder that began from the moment Cortés and Pizarro toppled the Aztecs and Incas. We were taught that Spain and Portugal bled their New World colonies of their natural riches continuously for three centuries. Instead of reinvesting their fortunes in the colonies, the Iberians stood accused of sending the bulk of their treasure back to Europe and using most of what remained to prop up their cities and estates in the New World.

The vast interior of the South American continent—where potential agricultural lands were too distant from ports and where cursory exploration had failed to uncover mineral riches—remained an empty frontier. From the earliest days of the conquest, we were

taught, Latin America, and particularly its huge southern continent, divided into two distinct types of society. One flourished in the cities, coastal plains and around the mines, which became the strongholds of colonial rule. The other—much greater in territory and sparser in population—languished in the remote hinterlands, never losing its backwardness.

But the question always left unanswered by my teachers and textbooks was why, even after the Spaniards and Portuguese were expelled and independence achieved, there never was a lasting frontier drive in South America, that incredible land mass almost as large as Canada and the contiguous United States combined.

If I plunked down the point of my school compass somewhere in the highlands of the Mato Grosso in central Brazil, and then swung the free arm of the instrument over the map in a thousand-mile radius, I could exclude most of the human activity on the vast South American continent from the arrival of the conquistadores 450 years before to their mixed race of descendants in the last half of the twentieth century. Beyond this periphery are most of the great urban centers—São Paulo, Rio de Janeiro, Buenos Aires, Santiago, Lima, Caracas—with their industries and farmlands spreading out in progressively weaker concentric circles. Within my compass arc is the lightly populated, undeveloped, still mysterious, inner frontier stretching over almost half the continent, a terrain of rain forests and tropical savannas.

South Americans feel extremely defensive about this huge "hollow frontier," as some scholars have dubbed it. They cite various justifications for this immense gap in the middle of their continent. I had absorbed some of these arguments in my school days in Mexico. Others I would hear about years later.

Geography is the reason most often advanced by South Americans to explain the persistence of these sprawling frontier lands. The temperate climate and easier landscape of the United States and Canada never presented the English settlers with the special obstacles the Iberians and their descendants faced in the tropics. How much more impenetrable these Amazon jungles were than the North American plains and woods. The heat, the lashing rains, the relentless insects, the stubborn underbrush and the densely packed rain forests could seemingly overcome the most determined pioneers. But the argument conveniently overlooks the fact that tropical Indonesia became one of the most populated regions in the world. The jungles of Zambia and Zaire, located at the same latitude as the South American hinterlands, are far more inhabited than the Amazon basin and its periphery.

It isn't necessary to look to Asia and Africa to find fallacies in the geographical determinism that South Americans have embraced. At least three sustained drives occurred into the hollow frontiers of South America before the modern era, and none of them failed for reasons of geography.

First, there were the Spanish conquistadores and their Portuguese counterparts the *bandeirantes*. Appallingly ill-equipped and poorly financed, they set out from the coastal regions of South America and penetrated from north, south, east and west into the deepest recesses of the continent in search of gold and precious stones and Indian slaves. No terrain was terrifying enough to abort their forays. Weighted down by cumbersome armor, drenched in perspiration, they hauled themselves over mountains, forded streams, hacked through jungles and floated down rivers without the remotest notion of where their waters would take them. They had no timetables, no concept of how long their journeys might last. Their provisions disappeared long before they returned home, forcing them to live off the inhospitable land and scavenge for animals and plants that often were not edible. Perhaps they might replenish their supplies by raiding Indian villages along the way. If not, they were even ready to eat their horses. And always, they knew that their odds of survival were slim. To mention only one example, not an unusual one at that, Gonzalo Pizarro set out with four hundred men in search of treasure in 1541 from his Andean stronghold in Quito (now the capital of Ecuador) to the Amazon jungles, and returned two years later with only eighty haggard, starving and sick men.

When the expeditions of the conquistadores ended in the late 1500's, and those of the *bandeirantes* almost 150 years later, it was not because men could not be found to undertake the perilous odysseys. Rather, the Spanish and Portuguese courts had become convinced that no treasures existed in the jungles and that the conquistadores and *bandeirantes* were too unfettered and headstrong to be allowed free rein.

The second sustained drive into the South American frontier lands was led by the clergy. Here again, contrary to the claims of modern South Americans, geography did not prove an insuperable obstacle to the penetration of the hinterlands. Priests had accompanied the Spaniards from the very moment they set foot in the New World, and they remained at the side of the conquistadores throughout their hazardous forays into the heart of South America.

When the Spanish court authorities decided to end the era of the conquistador, they entrusted the exploration and settlement of the New World frontiers to the clergy, particularly the Jesuits. Beginning in the late sixteenth century and for almost two hundred years thereafter, the Jesuits established Indian missions throughout the Amazon basin of Brazil and Peru, in the savannas of southern Colombia and Venezuela, in the wet plains of northern and eastern Bolivia and in the dense forests of eastern Paraguay.

For the Spanish Crown, these missions were an ideal method of securing the far-flung boundaries of the empire against the encroachments of the Portuguese from the eastern half of Brazil. Unlike the conquistadores, the missionaries wanted no personal wealth and were prepared to spend their entire lives in the frontier lands. Their missions were economically self-sufficient and often produced sizable tax revenues for the Crown and its viceroys. The primary concern of the priests was to convert the Indians to Catholicism and protect them from Spanish and Portuguese slave raiders. Deep in the western Brazilian Amazon region, Jesuits were able to found scores of missions, each with hundreds of Indian inhabitants, and sustained by agricultural plots along riverbanks. In Paraguay, the Jesuits recorded their greatest frontier achievements, banding together one hundred thousand Indians in prosperous missions where crops, livestock and crafts thrived. When the Jesuit missionary effort finally came to an end in 1767, it was because of political intrigue, not geographical considerations or economic hardships. The Spanish court, wary of the independence and power of the Jesuits, decided to banish them from its overseas empire. With the departure of the Jesuits, their missions swiftly collapsed or dwindled in economic importance, and the vast South American frontier lands became hollow once again.

There was yet a third sustained drive into the continent's interior. And this one took hold under the aegis of the independent South American republics when rubber boomed throughout the Amazon basin at the start of the twentieth century. Once automobiles became fashionable, there were no jungles that were too impenetrable, no insects too bothersome, no rains or temperatures too oppressive to dissuade hordes of adventurers from scouring the Amazon basin in search of latex for rubber tires. The Amazon River and its tributaries became the highways and byroads of a lively commerce. Ocean liners reached the heart of the continent, and when they could go no farther, they turned their cargoes over to flat-bottom steamers and canoes. Even cataracts and rapids could not obstruct the rubber trade. The foolhardy gunned their rafts over watery precipices and through boiling narrows. The patient organized elaborate portages around these bottlenecks, hoisting boats laden with cargoes out of the rivers, over high, slippery embankments and then back again into calmer waters.

Villages like Iquitos in Peru and Manaus in Brazil, blessed with deep harbors on the Amazon River, were transformed into thriving cities that rivaled their nations' capitals in luxury and services. The entire Amazon basin became an integral part of an elaborate and sophisticated international economic system. Powerful commercial houses in London and Paris raised financing for the merchants and rubber gatherers in the South American jungles, and they in turn sent their smoked latex to the factories of the United States and Europe.

Then the rubber boom collapsed in South America in the second decade of this century. The cause was the rise of cheaper rubber in Southeast Asia. The rubber producers of Ceylon and Malaya were at least as distant as the Amazon basin fron the industrial markets of Europe and the United States. But in Asia, investments were made to develop better strains of rubber trees that were more productive, more disease-resistant and densely grown on plantations. In South America, rubber trees remained wild and spaced widely apart, raising labor costs and slowing the collection of the latex.

The third great surge into the South American hinterlands had not collapsed because of geography. It foundered on economic shortsightedness. Not only did South Americans fail to set aside some of their rubber revenues to ensure the continued competitiveness of the industry; they also neglected to reinvest rubber profits into other productive ventures in the frontier regions. The continent's interior again lapsed into slumber. South Americans had been guilty of the same mentality of plunder that they found so reprehensible in their former Spanish and Portuguese rulers.

Conquistadores and *bandeirantes* hunting for gold. Missionaries seeking souls. Traders in search of rubber. A supposedly unyielding geography had been overcome by three powerful waves of frontier expansion led by dissimilar protagonists, using varied techniques and living in distinctly different eras.

When geography arguments wane, apologists seek refuge in history to explain the persistence of that giant, undeveloped core in the South American continent. And this history begins with the differences they attribute to the English colonist in North America and the Iberian conquistador to the south.

The North American pioneers, it is pointed out, were hardworking farmers, determined to turn their backs on Europe and build a new, moderately prosperous society of their own. When they achieved independence from Britain, their government encouraged them to push into the western frontier where free land was available for the small, free farmer.

The conquistadores, on the other hand, were a more predatory breed. They were soldiers of fortune, recruited from the battles against the Moors and the Mediterranean wars. With imaginations fired by medieval versions of ancient Greek mythology, they rampaged through the New World in search of treasure-hoarding Amazons, the Seven Enchanted Cities, the Golden Fleece, the Fountain of Youth and the River of Silver. Above all, there was the legend of El Dorado, the man of gold, the Indian chieftain who every day covered his body with the yellow dust and washed it off in a lake whose bottom had become caked with glittering treasure.

There can be little doubt of the power of these myths on the conquistadores. Spain, in the fifteenth and sixteenth centuries, had a vast audience for these so-called Romances of Chivalry, accounts of strange, opulent kingdoms in distant places, waiting to be pillaged by knights courageous and determined enough to find them. Monarchs, aristocrats, clergymen, adventurers and foot soldiers, if they were literate, devoured and believed these Romances of Chivalry. When Columbus, looking for a passage to Asia, discovered the New World, it seemed to confirm the myths. Where else could those enchanted kingdoms be if not here? The correspondence between conquistadores and the Spanish court is littered with references to characters and places mentioned in the Romances of Chivalry. So convinced were the first explorers of the reality of these legends that their eyes could conjure up mirages. Father Carvajal, the chronicler of Orellana's expedition down the Amazon, claimed to have seen white women warriors. Another priest mistook some shabby mountainside Indian villages glinting in the sun for the Seven Enchanted Cities, and his vague assertions were enough to send Francisco Vásquez de Coronado on a futile expedition in 1541 from Mexico City into what is now the American Southwest. Bernal Díaz del Castillo, the scribe of the conquest of Mexico, was so awestruck upon first setting eyes on the Aztec capital that he wrote, "It was like the magical things related in the book of Amadis"— perhaps the best known of the Romances of Chivalry.

The enormous wealth of the Aztecs and Incas only whetted the appetite of the conquistadores and spurred them deeper into the mountains and jungles on journeys with little respite. For unlike the pioneers of North America, these Spaniards and Portuguese came to plunder, not to stay.

"I am here for gold, not to scratch the land like a peasant," Cortés bragged to his lieutenants. And he was echoed by Portuguese adventurers in Brazil who vowed to observe their king's edict "not to devote thyselves to tasks that detract from the search for precious metals." It was not by accident that the Iberians ignored the more fertile and accessible lands of North America in favor of the rougher terrains of Central and South America, which were more distant from Europe. Their science and mythology taught them that gold proliferated more in warmer climates.

Long after the quest for El Dorado ended, the mentality of quick profit and plunder prevailed. The most fortunate and renowned of the conquistadores were given *encomiendas*—huge, feudal estates with numerous Indian serfs. And although the *encomiendas* could be owned for only two generations, agriculture came to be dominated by immense properties in the hands of private individuals and the Church. What remained was held by the Indians either individually or communally.

Not even demographic catastrophe among the Indians altered the dependence of the Spanish and Portuguese colonies on large agricultural estates staffed by cheap or slave, nonwhite labor. Plagues and other diseases brought over from Europe devastated the Indians. According to some estimates by historians, Mexico at the time of the Spanish Conquest in 1519–21 had more than twenty million inhabitants. But by 1600, the Indian population had declined to fewer than two million because of pestilence and malnutrition brought on by the widespread disruption of the Indians' own system of agriculture. In the South American Andean countries, the Indian population tumbled from 6 million to 1.5 million only three decades after Pizarro overcame the Incas, and continued to drop until 1800, when it reached its nadir at about six hundred thousand. In the Amazon basin, where an estimated two million people lived before the conquest, only a million survived after a century of Spanish and Portuguese incursions for treasure and Indian slaves.

(It was not until the twentieth century that the Indians of Mexico and the Andean countries reached and then surpased their preconquest population levels. In the Amazon, the Indian population has continued its decline to the verge of extinction.)

To replenish their dwindling pool of Indian labor, the Spanish and Portuguese colonies imported African slaves. There was no thought given to breaking up the large agricultural estates or opening the frontier lands to smaller, family-size plots for new immigrants from Spain and Portugal. The people who flocked to the Iberian colonies did not want homesteads anyway. They despised manual labor, for like Cortés they had not come to the New World "to scratch the land like a peasant." Many were minor gentry who dreamed of Indian servants and leisure in the colonies. If they could not have a huge rural estate or a mine, they would settle for a secure, easy bureaucratic niche in a city or town. Then, with luck, they might trade on their superior social status as true Spaniards and Portuguese and deign to marry into wealthy families of Creoles—as the Europeans born in the New World were called.

By 1565, Martín Cortés, the son of the conqueror of the Aztecs, was writing to his king, Philip II, to complain of the shiftlessness of Spaniards arriving in Mexico City:

> In this city the number of Spaniards is increasing daily, and there come great quantities of them from Spain every year, and no one works, and there are a great number of loafers; and the viceroy told me himself that every day in Mexico eight hundred men rise in the morning without having any place where they can eat; and nothing is done to see to it that the Spaniards work.

Similar complaints were forwarded from Peru and Colombia and Brazil over the next two hundred years. Until the twentieth century, work for most people in the world meant farming. Yet in the New World empires of Spain and Portugal—territories almost twenty-five times as large as the mother countries—there was not enough work for immigants!

It might be difficult to swallow a historical theory that blames the absence of frontier expansion on a lack of pioneering spirit and work ethic among the Iberians who sailed for the New World. To make the theory more palatable, some historians link the character flaws of the colonists to the institutional defects of their government.

The Spanish court was Europe's most authoritarian monarchy. It evolved an efficient, centralized government, an elaborate bureaucracy and rigid legal system that were foisted upon the Crown's subjects in the New World. Administrators appointed by the court soon grabbed power from the more independent-minded conquistadores. Colonists were encouraged to settle in the towns and rural estates that were established by the first invading hordes as their base camps, mostly along the South American seaboard or around the important mines. Long before the industrial age, Latin America became relatively urbanized. By the seventeenth century, Mexico City, Lima and Salvador de Bahia were bigger than most Iberian cities and any town in North America.

Already separated from their New World possessions by an ocean crossing that could take six to twelve weeks, the Spanish and Portuguese courts did not want to make their political and economic control over their colonies any more difficult than it had to be. It was easier to rule towns and cities located whenever possible near the coasts, where troops could be garrisoned and tax collectors could carry out their work more efficiently. Industry and agriculture were encouraged close to urban centers.

The small homesteaders or pioneers willing to venture into the wilderness had no place in these colonial schemes. If they had settled in large numbers in the backlands, they might eventually elude the court's already overextended reach. Then maybe these self-reliant pioneers might create rival, autonomous centers of power on the geographical periphery of the empire and threaten the colonies with disintegration. No matter how remote that risk, it was still safer to hand over the settlement of the frontiers to the missionaries and their disciplined Indian wards. In the end, even these missionaries became suspect in the eyes of the Spanish and Portuguese rulers, who cast them out of the New World in the second half of the eighteenth century.

These then are the explanations most often put forth by South American apologists to account for the existence of the enormous, unoccupied frontier land in their continent after three hundred years of colonial rule: a geography that was allegedly insurmountable; settlers who came for booty and not to till the land; rulers who took far more treasure from their empire than they invested in it; institutions that oriented the colonies toward the sea and away from the continental interior; a willful neglect of the hinterlands.

And all these flaws became the heavy legacy that the Iberians bequeathed to the South American republics in the nineteenth century. Three hundred years of misguided colonial rule was long enough to forge traditions, habits, thought patterns, institutions that supposedly could not be erased even by the violent wars of independence and many decades of self-rule thereafter.

Like the Spanish and Portuguese viceroys before them, the newly independent South American governments tied the destinies of their countries to the cities and towns and the coastal plains settled during the Iberian Conquest. Agriculture and industry continued to revolve around these urban centers. Huge estates prevailed in the rural areas. Pioneering continued to be discouraged, and in any case, there were no volunteers.

Since rural life offered few prospects for land-hungry European settlers, South America failed to attract immigrants on the scale of the United States. Between 1820 and 1920, fewer than seven million Europeans emigrated to South America, compared to the more than thirty-three million who moved to the United States. In South America, these immigrants settled almost entirely in the cities and coastal zones, while in the United States many of them headed to the frontier lands.

At this point, a pause is in order to question the inexorability of the arguments put forth by the South Americans justifying the failure of their countries to conquer the frontier wilderness. The issue begins to resemble the old religious debate over free will and predestination. Were the South American nations so shackled by their Iberian inheritance that they could not break free in dramatic new directions? Didn't independence offer them the opportunity to forge a radically different vision for their countries? Or were South Americans in fact responsible for placing new obstacles of their own in the path of frontier development?

Both the United States and South America entered the nineteenth century with enormous, unsettled territories unfurling before them. But while the pioneers in the United States marched across the

West, the vast frontier lands of South America continued to stagnate. They were so unexplored that countries were unsure of their own boundaries. Who could draw with any confidence the line between the Amazon possessions of Brazil, Bolivia, Peru, Ecuador and Colombia, or between the Chaco plains of Paraguay and Bolivia, or between the subtropical forests of Brazil and Paraguay?

In the nineteenth century, North Americans became convinced that it was the conquest of the frontier that set them apart from Europeans and other people. Manifest destiny—the belief that the United States should inevitably span the continent between the Atlantic and Pacific oceans—gave North Americans a self-sufficient, nationalistic ideology and identity. In 1893, the American historian Frederick Jackson Turner presented a paper that came to be considered a manifesto on the importance of the frontier.

"Up to our own day," wrote Turner, "American history has been in a large degree the history of the colonization of the Great West. The existence of an area of free land, its continuous recession, and the advance of American settlement westward explain American development. . . . This expansion westward with its new opportunities, its continuous touch with the simplicity of primitive society, furnish the forces dominating American character. . . ."

Turner's thesis, though disputed, debated and refined by other historians, was taken up in its simplest form by hundreds of western novels and films, and has become deeply rooted in every American's psyche.

But almost fifty years before Turner, South America had produced its own manifesto on the frontier. Its author was Domingo Sarmiento, the continent's foremost political thinker at the time, and he presented ideas that were diametrically opposed to Turner's theories. Where Turner found opportunity, material development and spiritual growth in the wilderness, Sarmiento saw only danger, impoverishment and brutality in the frontier lands.

Sarmiento set forth these notions in his masterpiece, *Facundo*, published in 1845. The book was a stinging critique of the rise of an Argentine dictator, Juan Manuel Rosas, a man who forsook Buenos Aires for the pampa grasslands of the interior and then stormed to power with an army of gauchos and a deeply anti-European outlook. Rosas was a metaphor of the evil lurking in the frontier lands. The subtitle of Sarmiento's book, *Civilization and Barbarity,* posed the choice between a European orientation found in the cities and coastal plains of South America and the native isolationism and know-nothingness of the backlands. He wrote:

> There is something in the wilds of the Argentine territory which brings to mind the wilds of Asia. The imagination discovers a likeness between the pampa and the plains lying between the Euphrates and the Tigris; some affinity between the lonely line of wagons which crosses our wastes, arriving at Buenos Aires after a journey lasting months, and the caravan of camels which takes its way toward Baghdad or Smyrna. . . . The head of each party is a military leader, like the chief of an Asiatic caravan; this position can be filled only by a man of iron will, and daring to the verge of rashness that he may hold in check the audacity and turbulence of the land pirates who are to be directed and ruled by himself alone. . . . It is necessary to see their visages bristling with beards, their countenances as grave and serious as those of the Arabs of Asia, to appreciate the pitying scorn with which they look upon the sedentary denizen of the city, who may have read many books, but who cannot overthrow and slay a fierce bull, who could not provide himself with a horse from the pampa, who has never met a tiger alone. . . . Moreover, the countryman, far from attempting to imitate the customs of the city, rejects with disdain its luxury and refinements. . . . The European is in [his] eyes the most contemptible of all men.

When I was growing up in Latin America, Sarmiento was as widely read as Turner once was in the United States. But how to explain his enormous popularity beyond his native Argentina? True, he was an elegant writer, and his stirring crusade against a tyrant like Rosas had a universal appeal. Perhaps more important, though, Sarmiento touched a raw nerve that makes South Americans quiver even today. South Americans, he asserted, must continuously strive to maintain European civilization in their continent, or risk being overwhelmed by the savage natives and natural forces of the backlands. He portrays the gauchos—those dark-skinned, mixed-blood cowboys of the pampas—as cruel, ignorant bedouins, ill-dressed and ill-mannered horseback marauders incapable of living a settled existence. And Sarmiento's pampa is a brutish landscape, windswept, barren, unbearably lonely and dehumanizing.

Sarmiento's readers were mostly the urbanized whites of South America, who shared his revulsion over the continent's interior and its inhabitants. His audience was the Creole elite—the Europeans born in the New World. They had led the struggles against the

Spanish and Portuguese colonial rule, and they monopolized political and economic power in the aftermath of independence. But barely a generation after achieving self-rule, they were overcome by an intense nostalgia for Europe. Not that they wished for a return to colonial status; but they wanted to recreate and preserve European civilization in the New World.

To the long list of grievances against three centuries of Iberian rule, they would add one more: abandonment. The Spaniards and Portuguese had forsaken them in an unformed, inhospitable land populated by an Indian and mestizo majority. How recognizable to these Creoles were Sarmiento's brutish pampa and uncivilized gaucho half-breeds. The white, urban Brazilian could find their counterparts in the arid backlands and wet jungles of his country. The Peruvian Creole living in Lima could point them out in the lofty Andes and steamy Amazon valleys beyond the mountains to the east.

In the United States, the Indians were killed off or hidden away in reservations. In much of South America, they survived the diseases, malnutrition, brutal labor conditions and massacres. And as pure-blooded natives and mestizos, they always remained the largest population sector. The history taught in schools might portray them as victims of an Iberian Conquest that destroyed flourishing Indian civilizations. But side by side with these official versions of history, a stubborn racism prevailed among the Creoles, who clung to their European ideals. They had the power and money to build the cities of South America into rough replicas of Europe. But they were far less confident that they could Europeanize the vast interior of the continent. What a risk it would be to migrate into the backlands and expose themselves to a harsh nature and a crude frontier society. Who could say with certainty that coastal and urban civilization would overcome frontier barbarism?

Thus South America not only absorbed the Iberian prejudices and fears about the frontier lands; it created even stronger prejudices and fears of its own. Through the centuries, the South American descendants of the Europeans—that upper and middle class of businessmen and commercial farmers, bureaucrats and military officers, professionals and intellectuals—have turned their backs on their continent's interior and set their gazes firmly overseas. Commerce has become directed not with neighboring countries nor across land corridors, but toward markets in Europe and North

America across the oceans. Europe and the United States have become the inspiration for ideas and life-styles. When South Americans travel, it is still to New York and Los Angeles, Paris and Madrid and London—not to the Mato Grosso, Iquitos or Bolivia's northern savanna.

As late as the mid-twentieth century, there was still no frontier myth to embrace in South America. And without it, there lingered a feeling of imcompleteness, a confusion over identity, a sense of isolation that could end only when South Americans finally turned inward and took full possession of their hinterlands.

3

I was fortunate to have moved to South America as a journalist in the 1970's, when the isolation of the continent's interior was being challenged by the most serious frontier drive since the Iberian Conquest. This thrust has continued to gain momentum in the 1980's.

The long-delayed development effort is taking place now because South Americans can no longer afford the luxury of confining themselves to the old colonial redoubts. The already overcrowded cities are bursting at their seams. Their population-growth rates are the largest in the world. Lima, which had a population of five hundred thousand in 1940, now harbors almost a third of Peru's eighteen million inhabitants. São Paulo has about twelve million people now; in fewer than three decades, it will grow to more than twenty-five million. By the dawn of the twenty-first century, the United Nations predicts that five South American cities—São Paulo, Rio de Janeiro, Buenos Aires, Lima and Bogotá—will have more than ten million inhabitants. A yellow or silvery haze of smog shimmers every day over the larger urban centers. In the suburban slums that ring every major city, the permanent odor of uncollected garbage lingers in the air. Water and electricity are often scarce. Transportation is so woeful that four hours of daily commuting is not unusual for the suburban poor who are fortunate enough to have jobs.

Conditions are often bleaker in the established agricultural zones. After all, it was agrarian poverty that sparked the massive exodus of the last four decades and transformed South America from an essentially rural continent to the most urbanized region in the Third World. More than sixty percent of South Americans now live in cities, compared to twenty-seven percent of Asians and twenty-six percent of Africans. Mechanization of farming has chased millions of South American peasants and laborers out of rural areas. Many others migrated to the cities because growing families relentlessly subdivided land into plots too tiny to remain viable. Unlike the North American agrarian scene, the rural exodus has not meant that South American agriculture has attained a mechanized self-sufficiency. In most of the continent, farming has not kept pace with the food needs of the increasingly urbanized population. South America, which for most of this century was a net agrarian exporter, has in several recent years bought more foodstuffs than it has sold abroad.

Worsening trade balances and mushrooming foreign debts have also rekindled interest in the frontier lands. By mid-1982, South American countries had piled up about $200 billion in debts abroad, according to the World Bank annual report. This foreign debt is two and a half times the size of South America's exports. In the long run, many South American governments have concluded, the untapped riches of their continent's interior hold an important key to repaying their foreign loans and redressing their trade imbalances. Only by rushing to uncover new mineral deposits, energy reservoirs and other natural resources in the wilderness can South America hope to maintain industrial growth and finance burgeoning imports.

Thus, during the past decade, throughout the Amazon basin and its rimlands—an expanse more than ten times the size of Texas—people and resources have been moving into virgin territories on a larger scale than anywhere else in the world. Petroleum companies are probing the deepest recesses of the rain forests of eastern Peru and Ecuador. Brazil is lacing its Amazon region with thousands of miles of roads, gouging remote jungle mountains for their mineral treasures and turning over huge chunks of virgin tropical land to many thousands of pioneers. In the long-forgotten eastern frontier lands of Paraguay, enormous quantities of hydroelectric power are being harnessed and dense forests are being stripped away to make available rich new farmland. The savannas and plains of northern and eastern Bolivia are producing a cornucopia of cattle, grain, oil, natural gas and illicit narcotics.

For the most part, the new frontier drives are intensely nationalistic efforts. South Americans have invited relatively few Americans and Europeans, primarily engineers and technicians working under limited-term contracts for multinational companies. With one or two glaring exceptions, the push into the wilderness has carefully observed national boundaries, and countries have drawn their pioneers from among their own citizenry.

The people thrusting into the backlands have been lured from the entire social spectrum—farmers, peasants, unskilled laborers, businessmen, professionals, priests, prostitutes, hired gunmen, thieves, con artists, charlatans and dreamers.

Hordes of dirt-poor dark-skinned settlers cram their families and meager possessions on the backs of flatbed trucks and head for unknown destinations in the hope that fertile homesteads lie at the end of their thousand-mile journeys. White, middle-class planters who have outgrown their parents' farms are searching for land of their own on the frontier. Less numerous but infinitely more powerful are the big entrepreneurs, who employ batallions of itinerant laborers to hack, burn and raze vast jungle tracts for large-scale cattle ranching or for resale to smaller settlers.

There are young engineers, doctors, lawyers, accountants who are gambling that their careers will advance more quickly in the frontier lands than in cities crowded with established competitors. There are merchants who began hawking their wares from the backs of trucks parked amid fetid tent towns and in a few years built chain stores and warehouses in booming pioneer cities.

The wilderness has also drawn violent criminals on the run who quickly discovered that they could hire themselves out as gunmen for big landowners fighting off squatters. And in the remoteness of the frontier lands, narcotics traffickers have found the seclusion, manpower and raw materials to build a multibillion-dollar smuggling operation.

In the United Sates, where the conquest of the wilderness ended almost a century ago, we are constantly inspiring ourselves with metaphors of new frontiers—in medicine, basic sciences and outer space. Yet we have remained largely aloof or hostile to South America's massive push into its hinterlands, which is exploding with as much energy, hope, greed and savagery as marked the surge westward of American pioneers in an earlier era.

The aboriginal Indians of South America, clinging to their last refuges deep in the jungle interior, are still being annihilated by white men's diseases, forced integration and outright massacres. Repeating the history of the American West, government agreements creating Indian reservations are violated almost as soon as they are signed.

The caravans of battered trucks rumbling into the new South American frontiers recall the horse-drawn wagon trains of the nineteenth-century United States. The shotgun casually slung over a settler's shoulder is the modern-day equivalent of the American Colt .45. The Amazon land battles between cattlemen, homesteaders and squatters are a throwback to the prairie wars of an earlier North American epoch. The muddy main streets and wood shacks of the newer South American frontier towns invite comparison with old Dodge City and Abilene.

Perhaps our vision of what is happening in South America is clouded by the dizzying procession of military governments, the endless cycles of revolution and repression, the violent political swings between left and right. Or perhaps the contemporary frontier experience in the southern continent is one which North Americans nowadays find too painfully cruel and disorderly to be reminiscent of the conquest of the Old West. All the revisionist histories of Indian massacres, robber barons, despoliation of nature have somehow not shaken the nostalgic conviction among North Americans that their own frontier expansion was a uniquely heroic, enriching and formative national experience. But they have made us more sensitive to similar injustices and mistakes now being committed in the South American hinterlands. The environmental dangers posed by the destruction of large tracts of Amazon rain forests, the persecution of Indians, the absence of law and order, the unequal struggles for frontier land between the wealthy and the poor, all seem to outweigh the potential benefits of the wilderness crusade in the minds of many North American observers.

Many South Americans themselves have greeted the new assault on their frontier lands with a mixture of disbelief and distrust. The jungles and savannas of the interior still seem to them too impenetrable and distant to support civilization. Some argue that with so much poverty plaguing the older cities and coastal plains, their nations can ill afford a quixotic, expensive frontier drive. Others maintain that the conquest of the hinterlands is a cynical attempt by beleaguered governments to deflect attention away from more pressing political and economic dilemmas.

How much easier it is, they point out, to coax landless peasants into the wilderness than to carry out agrarian reform in valuable farm zones closer to domestic markets and ports. How convenient it is for an unpopular government in Lima or Brasília to fan nationalism by trumpeting victory over the frontier. How simple it is to cover gross inequities in income distribution by holding out the promise of boundless wealth in the hinterlands for those ambitious and courageous enough to settle there.

Well aware of this pervasive skepticism, but still harboring my own secret enthusiasm for the South American wilderness, I began in the early 1970's to seek out the planners and overseers of the frontier drives. In their majority they were uninspired bureaucrats, hoping for more promising posts but meanwhile occupying small offices in the most hidden recesses of ministry buildings in the capitals of Brazil, Peru, Ecuador, Bolivia and Paraguay. Few of them claimed to see a continental strategy in their countries' frontier efforts. They could offer vague maps, glossy publicity brochures and outdated statistics more easily than a sweeping vision of the settlement of the hinterlands. Many of them doubtless were horrified at the chaos and violence and discomforts they encountered on trips to frontier zones and much preferred to be briefed in their own offices by subordinates called in from the field. In La Paz, the Bolivian capital, I once met a colonel in charge of regional planning for the northern frontier province called the Beni, who had never visited the area. In Brasília, a ranking official in the land colonization agency pouring over a map with me mistakenly pointed out a pioneer zone that turned out to be an Indian reservation. And in Asunción, the Paraguayan capital, the head of the agrarian reform agency candidly admitted that no one in his office could say with any certainty how many people had settled in his country's eastern frontier lands, where they had come from and how many among them had legitimate land titles.

During my first three years in South America, my image of the frontier drive resembled a jumble of jigsaw pieces. Dozens of mining, road and land colonization schemes dotted the continent's interior in an isolated and disjointed pattern. The puzzle began to take recognizable shape only after a trip to Lima in 1976 when I met with Fernando Belaúnde Terry, at the time a former president of Peru plotting his return to high office. Belaúnde had long been pointed out to me as an early modern visionary of the South American frontier. But he had only recently returned to Lima from a lengthy exile, mainly spent in the United States.

I was vaguely aware that Belaúnde had once proposed and lobbied unsuccessfully in Peru and abroad for a long, expensive highway through several South American countries to open up the interior of the continent for settlement and commerce. But I had really sought out Belaúnde for an interview to discuss politics. He had been deposed as president of Peru in 1968 by a left-wing military coup, and now that same military government was becoming increasingly unpopular. After hearing Belaúnde give his assessment of the government's deteriorating political situation, I asked him what sort of vision he was offering the country if he ever made it back into power.

Looking around the large living room of his suburban Lima home as if hidden cameras and microphones were recording us, he lowered his voice to a conspiratorial whisper and gestured over to his library. Practically tiptoeing, he led me silently into the dark room and turned on the lights. Sprawled on a large, heavy table was a huge topographic map of South America. Tan mounds indicated the mountain ranges. Green felt marked the jungles. The rivers were blue veins. The plains were dabbed in yellow swabs.

What made the map even more distinctive was a long, thick, red undulating line—with many smaller capillaries radiating from its axis—extending through the highland jungles of Colombia, Ecuador and Peru, skirting the western Amazon territories of Brazil, then slashing across northern and eastern Bolivia and bisecting Paraguay to its eastern border with Brazil.

Belaúnde called this imaginary artery the Marginal Highway of the Jungle. He asserted that, once built, it would transform the continent, open the last frontiers, draw people and resources toward the empty interior and finally fulfill South America's immense economic potential.

"It will only be by turning our vision to the interior and conquering our wilderness the way the United States once did that South Americans will finally achieve true development," he said. "The game is being played on the frontier, not in the cities. And it is my dream to make Peruvians, then others, realize where their real destiny lies."

The highway was supposed to run thirty-five hundred miles, the distance between San Diego on the Pacific coast of the United States to Halifax on the Atlantic coast of Canada. With numerous smaller roads feeding into it, Belaúnde's highway would exert a sphere of influence over an enormous territory about six times the size of California. This inner frontier of mountains, jungles and plains would

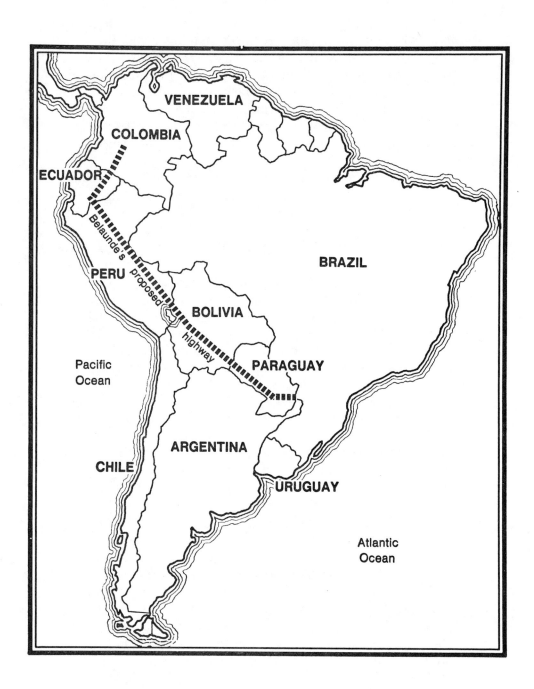

be as long as the highway and would span seven hundred miles at its widest point, the distance separating Chicago from Washington, D.C.

The mythical road drew a rough crescent as it swept through the interior of South America from the northwest to the southeast. For about half its length, it hugged the eastern jungle slopes of the Andes in Colombia, Ecuador and northern Peru, crossing dozens of streams and Amazon tributaries. Midway through Peru, the highway dipped into the lowland rain forest close to the Brazilian border. Here it would encounter its most difficult engineering dilemma because of constant floods during the rainy season. Traveling through more lowland jungle, the road exited Peru into northwestern Bolivia. Avoiding the Andes to the south, it crossed Bolivia in a southeast direction through the wet savannas of the Beni, through the more temperate, lush plains of Santa Cruz and then through the hot Chaco scrublands to the border of Paraguay. Still heading southeast, the highway cut across the Paraguayan Chaco that covers half that country. Then, reaching Asunción, the Paraguayan capital, the road would run a straight eastward course through farmland and, finally, through thick, subtropical forest to Paraguay's eastern border with Brazil. There, at its terminal point, Belaúnde's grand highway was supposed to join the already heavily transited road system south to Buenos Aires, the Argentine capital, and east to the industrial Atlantic ports of Brazil.

All along its transcontinental course, Belaúnde's highway would have feeder roads connecting it to farmlands, mining districts, provincial towns and major cities. Unlike any other visionary proposal to conquer the continent's interior, it completely bypassed the Amazon River, whose long west-to-east course from the Andes to the Atlantic had always been considered a natural passageway and blueprint for the development of the South American hinterlands. Belaúnde's main objection to using the Amazon as an axis was that it benefited Brazil almost exclusively because most of the giant river's navigable portions lay within that country. Brazil, Belaúnde suggested, should build a trans-Amazonic road system of its own that could link up with the Highway of the Jungle at various points in eastern Peru and northern and eastern Bolivia.

Belaúnde came from an aristocratic family that traced its roots to Pizarro's conquistadores. In his youth, he once fought a saber duel with a political rival. On another occasion, he swam several hundred yards under rifle fire in a failed attempt to escape from an island where he was being held as a political prisoner. By the time we met, late middle age had given him a subdued, scholarly aura. The athletic gait and shirt-sleeved look of his earlier political campaigns had been replaced by a tweedy, avuncular image. The old passion flared only when he spoke of his highway and the frontier. Then, the slow, soft voice picked up in cadence and volume, and the eyes tilted skyward out of focus, oblivious to interruptions.

The vision was born, he said, while he was studying architecture at the University of Texas in the 1930's. There, he absorbed the legends of the American frontier and witnessed the beginnings of ambitious, new highway construction programs. Years later, when Belaúnde became dean of architecture at a university in Lima, he invited his students on expeditions into the Andes to retrace the remnants of the long, stone-paved roads that the ancient Incas had constructed as the backbone of their empire. His idea of the Marginal Highway of the Jungle—located even farther inland than the Inca roads—took shape during those university forays. Belaúnde eventually turned the concept into the centerpiece of his presidential campaign during the early 1960's.

The Inca highway system, which had been built in the hundred years before the Spanish Conquest, tied together an Indian empire that stretched from southern Colombia, through Ecuador, Peru and western Bolivia, then south to the waist of Chile and into western Argentina. These narrow, elongated territories covered about four hundred thousand square miles, an area almost the combined size of France and Spain.

The main Inca road ran north and south through the Andes for 3,250 miles from Quito, through Cuzco, the seat of Inca power, and down to Talca, a modern-day city in the middle of Chile. Parallel to this highway, along the Pacific coast, ran another great road, some 2,520 miles long, from the northern Peruvian port of Tumbes to the outskirts of Santiago, the capital of Chile. And between these two arteries was a web of smaller roads that ran east to west and connected the coast, to the mountains and highland jungles. In all, the formidable Inca highway system stretched 9,500 miles, more than three times the breadth of the United States from San Diego to Boston.

The chief purpose of such an enormous road system was almost certainly more political than economic. Aside from tribute from vassal tribes in the form of jewelry, cloth and pottery, there was little commerce on these highways. The Incas emphasized self-sufficiency among their subjects whether they lived in the mountain valleys, along the Pacific coast or on the fringes of the Amazon rain forest. But the roads did facilitate the rapid movement of messengers, armies, officials and the Inca rulers themselves, who often visited their outlying domains. The highways were built and maintained by huge numbers of conscripted or voluntary laborers, and served to transport these work forces to large-scale construction projects in Cuzco and other urban centers. For example, the mammoth stone fortress of Sacsahuamán, which dominates Cuzco, reportedly used thirty thousand laborers, many of them drawn from vassal villages hundreds of miles away and brought to the Inca capital by the royal highway system. The roads also enabled the Incas to quickly exile thousands of politically suspect vassals to other locations in the empire, or to implant large communities of loyal followers in troublesome domains.

The entire highway system was provided with granaries and inns, called *tambos,* spaced every eight to fifteen miles apart. Undoubtedly, by their sheer size and quality, the roads themselves were intended to impress upon the Incas' subjects the power and grandeur of their rulers. The Spanish conquistadores expressed astonishment that the highways, paved in stone and bordered by high stone walls, were wide enough so that eight horsemen could ride abreast. The proportions seemed far too large for Indians who traveled on foot.

In the aftermath of the Spanish Conquest, the Inca highway system soon fell into disrepair. The Spaniards preferred the coastal plains to the Andean highlands, and established their capital at Lima on the Pacific. Their main interest in the interior was to build and maintain a reliable road to the bountiful silver mines of Potosí, in the Bolivian Andes. The decimation of the native population by smallpox, plague, common colds and other diseases brought over from Europe greatly reduced the pool of Indian labor. Those who survived were conscripted for work in the Andean mines and the coastal plantations and ranches. There was no surplus labor force to maintain the bulk of the Inca road system or the intricate irrigation networks and terraced fields which had made the Andean highlands so agriculturally prosperous. Cut off and abandoned, whole villages and towns disappeared in the mountains and jungle fringes.

Isolated remnants of the Incas' highway system still exist on the ouskirts of Cuzco, Catamarca and dozens of other former Inca strongholds. Sometimes they span many miles before becoming jagged stone obstacle courses. More often they are difficult to follow more than a few hundred yards, covered as they are by mud slides and overgrowth. But it is easy to see why even these skeletal traces could inspire Belaúnde to dream of a similar, modern road network through the interior of the continent.

"By means of a carefully planned network of roads, the Incas unified the Andean area from north to south, extending from Ecuador through Peru, Bolivia, Chile and Argentina. And by building other roads from east to west, they integrated the highlands with the coast and the edge of the jungles," Belaúnde explained to me. "After the Spanish Conquest, the political and economic structure of the old Inca empire assumed a completely different orientation. The Spanish colonist looked outward to Europe. And as a result, the coast gained in economic importance as an outlet to the sea. The effect, even to this day, has been that most South American countries have turned away from each other and have developed closer ties with nations on other continents. The only way to link the people and the land of South America together into an integrated whole is the same way the Incas accomplished the task—by roads. I am not proposing to resurrect the Inca highways. I want a highway system that runs even deeper into the interior, beyond the mountains and through the highland jungles. And I want a highway that runs much farther east across the continent than the Incas ever attempted. The Andes, as formidable as they may be, cannot block our way to the interior forever. The jungles may someday produce the El Dorado so many sought and never found, a treasure in agriculture and minerals and lumber far surpassing any yields of Inca gold. The human overflow from the cities and coasts and highlands must have an outlet to the jungles to avoid demographic catastrophe."

Belaúnde began strenuously pushing the jungle highway project in his country and abroad soon after he assumed the presidency in 1963. He convoked conferences in Lima that drew ranking government officials from Colombia, Ecuador, Bolivia and Paraguay. He accompanied presidents of neighboring countries on visits to sites of his proposed highway in Peru. And he flew planeloads of journalists and foreign bankers deep into those highlands and jungles on inspection tours which he often led personally. In Washington, he lobbied hard for loans from the Inter-American Development Bank, the World Bank and the Alliance for Progress. A leading American engineering company was commissioned to make a study of the entire thirty-five-hundred-mile route. The Peruvian Army Corps of Engineers began to bulldoze sections of road. Belaúnde also announced that volunteer labor brigades would be sought among peasants of the Andean highlands to contribute one or two free workdays each month for highway construction. Belaúnde claimed that the volunteer concept, like the highway itself, was inspired by the Incas, although in fact most road construction under the Indian rulers had depended on conscripted laborers or subjects who were volunteers only to the extent that they offered their services in place of tribute.

Despite the widespread publicity, the construction of the Highway of the Jungle soon ground to a halt. Some feeder roads were built, but little of the big northwest-southeast axis through the continental interior was completed. The project, so identified with Belaúnde, was not a priority for presidents in neighboring countries. Financing lagged and then petered out.

Many Peruvians, even staunch loyalists of Belaúnde, had never lent much credence to the highway. They might have applauded the concept in theory, and certainly considered it a powerful campaign slogan, but its economic and social benefits seemed to lie in such a distant future. And meanwhile, more immediate problems were pressing upon the country. Anyone could see that the migration of Andean peasants was accelerating toward Lima and other cities rather than into the jungles as Belaúnde had hoped. Their cardboard-and-oil-drum shacks invaded the scarce, fertile fields on the capital's periphery and sprawled into the coastal desert strip. They clamored for industrial and construction and service jobs in the cities, not for pioneer agricultural plots in the jungle highlands.

Leftists and populists called for radical agrarian reform that would distribute existing farmlands. On the northern Pacific coast, a handful of families and corporations owned sugar estates, each as large as Rhode Island with ten thousand or more workers. There were ranches in the Andean valleys that would take a cattle herder on horseback three full days to cross. Small but troublesome guerrilla bands roamed the southern mountains. The government was under rising pressure from nationalists in the military to demand greater revenues from foreign companies for their mining and petroleum concessions. And beyond this explosive agenda of current problems was the centuries' old, pervasive distrust of the frontier.

Neither conservatives nor progressives believed in a new El Dorado in the jungles. They knew of no businessmen anxious to invest there. No cadres of idealistic university students were ready to lead pioneer bands into the backlands.

As years went by, the project sank from public view, and Belaúnde's dogged insistence on the merits of his frontier highway gave him a somewhat quixotic reputation. He had been nicknamed affectionately "El Arquitecto" when he first unveiled his visionary proposals to build up the interior. But now it became a term of derision, a shorthand way of describing a president who clung to utopian concepts while losing grasp on political power and administration. In 1968, a left-wing military coup deposed Belaúnde and sent him into exile.

During his dozen years out of power, Belaúnde remained a popular figure. His personal honesty and good intentions had never been questioned. His many supporters were always ready to blame any failings in his first presidency on incompetent cabinet ministers, not on Belaúnde himself. But even his most loyal followers continued to scoff at his frontier project.

"It's a highway that goes from nowhere to nowhere," an editor of a Lima journal sympathetic to Belaúnde assured me after I recounted my interview with the former president. "But he hasn't changed his mind about it. If he ever moves back into the presidency, you can bet he will bring his highway map along."

The editor was at least partly correct. When the military government fell in 1980 and Belaúnde was reelected president, he did cart his huge map back to the palace and, once again, reeled out his grand project to visitors.

But I never thought Belaúnde's Highway of the Jungle was a flight of fantasy. In the early 1960's, he had instinctively traced a northwest-southeast route that would later emerge as the true axis of South America's frontier development—from the jungles of Colombia, Ecuador and Peru, along the western Amazon periphery of Brazil, through the tropical flatlands of northern and eastern Bolivia and into the woods of Paraguay. Today, the assault on the continent's wilderness is also taking place elsewhere, mainly in the northern Brazilian rain forest, closer to the Amazon River. But these projects, some of them huge and costly mineral and agricultural ventures, are like isolated buoys in an ocean of jungle. Belaúnde's highway is a far more useful thread to make sense out of the disorderly, explosive frontier push. It remains the most plausible blueprint for the eventual integration of South American's backlands.

The moment I saw that sprawling topographic map in Belaúnde's library, I realized I had been inadvertently traveling along stretches of his imaginary highway for several years. And I determined to continue to follow it—by plane, Jeep, bus, boat and on foot. Sometimes I would wander quite far off its actual course. But always I would stick to the general northwest-to-southeast trajectory it traced through the continent's frontier lands.

It was an odyssey that took me through oil camps and Indian rituals in the Peruvian rain forest; the rubber groves, pioneer farming communities and land wars of the western Brazilian Amazon; and the construction site of a giant dam on the border between Paraguay and Brazil that will produce more energy than any oil field in the world.

4

I began my journey in 1982, two years after Belaúnde returned to the presidency, by going back to the oil fields of the Peruvian Amazon, partly because petroleum had become the most important resource in the country's frontier region, and also because I wanted to complete the excursion that had been aborted earlier by the tarantula bite.

The Peruvian oil camps, on the border with Ecuador, are located in territory that has long been contested by both countries. The dispute underlined the fact that Belaúnde's transcontinental highway project was challenging one of the basic tenets of South American history: undeveloped frontiers are the best guarantee of stable relations between neighboring countries.

Ever since the Iberian Conquest, South America has been plagued by numerous conflicts over unclearly defined borders. The Spaniards and Portuguese constantly tested the limits of each other's empires, in the Amazon basin and its periphery, and in the southeast corner of the continent where the territories of modern-day Brazil, Argentina, Paraguay and Uruguay converge.

Independence from Spain and Portugal in the nineteenth century created ten South American republics out of the two empires, and served to multiply these frontier disputes. Often, tacit understandings were reached not to develop frontier lands under contention. The links between South American nations were weakest along their mutual borders. The frontiers were zones where economic activity petered out, population became sparse and commerce was minimal, except for contraband. But sometimes, with the discovery of real or imagined sources of wealth in these hinterlands, wars erupted between neighboring countries, leaving legacies of distrust that have persisted to today.

All along its northwest-to-southeast axis across the interior of the continent, Belaúnde's imaginary highway crosses or runs near areas of frontier battles that have been fought during the last 120 years. In the upper Amazon basin (near the first stretch mapped out for Belaúnde's route), Colombia, Ecuador, Peru and Brazil have had several territorial disputes during the last century. Not far to the north of the next span of the highway, Brazilian forces took possession of Bolivia's rubber-rich province of Acre in 1902–03. Farther to the southeast, Belaúnde's proposed road cuts across the Chaco, where Bolivia and Paraguay lost a hundred thousand men in their 1932–35 war over this hot scrubland. Eastern Paraguay, where Belaúnde's mythical highway ends, was the main battleground of the bloodiest conflict in South American history—the war of 1864–70 in which Paraguay lost more than half its population and one fourth of its territory to the invading armies of Brazil, Argentina and Uruguay.

Belaúnde campaigned hard to dissolve this bitter heritage in the frontier lands. But neither regional conferences nor summit meetings with other South American presidents could overcome the political obstacles that his transcontinental highway project encountered almost immediately in neighboring countries.

The first of these political obstacles involved the initial segment of the highway. After slicing through the heart of Colombia, this section of the road was supposed to be bulldozed across the mountainous jungles that straddle the border between Peru and Ecuador. But the lengthy territorial dispute between these two countries proved as intractable as the terrain. In 1941, Peruvian troops had swept into these tropical forests and overwhelmed hapless Ecuadoran garrisons. A treaty signed a year later gave Peru possession of seventy-seven thousand square miles stretching eastward into the Amazon basin, an expanse the size of Kansas. Coming in the midst of World War II, the conflict drew little attention outside of South America.

But the Ecuadorans have never accepted this loss of about forty percent of their lands. To this day, their maps differ from any other maps of South America. Even Iquitos, far to the east, is marked down in their school textbooks as an Ecuadoran city.

While the prestige of being a larger nation has undoubtedly been the key factor in this protracted frontier dispute, oil has also played a major role. Throughout the 1920's and 1930's, many geologists speculated that the jungles east of the Andes, in a crescent that extended south through Colombia, Ecuador, Peru and Bolivia, were destined to become the world's third great petroleum realm after the Middle East and the Caribbean basin. Teams of surveyors discovered large beds of sedimentary formations more than twenty thousand feet below the surface that could conceivably contain hydrocarbons. But with plentiful, cheap and accessible supplies available elsewhere in the world, drilling so deeply into the remote Andean and Amazon regions seemed too expensive a venture, and excitement waned in the three decades that followed the 1941–42 war between Peru and Ecuador.

The steep rise in oil prices after 1973 renewed interest in the Amazon basin and its mountainous periphery. Thanks largely to the experience gained with helicopters in the Vietnam war, prospecting and drilling for oil became feasible even in the most isolated jungles. Using helicopters capable of ferrying heavy equipment and supplies deep into the Amazon rain forest, surveyors and engineers were able to establish base camps far away from the navigable rivers which had, until then, provided the only access to the interior. By the mid-1970's, Ecuador was pumping two hundred thousand barrels a day from new wells in its eastern jungles. A few years later, just across the border in the same terrain, Peru also began producing oil, though in smaller quantities.

In both countries, hopes over the potential wealth of the Amazon frontier lands soared again, reopening the old territorial dispute. In 1981, Peru and Ecuador waged a month-long, indecisive war. Because the landscape was so inaccessible to foot soldiers, the battles were mainly confined to bombing and strafing of supposed enemy emplacements, most of which turned out to be virgin jungle. Casualties on both sides probably did not exceed a few score before a truce was declared.

To visit the Peruvian oil fields in the disputed borderlands, I needed permission from both the Peruvian government and the Occidental Petroleum Corporation, the American company that was pumping most of the oil out of the Amazon jungle. But even before the 1981 war, journalists were not welcomed in the petroleum fields. Part of the reason was that the left-wing military government that held power between 1968 and 1980 had vastly inflated its estimates of an oil bonanza in the Amazon. Of the seventeen foreign companies that carried out surveys in the Peruvian rain forests during the 1970's, only Occidental uncovered commercial quantities of oil.

And "Oxy," which had constant skirmishes with the military government over profits and expenditures, wanted a low profile for its jungle ventures.

For years Oxy had turned down my requests to inspect its Amazon oil fields. So I was pleasantly surprised when I was informed in early 1982 that arrangements for my visit to the petroleum zone would be approved as soon as I met with Gerhard Jensen, Oxy's chief representative in Peru.

"I gave guys like you the brush-off for such a long time because a few lines of publicity weren't worth the risk of annoying the military government," said Jensen, a tall, lanky vice-president who supervises Oxy's Peruvian operations from his office in Lima. "All we had to do was keep a couple of generals happy. And I think we played our hand well. We survived the generals without becoming so identified with them that we couldn't get along with Belaúnde when he got back into office. We even helped Peru out in its war with Ecuador last year. We let the Peruvian Air Force use our airfields in the jungle. A few of our guys actually got decorated as war heroes."

Since 1971, Oxy had spent more than $700 million in its Peruvian Amazon operations, an investment that had been fully recovered by 1979. The company was producing an average of 105,000 barrels a day in 1982. Most of it was light oil. But some of the petroleum was so heavy that a bottled sample that Jensen had inverted on his desk had not dribbled down in three years.

Oxy pumped its oil into a five-hundred-mile-long pipeline which the Peruvian government had built in order also to transport its own petroleum from the jungles and over the Andes to a shipping terminal on the northern Pacific coast of the country. About thirty-five hundred foreigners and Peruvians worked in Oxy's twelve oil-producing sites on the border with Ecuador. The installations were connected by three hundred miles of roads, which the company had built mainly with equipment and supplies brought into the jungle by helicopter.

This network was both a source of astonishment and irritation for Belaúnde and supporters of his frontier vision. In a sense, Oxy's roads stood as a rebuke to the president's failure to press ahead with his own highway through those jungles. Up until then, the Amazon frontier had failed to attract significant numbers of Peruvian pioneers and had largely remained the province of foreign oilmen and technology.

Belaúnde toyed with the idea that perhaps the Oxy roads could be used to create agricultural and industrial communities in those distant jungles for the time when the oil operations inevitably would dwindle. It was a notion that Jensen and the other Oxy executives found annoying. One of the few advantages of their costly Amazon venture was its remoteness. There was no need to mount an expensive community relations program. Labor was more tractable in the isolation of the rain forest. It was the company's chain of command, not a local government, that ruled over a 3.8 million-acre block of jungle three times the size of Delaware. If pioneer communities were built, Oxy would almost inevitably have to share its airfields and river ports. Already the company was irked by the several thousand Peruvian squatters who had settled on the periphery of the oil region, peddling bootlegged liquor and prostitutes.

The day after my interview with Jensen, I showed up before dawn at Lima's international airport to catch a flight to Andoas, Oxy's jungle headquarters, about 670 miles north of the capital. Most of the oil company's American personnel worked twenty-eight consecutive twelve-hour days and then took twenty-eight days of vacation back in the United States. Many of the passengers gathered in the airport's waiting room were returning from their four-week respite, and some of them were obviously hung over from one last spree in Miami the night before.

Sitting next to me were two young, blond and bleary-eyed Oklahomans with scarred hands and indecipherable tattoos on their forearms. Our plane was an aging Russian Antonov, a twin-engine turboprop that was a relic from the days when the former left-wing military government had enjoyed better relations with the Soviets. I must have been looking at the aircraft uncertainly because one of the Oklahomans said to me, "Don't worry, they never let it fall on the way into Andoas 'cause they want your twenty-eight days."

When a loudspeaker invited passengers to board, everybody inexplicably dashed down the tarmac to the plane. The mystery was resolved as soon as I entered the craft: only a few seats had windows. For more than two hours, I sat in darkness, not once catching a glimpse of the skies or terrain below. Because the Antonov is built out of fiberglass, it vibrated so loudly that any conversation was impossible. When we landed, thick fumes of water vapor hissed from

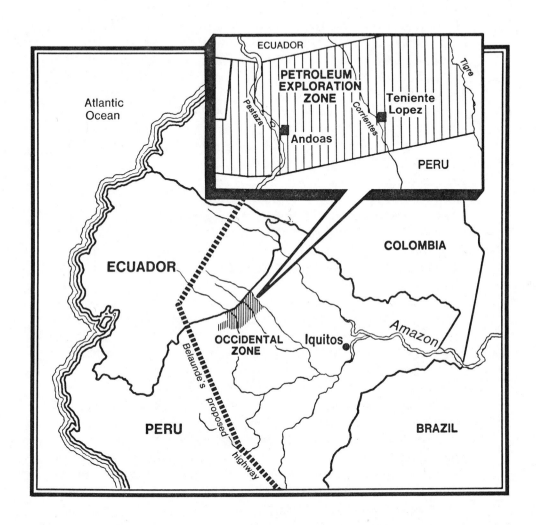

Atlantic
Ocean

ECUADOR

PETROLEUM
EXPLORATION
ZONE

Pastaza

Corrientes

Tigre

Teniente
Lopez

Andoas

PERU

COLOMBIA

ECUADOR

Amazon

OCCIDENTAL
ZONE

Iquitos

Belaunde's proposed highway

PERU

BRAZIL

the aircraft's ceiling, engulfing the cabin so completely that I was unable to see the passenger in front of me.

Andoas is situated on the edge of the coffee-colored Pastaza River, only a few miles south of the border with Ecuador. The terrain is highland jungle, row upon row of hilly rain forests drained by dozens of coiling streams and rivers that surrender their waters into the Amazon 220 miles to the east. At Andoas, the jungle has been pushed back to a distant periphery and is lighted up by yellow flares burning the gas that seeps up from the oil wells. The settlement and its airstrip are built on black sand dredged up from the bottom of the Pastaza River. The dark sand is so porous that it quickly absorbs even a torrential rainfall.

Andoas looks like an old-fashioned military camp. There are no women. The buildings are low-slung barracks of plywood and cinder block. The offices are so coldly air-conditioned that even the tropical heat is more comfortable. Outside, there is a steady cacophony of mechanized sounds. Jeeps, bulldozers and heavy trucks rumble through the base while helicopters whir overhead.

I was dropped off at the living quarters of Roy McDonald, superintendent of the entire jungle operation. It was a three-room, thatched-roof, cinder-block house with linoleum floors and equipped with a refrigerator, washing machine, dryer and stove—all electric. Boxes of American cereals and peanut butter jars were crammed into the pantry. The bookshelves were stacked mostly with cowboy novels. The big shortwave radio was tuned to the Voice of America.

McDonald, fifty-five years old, is a husky six-footer built like a former linebacker, with white, thinning hair and deep-set, pale eyes that seem to hide behind the lower rims of his metal-framed glasses. Tight-mouthed and unsmiling, he succeeds admirably at projecting the image of an austere, tough but fair-minded boss.

He was born and raised near the Oklahoma oil fields, and as a teenager he moved to California, again to the oil fields. Then it was on to Venezuela, Nigeria and Libya. He came up through the ranks as a laborer and foreman, without a formal engineering education or business administration degree, and he was proud of it. For the last four years, he has been in charge of Oxy's production in the rain forest. He spends ten straight days at the jungle base, and then ten more days back in Lima, where he lives with his wife and two children.

"I'm a dying breed in the oil business," he said, his fingers fidgeting nervously on his dining-room table as he tried once again to kick his cigarette habit. "The guys who end up as senior managers nowadays are all engineers or accountants or lawyers. I started at the bottom. I was a pusher at twenty-five—in charge of a well. That's good-paying but dangerous work. Almost everybody I know ends up missing a finger, a toe or worse. Anyway, there isn't anything I haven't done in an oil field. So when I ask one of my guys a question, he better come up with the right answer. No baloney about tools and parts missing, or how busy he was doing something else. If he doesn't come up with the right answers, he's going to have some very embarrassing moments, because I'm going to dress him down in front of a whole bunch of people. A lot of these guys are better off here than in the States. I guess you could call some of them social misfits. They never could stand the lack of discipline back in the States. Over here, though, they're real good. They're not going to raise hell here in the middle of no place. They put in their twelve hours a day, and there's not much time for anything else besides eating and sleeping."

At times, McDonald conceded, the routine of his job and the power that came with it made him ornery. The year before, during the brief war with Ecuador, a Peruvian major and his troops had descended on Oxy's camp and ordered that all lights and flares be shut down so as not to provide inviting targets for Ecuadoran bombers on night missions. In effect, the order would have brought oil production and pumping to a standstill. And McDonald, concerned over lost revenues for his company, refused to obey the major's command.

"I told him I wanted it in writing, and I wanted it from my own headquarters," said McDonald. "Hell, besides Oxy, Peru stood to lose millions of dollars a day in lost production and revenues. But in the end, some of my own people here talked me into giving in. Afterward, I got a medal from the Peruvian government. It was either that or face a court-martial for treason."

The man who talked McDonald into temporarily shutting down the oil operations is Oscar Zavala, his Peruvian-born second in command. "I think for a while he just lost sight of where he was," said Zavala, a low-key, elflike man with a mouthful of gold fillings. "I mean out here the only thing that counts is Oxy. You can easily forget you're in a foreign country. And suddenly, here we were in the middle of a war, and a military officer we never saw before comes storming into the base and takes over. Roy was bellowing that he was in charge and no one but his bosses were going to tell him what to do. I had to bring him around, reason with him a bit, remind him that he was the one who was always saying we're guests in a foreign country. Well, he came real close to getting put up in front of a firing squad. In the end, when he got his medal, he turned to me and said, 'Oscar, you saved my ass. You got me to do what had to be done, and you're the one who deserves this medal.' "

McDonald spends his time touring the score of installations connected by the extensive, dirt-road network that Oxy has built for its jungle fiefdom. Often this means driving 100 to 150 miles a day. Usually he visits supervisors who are encountering technical problems. But he also likes to drop in unannounced on isolated operations, just to monitor their performances.

I have rarely seen better maintained roads in the South American wilderness. The frequent rains make asphalting unfeasible. But an hour after a squall ends bulldozers skim the mud off the roads and smooth out the ruts. All heavy vehicles, some of them seventy-five-ton behemoths, are equipped with huge balloon tires. Their air pressure is so low and their surface area so great that they cause little damage to the fragile, dirt highways. In fact, the tires distribute a vehicle's weight so evenly that once a worker standing behind a heavy truck had his foot run over and suffered so more than a slight limp for a couple of days.

As extensive as the road network is, it does not lessen the isolated existence of most oil workers. McDonald is one of the few people who ever gets to visit more than one or two installations. Most employees are familiar with the Andoas base camp because it is their gateway into and out of the jungle. Otherwise, they confine their lives to their oil field and its nearby barracks, mess hall and recreation room, equipped with pool tables and a color television set showing tape-recorded American films, with Spanish subtitles for the Peruvian workers. The engineers and technicians, most of them foreigners, live in mobile units equipped with four beds. The laborers, most of them Peruvians, sleep in large dormitories. But everyone eats the same food—American and Peruvian dishes served cafeteria style and concocted from relatively fresh vegetables and frozen meats and fish flown in from Lima and Iquitos several times a week.

Accompanying McDonald on his daily route, I stopped off first at the largest oil-producing plot, not far from the outskirts of Andoas. It accounts for about half of Oxy's jungle output. The man in charge is Rick Langford, a thirty-three-year-old Louisianan who is tall, thick around the middle and has stringy hair and a reddish beard framing his boyish face. As senior production foreman, he supervises thirty-five people.

On most days, Langford gets up at five A.M. and checks the overnight production figures. When it is light enough, he tours the installations: first, the oil wells on a knoll that swells above the jungle floor, and then a labyrinth of colored pipes and pumps that reeks of combustion in a large clearing next to his plywood offices. The red pipes carry oil. Water that has been separated out of the petroleum flows through white pipes. And blue pipes carry gas. The gas is used to pump the oil out of the ground and into huge storage tanks. From there, the oil is pumped into the network that feeds into the pipeline that runs all the way to the Pacific coast. The gas that is not used to lift petroleum to the surface is flared off near the oil wells.

"Most of the problems involve the gas lift valves," said Langford. "The worst thing that can happen is that the gas will circulate in the well instead of in the casing around it so the oil won't lift to the surface. For some reason, the gas lift valves always seem to fail about two A.M., never in the daylight shift. So every once in a while, I'll get up in the middle of the night and make my rounds to make sure that nobody is sleeping on the job."

Some of the Oxy employees enjoy hunting in the jungle. But Langford dreads the rain forest and keeps to the roads and clearings. Only occasionally does his work take him more than a few hundred yards from his office, to a new well that is being drilled.

"It's one of the deeper ones," he said, as we walked around the drilling rig. "Eventually, we'll dig down to fourteen thousand feet. If all goes okay, you never see any oil or fluids at all. No gushers, like in the movies. That's a blowout, and you don't want that to happen. I was in a blowout once in the Gulf of Mexico. A few people died, and we had to call in an expert to cap the well. The key is to work up a rhythm. You connect three pieces of pipe into a section ninety-six or ninety-seven feet long, and you ram it into the hole and follow up immediately with another three pieces. That's called 'tripping in.' Then, every once in a while, you have to bring all the pipes out of the hole and change the drill bit. That's called 'tripping out.' "

Unlike most of the other oil employees, Langford is a college graduate. He had no money to continue his studies at law school, so he joined a small oil company owned by the Hunt family, the Texas billionaires.

"I started at the bottom, as a roustabout, painting and sweeping," he said. "Then I got a job on a drilling platform in the Gulf of Mexico. Then I moved to the North Sea off of Holland. And now I'm a senior production foreman. I don't work with my hands that much anymore. I'll do it when supervising gets boring, just so I don't lose the touch. I'm not overly ambitious. I don't live for my job. Eventually, I'd like to be production superintendent for a small- to medium-sized independent oil company. Someplace small enough to have direct contact with all the people under me."

Langford mentioned the two reasons most Oxy people give for agreeing to work in the jungles: the good salaries, which are made even more attractive because the company agrees to foot the bill for both American and Peruvian taxes and to pay every living expense incurred by employees in the rain forest; and a feeling that work in the jungles is more varied and interesting than a slot in an oil field back in the United States.

"There is a really low turnover among Americans here," said Langford. "We get all types. The whole spectrum from devout Christians to Attila the Hun. A lot of our drillers live up to the industry standard, if you catch my drift. I guess I fall into the devout Christian category. Basically, I do a lot of reading in my off time. I spend every other month in my hometown with my wife. There are only six thousand people living there, in northern Louisiana, and there's no way I could find work there. We have a small plane of our own, and we'll fly out to hunt and fish. We get involved in a lot of church activities. A real laid-back existence."

McDonald, who had been checking the production figures at Langford's installation, said it was time to move on. The next stop was a few miles down the road at an oil well that had a defective valve. Normally, wells erected on dry land are drilled vertically, straight down. But in the Peruvian jungle, the underground pools of oil tend to be too small and construction costs too large to merit dozens of individual wells. Instead, a well is dug vertically for the first thousand feet. Then, from this main stem, networks of pipe branch out diagonally downward until they each tap a pool of oil.

Thus what looks like a solitary well in a jungle clearing may, in fact, reach out to a half dozen underground reservoirs, some of them more than four miles away and another two to three miles beneath the surface.

The man who maintains this underground maze of well pipes is Jack Hager, a roly-poly, tobacco-chewing, middle-aged Texan with a baseball cap squeezed on his large head. He told McDonald that he was trying to locate a defective valve in one of the oil pipes a mile or two beneath the surface. His crew was manning what looked like a stripped-down bulldozer topped by a lengthy coil of wire and a motorized winch.

"We're tryin' to fish out the valve with this here wire line, and replace it with another one," he explained. "Damn thing is stuck thousands of feet below here someplace. I tell ya, it takes more than your ordinary guitar-picker to pluck it out."

Leaving Hager, we visited another oil well where a German chemical engineer, after weeks of experimenting, had discovered an emulsifier to rid the crude petroleum of some of its more troublesome impurities. Then McDonald met with his transportation chief to discuss a new fleet of pickup trucks, with an epidemiologist who was studying the camp's techniques for controlling malarial mosquitoes, with the production manager of a new well and, finally, with the young boss of a drilling crew who had recently been separated from his wife.

"Usual story, happens all the time," said McDonald, after offering his condolences to the man. "The guy spends half his life away from home, goes back to the States on his month off and his wife doesn't show up at the airport to meet him. He gets back home and finds the note telling him the she just couldn't take the loneliness anymore. Who you gonna blame? Maybe it would've worked out if he spent more time with her. Maybe not."

Parting company with McDonald, I hitchhiked on a company truck heading west about fifty miles to Teniente López, another large base camp in the Oxy fields. We looped up and down hills, along the red ribbon of highway in a green universe. For centuries, there was a widespread conviction that the South American jungles were almost entirely flat—probably because the earliest explorers journeyed through the wilderness along the Amazon River and its tributaries, where the terrain was, in fact, mainly level floodplains. But whenever I traveled in the rain forest by road, I rarely encountered long, flat stretches. The highways invariably dipped and bobbed and curved so much that it was hard to figure out the vehicle's direction.

Teniente López is smaller and less tidy than Andoas. Its barracks and staff quarters are flimsier and unpainted. Barrels and equipment are strewn about the camp. Only a hundred yards away, the Peruvian Air Force has carved out a base, and the roar of helicopters is deafening and constant.

In the cramped base-camp dining room, I lined up for food next to a short, bearded American whose plate was piled high with rice and vegetables. "Melton's the name, and I'm a vegetarian," he said by way of introduction. Looking at the grayish, rubbery filets, their sides curling upward, I decided to forgo the meat also.

Melton is a printer from California. His business went flat, so he signed up for a tour with Oxy to manage their huge tool and parts depot in Teniente López. He has always been a city person, and this is his first sojourn in the jungles. His awe of the veterans who have spent years in the wilderness is balanced by his sheer terror of the red-necks among them.

"I mean some of these guys are as crazy as anybody I've ever seen. They'd be put away in California. I've seen guys who are supposedly best friends get drunk and practically kill each other. Fists, beer cans, bottles, crowbars, anything they lay their hands on. And the next day, they're best of friends again, like nothing ever happened. I just smile at them a lot, agree with anything they say. They probably think I'm stupid. But I'm going to get out of here alive, all of me, nothing missing."

After dinner, Melton suggested we drive four miles over to a bulldozer depot run by an old-timer, a Texan named Jim, who mysteriously had a constant supply of cold beer. "Jesus, I just hope Lem isn't there," said Melton as he shifted gears. "He's the craziest one. If he shows up, look out for him. He seems calm one moment, and the next he's a bomb."

Jim is a slow-moving, big-bellied man about sixty years old, who seems to speak without actually moving his mouth. Catching only fragments of his words and phrases, I gathered he has spent more than thirty years in the South American frontier lands, working in mining camps, railway construction and oil fields. He has at least two wives, one in Texas and another in a ranch he owns in Colombia. And he lives with two peasant women here in his road maintenance depot. They call him *papito*—"daddy"—and hover over him, massaging his back, passing him cans of beer, scurrying to his quarters to run his bath. They apparently come from the squatters' settlement on the outskirts of Andoas, and I guessed *they* were the source of the bootlegged liquor.

We were soon joined by three other oilmen, including Lem, whose appearance caused Melton to stiffen momentarily. Lem is a tall, beanpole Texan with a mean, cadaverous face that is distended on one side by a huge lump of chewing tobacco. He is almost as old as Jim, and has worked with him in several other outposts in the South American interior. I remembered Langford's description of the various types of characters among his colleagues. And I quickly placed Lem in the Attila the Hun category.

With a full moon lighting up the depot's yard and the jungle beyond, we sat on the porch, drinking beer and swapping stories, much like I imagined a group of good ol' boys back in the American South. Taking my cue from the others, I balanced my chair on its two back legs and stuffed a wad of tobacco into my mouth. They took turns spitting out the juice five, ten, fifteen feet away. I drooled over my boots and finally removed the foul-tasting lump, surreptitiously dropped it off the porch and stuck to beer.

Lem, who was sitting next to me, started recounting his travels through South America. Trying to find common ground, I let him know that I had visited many of the same spots. But that seemed only to annoy him. I was perplexed that none of the places he mentioned even remotely matched my recollection of them. He misplaced rivers, confused countries and got the climates all wrong.

"Yeah, and I remember Yacuiba," Lem was saying about a tropical town in Bolivia. "Colder than a witch's tit. Why, it was so cold that when I woke up in the morning I had to punch my fist through a layer of ice over the water barrel just so's I could wash my face."

"But Yacuiba is hotter than this jungle," I blurted out. There was a stony silence. I felt Melton jab my side with an elbow. Working his jaw furiously, Lem glared down at me.

"I really don't believe you've ever been to Yacuiba, have you now?" he said. I heard a crackling, metallic sound. I looked down and saw a horribly crumpled beer can slip out of Lem's hand and bounce on the porch.

"Well, actually," I said, clearing my throat, "I just passed through it briefly. Didn't even stop because it was so cold."

The other good ol' boys mercifully guffawed. And taking advantage of the lull in the tension, Melton loudly suggested that it was getting late and we would have to drive back to Teniente López.

I woke up at dawn the next day. The sun evaporated the early-morning mist, gently unveiling the silver-gray oil storage tanks, the drilling rigs thrusting upward like skeletal Christmas trees and the dense rain forest just beyond the perimeters of Teniente López. I would be spending a couple of days in the jungle with a seismic surveying crew. This is the only part of the oil operations that McDonald never visits in his peripatetic daily journeys through the Oxy concession. The seismic crews are the real trailblazers in this wilderness. The other Oxy men, already chaffing at their own isolated existence, view the seismic surveyors as slightly insane. They spend their working lives deep in the rain forest with their Indian and peasant bearers, and almost never surface at the base camps, except when they are about to fly back home on vacation. Using explosives, sensitive geophysical equipment and portable computers, they map out geological formations far underground that might contain oil. It is on the basis of their surveys that Oxy decides whether or not to erect new drilling rigs and build new base camps.

I was given a brief letter of introduction for Jim Carlisle, the leader of the seismic crew. I walked over to the Peruvian Air Force base next to Teniente López and joined some Peruvian laborers aboard a helicopter that was about to fly into the jungle. The craft whirled its blades to an ear-splitting roar. The pilot, a Peruvian officer in a bright orange jumpsuit, flicked a dozen switches, gave a thumbs-up signal to his copilot and began to lift off. Suddenly, the workers seated around me started to shout and gesture toward a small, plump, tight-jeaned woman dashing toward the helicopter.

The pilot eased the craft back down on the ground. A door slid open and the woman, out of breath, vaulted in and wedged herself between the cheering passengers. The helicopter lifted upward again, tail first, and then spun away from the base and over the rain forest.

Since I was the only stranger aboard, she gingerly introduced herself as Rosa. She was from a squatter settlement across the river from Andoas. In spite of her heavy makeup and overpowering perfume, she could not have been older than sixteen. She was a camp follower, in the long tradition that had been established in the Peruvian Amazon frontier even before oil exploration had gotten underway. For decades, the military has ferried prostitutes by boat and plane to its most distant outposts with the venerable excuse of improving the morale of its soldiers. The petroleum boom has only increased business.

Rosa said she had been visiting the oil camps for two years and preferred to have a girl friend along. At first, I thought she meant for company, until it dawned on me that she would be facing about forty young men in her one or two nights in the jungle. There was not a trace of the hard-edged city prostitute about her. She spewed forth an incessant, exuberant adolescent banter. She showed off her new radio-cassette recorder to the other passengers, pinched and elbowed back the workers who poked at her, and bounced up and down until the copilot barked in annoyance.

Wisps of clouds and fog floated below licking the thick jungle canopy. The dark brown Corrientes River looped like an intestine as it slithered through the forest. We overtook a flock of macaws, their brilliant blue plumage and long tails fluttering like kites above the verdant landscape. As we started our descent after fifteen minutes of flight, the dense foliage pulled slightly apart and I could make out individual trees: first, the stately silk-cottons, with tall, massive trunks and branches that reached out horizontally above their neighbors' heads; then, the slightly shorter palms with crowns of great pinnate fronds; and, in between, thin, long, white-barked trees that seemed almost denuded of leaves.

The helicopter banked sharply left and glided toward a hilly clearing. On the ground, a group of workers covered their ears and turned away to avoid the dust and wood splinters churned up by whipping blades. I jumped out first and was pleasantly surprised by a chorus of cheers, until I realized they were welcoming Rosa, who had stepped out behind me. A collective groan erupted as she got back on board after being told that this wasn't her stop, and the helicopter took off again. I walked up to the laborers, all of them young and swarthy, and explained I was trying to locate Jim Carlisle. A man said Jim and his seismic crew were not far away and that he would guide me to them.

His name was Fernando, and he spoke Spanish with a squeaky Indian accent. Barely five feet tall, he was clad only in shorts and knee-length rubber boots. In a smooth, loping gait, he started down a ravine along a narrow path that had been hacked through the underbrush. After a few steps, it seemed as if we had entered a huge, airy cavern. The voices and bright sunlight of the clearing gave way to semidarkness and a silence only occasionally punctured by the muffled shrieks of monkeys and parrots and the sharp cracking of branches. Thick vines wrapped tightly around tree trunks and dangled like tentacles from the upper reaches. Ferns as big as elephant ears bent over their thin stems. Giant cypresses were balanced aloft by their gnarled roots, which rose several feet above the ground like powerful stilts. Even fallen logs, dappled with green and russet and pastel-hued lichens, seemed alive.

After a hundred yards, Fernando looked back at me stumbling over tree stumps and bushes and sinking knee-deep into mud, and slowed his pace. I thought I was in good shape because I had been jogging three miles a day. But nothing had prepared me for the obstacle course I was now trying to negotiate. As soon as we would reach the bottom of a ravine, there would be another steep hill to climb. I gasped for breath in the moist heat, and my glasses fogged up and then washed over with perspiration. Fernando chuckled and repeatedly offered a hand as I staggered along the trail. "Try to walk in the footsteps you see ahead of you," he suggested. "That's it. Heel first, not flat-footed."

His instructions helped enormously. But I found I had to concentrate so completely on where I was stepping that I became oblivious to anything further than a few feet ahead. "Can't see the forest for the trees," I kept repeating to myself like an imbecile, giggling at the suddenly meaningful revelation. Fernando stopped short and held me back as I was about to wade through a thick column of black ants. They marched like a legion, hundreds of thousands, maybe millions of them, transporting their eggs to a new nest. They were so large, more than an inch long, and so numerous, that they made a clearly audible rustling sound across the leafy jungle floor. It took ten minutes for the column to pass, and only after the last of the stragglers disappeared into the bush did we trudge on.

It was all becoming a blur as I stared at my right foot and then my left, searching out the footprints ahead of me. We had hiked only about two miles, but I was near collapse when we came upon the seismic crew. They were gathered under a crude lean-to made of a green plastic tarp hung over branches and wooden staves. The seismic equipment—recorders, computers, printout machines and audio devices—was placed on a waist-high table of thin logs. The effect was of a weird band of musicians playing its electronic instruments for an unseen audience. Gulping for air, I was so fatigued that I could only stammer, "Got a letter ... for Jim Carlisle ... from headquarters."

Carlisle, a small, wiry Londoner dressed in blue shorts, a tattered T-shirt and baseball cap, arched his eyebrows over the unexpected visit. "A letter for me? Dear man, you really shouldn't have troubled yourself."

I tried to laugh, but wheezed instead. He looked over the message, nodded and motioned me over to a metal chest that I could use as a seat. "Not the jungle type, eh? We'd offer you some beer, but we don't carry any. There's a small stream over there."

Some pack carriers were lolling in the water, using their helmets to douse themselves. I took one look at the muddy pool alive with water bugs and decided I wasn't that thirsty after all. I went back to the metal chest and let my pulse and breathing return to normal while I tried to figure out what the seismic crew was doing.

The operation seemed simple enough. Some days before, machete-wielding trailblazers had chopped perfectly straight north-south and east-west paths through the jungle in a grid pattern. They then drilled 80-foot-deep holes spaced exactly 440 feet apart, and placed a seven-pound explosive charge in each hole.

Carlisle and his two assistants, Gil Young, a twenty-one-year-old redhead from Indiana, and Edwin Zamora, a thirty-six-year-old Peruvian electronics engineer with copper-toned Oriental looks, set off the charges and measure the seismic waves caused by the explosions. The refractions of the waves, down to a depth of thirty thousand feet, are registered on magnetic tapes and printed out in graph form after each explosion. The tapes and charts are sent off to Lima for preliminary analysis, and then fed into computers back at Occidental's offices in Bakersfield, California.

Here in the jungle, the Indian and peasant pack carriers in the seismic crew are strung out in small groups near the site of each explosive charge. The seismic equipment is so sensitive that the slightest sound—a footfall, voices, a helicopter or airplane overhead, a jaguar or tapir running through the undergrowth or even a strong wind—could distort the readings on the graphs. So before every explosion, Carlisle, Young and Zamora cry out for silence. *"Quietos! Quietos!"* they yell. And all along the path, the pack carriers answer back in a chorus, *"Quietos!"* I wondered what that column of ants might have done to the graphs.

The ground shook as the explosions drew nearer. The closest charges rattled my teeth and sprayed us with geysers of mud.

"If you look closely, you'll see some small portions on the graphs that are a bit less even than the rest," said Carlisle, holding up one of the printouts made during an explosion. "It means they could contain domes or pools deep underground that might indicate oil deposits. But I certainly can't predict anything from these raw graphs. For one thing, the terrain around here is so hilly that we have to wait for the computer analysis in Bakersfield to factor out the distortions. And even then, it's all very chancy."

It is hard, monotonous work. The crew—Carlisle, Young, Zamora, and about forty pack carriers—spend two or three nights at a makeshift base camp on a razed hilltop. They set out into the jungle shortly after sunrise and return in the late afternoon, without a lunch break. The Indian bearers—straining under eighty-pound packs harnessed to their backs and heads—cover about five miles a day, stopping three or four times to set up the equipment and record the explosions. Once an area is seismically charted, the men and supplies are relocated in several helicopter sorties to another nearby hilltop camp, and the operation begins again.

The pack carriers are recruited by labor contractors in Iquitos, the Amazon river port about 220 miles east. They are paid $120 a month for seven-day weeks, and their schedule calls for ninety straight workdays and nine days' vacation back in Iquitos. Most of them are short—between five feet and five feet six inches. But they have the thighs and shoulders of fullbacks. The turnover rate is high: as many as one third quit, most often during the first month of work, because they cannot withstand the heavy loads. Those who remain on the job are remarkable physical specimens.

Carrying nothing but a notebook and pen, I still straggled far behind these bearers. They deftly tiptoed across thin log bridges while I lost my balance and tumbled into mudholes and water pools. My stamina abandoned me completely at the foot of the last hill leading back to the base camp. I just collapsed into a nearby stream. Forgetting my fear of dysentery, I gulped down the muddy water and let it wash over me. As I lay in the brook slowly reviving, I heard shouting and whistling from the base camp on the hilltop. I dragged myself out of the water and climbed the last several hundred yards on my hands and knees. At the flat summit, I discovered the source of the commotion. About half the pack carriers had shed their eighty-pound loads to play soccer. Most of the rest were lined up outside a makeshift barracks waiting their turns for a few minutes with Rosa, who had arrived by helicopter while we were still in the jungle. It was only two hours later, as the sun started to set, that they stopped the match and the lovemaking and followed Rosa as she ran to the stream to cool down and bathe.

I hadn't eaten all day and I was famished. The beef was tough and overcooked, so I readily accepted a slab of monkey meat that many of the Indian bearers seemed to prefer. As it was being grilled, I spied the pile of eviscerated, skinned money carcasses. "I never tried the stuff myself," confessed Carlisle. "They look a bit too human lying there on their stomachs." I had to agree. But I still went back for seconds. The meat was not too stringy, and with onions and lemon, it had a pleasantly tangy beeflike taste.

The jungle surged to life as the sun began to fade. From our hilltop, the forest undulated into greens, grays and purples out to the horizon. Red-and-yellow-and-blue macaws fluttered clumsily, squawking loudly as they strained to reach the treetops. Luminous blue-and-violet birds darted far more gracefully between the highest branches. Monkeys shrieked, first in scattered voices, and then crescendoed in loud unison to the roar of a football stadium, before dying down to feeble cries and repeating the cycle. The sky turned yellow and then flaming orange and red as the sun slid behind the most distant western hills.

How incredible that one moment these jungles seem so infernal, and the next, almost lyrically beautiful. The rain forest is the mythical setting of so much literature to come out of South America. It has usually fared better in books by foreigners, seeking here a magical reprieve from dull, tawdry urban life. The English naturalist and novelist W. H. Hudson in his *Green Mansions* described the jungles as a Garden of Eden, swarming with lustrous butterflies and rainbow-hued flowers.

South American writers, perhaps reflecting the prejudices of the Iberian descendants who sought to recreate European civilization in the cities and coastal plains of the New World, have tended to view their continent's tropical interior as the ultimate parable of evil. People relinquish their humanity when they enter this dreaded green hell. Typical of this bleak vision is the novel *The Vortex,* by the great Colombian writer José Eustasio Rivera.

"Where is the solitude poets sing of? Where are those butterflies like translucent flowers, the magic birds, those singing streams? Poor fantasies of those who know only domesticated retreats!" he wrote in a stinging rebuke to Hudson's idyll. "No cooing nightingales here, no Versaillan gardens or sentimental vistas! Instead the croaking of dropsical frogs, the tangled misanthropic undergrowth, the stagnant backwaters and swamps.... At night, unknown voices, phantasmagoric lights, funereal silences. It is death that passes, giving life.... Warning whistles, dying wails, beasts belching. And when dawn showers its tragic glory over the jungles, the clamor of survivors begins again.... This sadistic and virgin jungle casts premonitions of coming danger over one's spirits.... Our senses confuse their tasks; the eye feels, the back sees, the nose explores, the legs calculate, and the blood cries out: 'Flee! Flee!' "

I retired along with Carlisle, Young and Zamora to a lean-to about a hundred yards away from the pack carriers' crowded barracks. Our flimsy shelter consisted of an overhead tarp shielding the sun and rain from light mattresses held several feet above the ground by crude wooden pegs. Each bed had a mosquito net tethered like a semitransparent veil above the mattresses.

Carlisle tuned his shortwave radio to the BBC, which was describing the cold wave and snow blanketing London and the English countryside. "Who needs that kind of life?" he said. "I've spent the last forty-five days in the jungle, and it's my kind of climate. Last time I was in England was two Christmases ago, and I'm not planning to go back anytime soon."

Carlisle is about forty, with thinning black hair and a sharply jutting chin. He spent nine years in the British Army as a communications and electronics expert, and for the last decade he has worked on seismic surveys for petroleum companies in the Sudan, Indonesia and several South American countries.

Like many of his colleagues, he is a loner. He is friendly and droll, and generous when it comes to sharing food, giving advice, shouldering a work load. Perhaps out of necessity, he seems to have a knack for getting along with almost anybody. But his dreams are those of a very self-sufficient man. There is no woman waiting for him back home. His friends, mostly other seismic surveyors, are scattered around the globe in isolated, inhospitable terrains like the Borneo jungles and the sweltering bogs of the southern Sudan. Vacations will not bring them together, only the vagaries of their profession. After a decade of tax-free income and minimal personal

expenses, Carlisle has stashed away a hefty bundle of savings—mostly liquid assets and some mining stocks. A few more years, he said, and he will retire to a house he will build on an island off southern Thailand. He will read, walk the beaches, drink and listen to the BBC to reassure himself that life is not getting any better in old England and the rest of the industrialized world.

Gil Young, the Hoosier with an unruly scalp of red hair that looks as if it has been plugged into a light socket, is in the jungles for adventure. His high school diploma probably would not have landed him anything more than a factory job back home. He has been in the rain forest for ten months and plans to stay another year or two. Then he will return to the States, enroll at an engineering college on a company scholarship and maybe marry his Indiana high school sweetheart.

Well over six feet tall, he towers over the Peruvian pack carriers. He suspects they are overly amused by his gawkiness, his freckled skin that turns lobster-red after a few minutes of exposure to the sun and his hopelessly mangled Spanish. "I bought a cassette and I play it almost every night, but I just can't hack a foreign language," he complained. "Every time I open my mouth those guys start laughing."

"Folks back home have some weird ideas about the jungle," he said. "They think there are snakes slithering between our feet, wild Indians, man-eating tigers. Hell, New York and Chicago and any American city are a lot more dangerous than this. I was just up in Miami on vacation, and a black kid whacked me in the face with a two-by-four and stole all my money. I still have this black eye and my nose is broken. Nothing like that ever happened to me here."

He keeps up with the hit parade on the shortwave radio and strains to hear the sports scores. He was reading a novel set mostly in the Brazilian Amazon. The jungle scenes did not ring true to him, but he was certain that the ribald descriptions of Rio and the carnival season were realistic. "Of course, I've never been there, but it sounds real exotic," he said.

Zamora, the Peruvian, is the only real engineer of the three. He spent eight years studying electronics on scholarship at a Budapest university. He married a Hungarian woman and learned the language. His commitment to the jungle is purely financial. He misses the time away from his family in Lima, but figures he can earn at least twice as much money in the rain forest. The years in Budapest, and traveling around Western Europe and Scandinavia, were evidently the best times of his life. He can describe in faultless detail the façade of a church in Bratislava or a boat journey down the Danube. We talked for hours about politics and history and literature.

He extolled the relative prosperity and relaxed political atmosphere he remembered in Hungary, but offered only derision for the other Eastern European countries he visited, and sounded more approving about Scandinavia and West Germany. He despaired about the economic situation in Peru under any sort of political system, and seemed to prefer working for an American company rather than a Peruvian firm. He exuded warmth and sympathy for the pack carriers, and whenever they approached him, he found time to listen to their small talk and complaints, without a hint of the usual castelike paternalism.

Zamora got up and suggested we walk over to the pack carriers' barracks. "Come on, you'll enjoy the conversations and music," he said, grabbing a flashlight to lead the way through the darkness. A campfire was burning brightly outside the barracks, and one of the men was playing a lively tropical serenade on his harmonica. "You can tell from the melody that he isn't from the highlands," observed Zamora. "There is none of the sadness or plaintiveness of the Andes in the music."

We had got only halfway to the barracks when I felt a large insect clinging to my neck, and I instinctively slapped it away. Zamora shined his flashlight on the ground, and a large spider scurried under a rock.

"Damned lucky!" he blurted out. "Damned lucky!"

It hadn't bitten me. But I was quivering. The gruesome hotel scene in Iquitos so long ago flashed before me. We walked back to our lean-to, and I tried to strike a cool, aloof pose as Zamora told Carlisle and Young about the spider. But my nervousness was apparent when I started remaking the sheets on my mattress.

"Yes, by all means, old boy, do check out all the corners," joked Carlisle. "Those creatures have a knack for hiding themselves, and we don't seem to have brought along any spider antidotes."

I forced a laugh. But I also checked under the mattress. I slept fitfully and investigated the bedding and mosquito net several times during the night.

When I awoke, the sun was already well above the horizon. Carlisle, Young and Zamora were eating oatmeal gruel as they pored over the seismic charts for the day's trek into the jungle. My limbs felt too stiff to withstand another five-mile foray, so I told them I would be heading back to the main oil camp in Andoas, which now had the aura of a civilized metropolis in my mind.

"Who knows, we might meet again in the Sudan or Asia," suggested Carlisle. I thanked them all for their hospitality, and waved as they made their way down the hillside leading a column of groaning pack carriers into the rain forest.

Besides myself, five workers and Rosa remained behind, waiting for a helicopter. Rosa was listless, obviously exhausted, her face pale and less sharply etched without its makeup. She sat on her haunches, cradling her large radio and smiling weakly in response to the jokes of the other youths.

The helicopter would be making several stops at the clearing to ferry supplies over to another makeshift camp a few miles away, where the seismic crew would spend the next few nights. We waited until midmorning before the craft was ready to pick us up for the flight back to Andoas. In the meantime, I stripped off my shirt, thinking that I would work on my tan. But the sun was so strong that my feet started to burn in my rubber boots. So I joined Rosa and the pack carriers in the shade of their barracks.

I struck up a conversation with Fernando, who had guided me through the jungles the day before. He and his companions had just completed their ninety-day work stints and would be flying back to Iquitos for a nine-day vacation as soon as they reached the main oil camp. Fernando is twenty-two years old, and this is his second hitch in the rain forest. Still a bachelor, he said that he hoped to save enough money after a few more years to start a small grocery with his older brothers on the outskirts of Iquitos. But he is afraid he will not be able to withstand the crushing work load much longer. His arms and thighs ripple with muscles completely out of proportion to his short, dark brown frame. For several months, though, he has suffered through bouts of dysentery which have only been partially alleviated by medicines he received at the oil camp clinic. He has decided to visit a *curandero,* a folk healer, during his vacation, at the suggestion of his father, a full-blooded Cocama Indian. Intrigued, I asked if I might accompany him to the rendezvous with the *curandero,* and Fernando readily agreed.

5

The skies were heavily overcast on the morning Fernando and I flew out of Oxy's camp to Iquitos toward the east. The plane was another Russian Antonov. Unlike the one that had brought me from Lima to the oil fields, this was a cargo plane. Virtually all the passengers were unskilled workers and pack carriers on home leave. There were no seats, only two long canvas benches bolted down on either side of the cargo hold. Instead of safety belts, there were overhead cables. Everybody grabbed them tightly as soon as the plane started to taxi down the runway.

It was a frightening flight. For almost an hour, the Antonov seesawed through a thick, leaden cloud layer. Some of the more inexperienced passengers used a one-armed grip on the overhead cable and crossed themselves furiously with their free hands. I myself preferred holding on with both hands. A few workers succumbed to nausea and vomited. Others relieved their tension by whooping loudly as if they were riding a roller coaster. One passenger lost his grip on a cable and stumbled backward down the hold until a friend caught him by the waist with a leg scissors.

Below us, the city of Iquitos and its surrounding jungles looked as gray as the sky. The plane touched down with a loud whack, and cheering broke out among the passengers. The door swung open, and we trotted a quarter mile to the terminal building through a lashing tropical rain.

I gave Fernando a lift in my taxi to the suburban slum where his family lived. The car stopped at the periphery of his neighborhood of mostly wooden shacks because the rains had whipped the unpaved streets into an impassable bog. Fernando agreed to meet me the following afternoon at my hotel in time to make the rendezvous with the folk healer.

The rains relented only in the morning of the next day. While waiting for Fernando, I read a book written twenty years before by Belaúnde. Called *Peru's Own Conquest*, it recapitulated the three previous attempts to settle the continental interior—led by the conquistadores, the missionaries and the rubber traders—and called for yet a fourth drive into the frontier lands, behind the wedge of the Marginal Highway of the Jungle. In the book, Belaúnde also recounted a visit he made to Iquitos in the early 1960's. He promised to restore the Amazon port to its rubber-era splendor by someday building a road that would connect it to his vaunted highway. But neither the highway nor its spur to Iquitos was ever constructed, and talk of an overland route leading out of this Amazon port had ceased.

Belaúnde was especially taken by the floating market and boathouses of Belén, in the corner of Iquitos's harbor where the Itaya River flows into the Amazon. He described Belén as "a primitive Venice without palaces. . . . It has a grand canal with many subsidiary branches, and its captivating beauty inspires artists to paint and poets to write. A sense of welcome, gaiety and optimism in the midst of poverty reigns in this aquatic community."

"Belén is one of the most genial human condensations in Peru, and even the best of artists would have trouble faithfully capturing the highlights and shadows of this picturesque port, where the tranquil waters duplicate its spectrum of colors and enhance its savage beauty," he wrote.

It was from Belén that Fernando and I hired a small motorized canoe to the folk healer's lodge. There were few traces of the "primitive Venice" that Belaúnde had found here two decades earlier. Thousands of vultures blackened the thatched rooftops of the floating boathouses as they waited their turns to scavenge among the mounds of garbage that had been dumped down the palisades to the river's edge.

Fernando and I elbowed our way through the crowds, noise and smoke of the market, past mosquito-infested stands of herbs, tubers, roots, prickly fruits, meat strips and armor-plated catfish wrapped in banana leaves. The putrid, rancid smells were suffocating.

We boarded the canoe and puttered way from Belén and the Amazon, heading up the Itaya River in a southwesterly direction.

The river was cluttered with branches, logs and other debris. The stench of raw sewage and garbage from the port abated after a few hundred yards. The current was so swift that the boat strained to make any headway.

Fernando explained that he had prepared for the session with the healer by eliminating salt, sweets and meat from his diet during the previous few days. The healer, whose name was Don Ramón, had known Fernando's father for many years. They were both originally from a small village farther down the Amazon. Like many of the villagers, Fernando's parents had moved to Iquitos almost two decades before in search of jobs. Don Ramón had followed several years later and was now a neighbor of Fernando's family. For isolation from the noise and bustle of the city, the healer kept a hut on the bank of the Itaya a few miles from Iquitos, and held his sessions there two or three times a week.

Fernando had been to Don Ramón once before, as a teenager, and claimed to have been cured of painful, recurring headaches. On that occasion, he had been given *ayahuasca*, a hallucinogen brewed from the woody vine Banisteriopsis, which is used in magical healing and religious ceremonies throughout the upper Amazon basin. Under the healer's guidance, Fernando said he discovered in a vision that his unhappy romance with a young girl in Iquitos was at the root of his headaches. The girl's father had ordered her to break off the relationship and paid a witch doctor—an evil folk healer—to cast a spell over Fernando.

"In my vision, I saw the father and his daughter and the witch doctor," said Fernando. "I had visited the girl's home, and I was served a soup that the witch doctor had prepared. The father argued with me over dinner and demanded that I stop seeing his daughter. She would not see me afterward, and a few days later my headaches started."

According to Fernando, once he realized what had happened, he was able with Don Ramón's help to purge the poison from his body and exorcise the evil spell. "The headaches never came back," he asserted.

Fernando was uncertain whether *ayahuasca* or other drugs would be used by the healer this time. It might depend, he said, on what had brought on his dysentery, whether it was induced by the ill will of another person or had natural causes.

Toward dusk, our canoe pulled alongside a sandbar in front of a small cluster of thatched-roof huts. The healer's lodge was about a hundred yards farther inland, at the end of a footpath cut through the jungle. It was set on thick wooden staves and open on two sides. Two blackened pots hung over a small fire on one side of the hut. There were other people inside when we arrived. Four of them— two men, a young girl and an older woman—were evidently patients and looked sicker than Fernando. The only one Fernando knew was a very fat shopkeeper, who was doubled over by a backache and grimacing with pain. A thin, younger man, with a pockmarked face, had a deep hacking cough. The two women sat listlessly against a wooden post that held up one side of the roof.

Nearest to the fire was the healer, Don Ramón. He was short and very old, perhaps about eighty, though it was hard to tell at first because his hair was jet-black, his body still sinewy and his bearing ramrod straight. His wrinkled face was fixed in an impassive smile. He was dressed in grease-stained khaki pants and a gray, long-sleeved linen shirt. By Don Ramón's side was his assistant, a man in his mid-thirties with a dark brown oval face and the downcast gaze of a deferential acolyte.

Fernando introduced me to Don Ramón and explained that I wanted to take part in the ceremonies even though I was not ill. The healer looked at me uncertainly, murmured some questions to Fernando and, finally, after a few minutes of discussion, turned to me with a broad smile that revealed several missing teeth. "You are welcome," he said in a choppy Spanish. "You will stay to the end."

Don Ramón had apparently already talked to his other patients before our arrival. He now took Fernando aside and asked him about his illness. I tried to listen to the conversation, but it was carried out in whispered tones. Don Ramón walked over to the fire and stirred the simmering pots. His assistant handed him a large rattle made of leathery brown leaves tied together at their base. The healer shook the rattle over the pots, while whistling and singing unmelodic, indecipherable incantations partly in Spanish, partly in an Indian dialect. He then instructed his assistant to remove the pots and let them cool.

Fernando told me that *ayahuasca* would be used in the ceremony. I had tried it twice before, during trips to Pucallpa, a Peruvian jungle city far to the south. There had been no healer or witch doctor present on those occasions, only some local businessmen and tourists I had befriended. The *ayahuasca*—the word comes from the

Quechua dialect spoken by the Incas and means "vine of the spirits"—had not been too strong. I remembered losing track of time and having a few lapses of consciousness, hallucinations that distorted the faces of my companions and the proportions of my surroundings. But I had never felt any sense of panic, or loss of psychological control. There was only a briefly discomforting nausea, which was more than compensated by a sharply heightened perception of colors, sounds and smells, and then a pleasant giddiness that lasted for several hours. So I was looking forward to *ayahuasca* again, and curious about trying it under a healer's guidance.

Don Ramón lighted up a fat, long cigar that he had rolled himself. He scooped out a large cup of warm liquid from one of the pots, blew smoke over it and handed it to the shopkeeper with the aching back. As the man drank the brew, Don Ramón rustled his rattle, whistled, chanted and whispered encouragement. The healer filled the cup again and repeated the ceremony for every visitor. When my turn came, I looked at the brown liquid a bit apprehensively. It smelled like bitter tea.

"Drink it, drink it all," Don Ramón whispered between whistles and chants. I sipped it tentatively, then gulped it down as Don Ramón and Fernando nodded at me. It had an acrid, oily taste and made my stomach growl.

Don Ramón was the last to drink the brew, downing it quickly with a burp. We sat without saying a word, listening to Don Ramón repeating his monotonous, slow-tempoed chants with his eyes closed. It was dark outside, the moon barely visible in the overcast, starless skies. About forty minutes had passed when the healer began to shake his rattle more firmly. He opened his eyes wide and began to whistle a different, faster melody. "Mother of the spirit, mother of the herb—she is coming, she is coming," he chanted over and over again.

I looked at Fernando. He was rocking on his haunches, his eyes staring distantly. The other visitors also seemed in a trance. I felt my heart beating wildly. My chest heaved as I gasped repeatedly for air, and I was sweating profusely. Overcome by nausea, I crawled to the open edge of the hut and vomited violently. The drug was far stronger than any I had taken before. I completely lost my sense of balance. I couldn't tell which direction was up or down. My eyes would not focus. Bright reds, purples, greens and blues flashed before me. The room expanded and contracted like a huge lung. I could hear the chanting of Don Ramón and the voices of the other people, but I couldn't seem to turn my head enough to bring them into my warped field of vision.

When the pulsating colors subsided, I stared out into the jungle. I felt I was being catapulted back and forth, back and forth, between the hut and the forest. One moment I was among the trees, brushing against the leaves, watching with fascination as the vines slithered like boas along the trunks. And the next instant I was flattened by an enormous gravitational force to the floor of the hut, barely able to lift my head and peer at the jungle, which seemed more than a hundred yards away. With great effort, I finally managed to turn around and find the other people. No matter how hard I tried to crawl toward them, I could not get closer because the floor angled upward. I called out to Fernando and Don Ramón, but no sound came out of my mouth, except a dry gasp. I was an unseen, far-off spectator.

Tapping his feet with great vigor and agility, Don Ramón was still chanting and shaking his rattle. His face contorted, and his head and arms took the shape of several animals in quick succession—a grunting tapir, a howling monkey and most often a snarling jaguar—while the rest of his body remained human. I squeezed my eyes shut and held my arms tightly around my knees. I rolled around the wooden floor, and when I stopped and opened my eyes, I was near Fernando, who was lying flat on his back.

Don Ramón chanted over him and blew cigar smoke at his stomach. Placing his mouth on Fernando's stomach, the healer sucked so hard that the flat belly was distended upward. Don Ramón, his cheeks bloated, pulled away from Fernando and drooled in the fire. The spittle turned into a long, thin snake that writhed and hissed as it burned to a crisp. Fernando lay so still I thought he was dead. His diaphragm did not move and his eyes were half-closed and unblinking. On my hands and knees I scampered backward in fright away from the others to the edge of the hut.

Don Ramón was kneeling over the shopkeeper, blowing smoke and sucking on the small of his back. The man clenched and opened his hands spasmodically until the healer rose and walked over to the fire. This time he spat thorns into the embers, using his fingers to remove a spine that had wedged between his teeth.

Having attended to all his patients, Don Ramón looked at me with a stony face for several minutes. He opened his mouth, but his voice sounded disembodied, as if it were emanating from loud-speakers on either side of me. There were gaps in his sentences, and I heard only disconnected phrases echoing around the room: "You want, want, want . . . lie still, still, still . . . where is, is, is . . . will come back, back, back."

He turned away and left the hut with his assistant. I saw them walking along the path toward the river and stared at them with relief until they disappeared, hoping they would not soon return. There was complete silence, interspersed with a high-pitched buzz. The patients looked dazed, but relaxed. Fernando and several others did not move, but I could see their chests rise and fall as they breathed. I seemed to be the only one in acute discomfort. The room's proportions still changed unexpectedly, lengthening and shortening, tilting up and down. Concentrating carefully, I managed to take regular, deep breaths, and my heartbeat slowed to its normal rhythm.

Everybody else claimed to be feeling better. The portly shop-keeper asserted it was the first time in a week that he had been able to straighten his back, and stretched out his heavy arms and neck to prove it. The pockmarked youth, who said he was a fisherman, was coughing less, but still looked frail enough to be suffering from consumption. I could not make out what illnesses the two women had. One of them was a teenager with a high-pitched voice who sounded cheerfully incoherent and rambled on about visions of flying above the jungle and river. The other patient, a square-jawed, middle-aged woman with large calloused hands, was a laborer at a flour mill and said she had been too tired and feverish to work during the last two weeks. Propping himself up on his elbows, Fernando announced that the pain in his stomach had disappeared.

I was feeling more relaxed, even lighthearted, probably because I was relieved that the drug had worn off. I told Fernando about my nightmarish visions. He and the others laughed as they recalled that I had scampered away from them and refused to join their circle. I protested that I had, in fact, been trying desperately to sit next to them, but the room had tilted so sharply that I almost fell out of the hut. They roared with laughter.

The shopkeeper said that on occasion he had also seen a healer metamorphose into different animals. "You can't fight the visions or fear them because it only makes matters worse," he said. "You have to let yourself be pulled along, without resistance. And you need Don Ramón to explain, to guide, to comfort." I asked him if he had seen Don Ramón pull out thorns from his back and spit them into the fire.

"Even though my back was turned away from him, I saw it all," he asserted. "It was as if I were hovering above myself, looking at Don Ramón removing the thorns from my body. In my vision, I saw that someone had stuck the thorns in me. I don't know who did it or why. But it was someone who has wished me ill for a long time."

After an hour or so, Don Ramón and his silent assistant returned to the lodge. The healer announced that the ceremony would go on and that we would be given another cup of *ayahuasca*. The whistling, chanting and tobacco smoke resumed. But when my turn came to drink, I declined. Don Ramón was not insistent and simply passed the cup to the next person. I glanced at my watch. It was almost two A.M. I was drowsy and very tired, and I fell soundly asleep at the edge of the hut before the others began to react to the drug again.

We awoke shortly before dawn. I had a dry, bitter taste in my mouth and a slight headache. Don Ramón had stepped outside. The bleary-eyed guests began to drop money into a small straw basket by the embers. I asked Fernando how much I should give, and he suggested fifteen hundred soles—about three dollars. We all walked to the river where a large dugout canoe with an outboard motor was waiting for us. We bid good-bye to the healer and waved at him as the boat, piloted by Don Ramón's tight-mouthed assistant, nosed away from the shore. The sun was barely over the horizon, but the river was already congested with boats of every size and shape laden with fish and produce on their way to the Belén port and market.

I asked Fernando if he had discovered the source of his illness. He said he was uncertain and would return in a couple of days for another session. Under the drug's influence, he had dreamed that a huge snake had forced its way down his mouth and into his stomach and intestines while he slept one night in the jungles. He was miserable working with the seismic crews, he said. The packs were too heavy to carry. He missed his family, and he hated the rain forest. Maybe, he suggested, his sickness had natural causes, by which he meant that spirits in the jungle had sensed his unhappiness and were trying to drive him away.

I never saw Fernando again. But I suspect that Don Ramón eventually advised him to get out of the jungles and find a job closer to home, and that his illness then miraculously disappeared.

Back in Iquitos, I napped most of the morning and woke up in the late afternoon still a bit dazed from the *ayahuasca*. I walked over to the towering "tropical Gothic" cathedral on the main plaza to seek out a Spanish clergyman, Father Joaquín García, who had been pointed out to me as an expert on the Indians and their rituals. A handsome, dark-haired, soft-spoken Augustinian priest of middling height, he had spent fifteen of his forty-two years in Iquitos. He was a scholar of the region's history, manager of an ample library and publisher of a magazine on the Amazon.

"In a town like this," said Father García, "it is difficult to know where Indian culture breaks off and Spanish culture begins. There are witch doctors and healers. People believe that the spirits of the dead linger around them for years. Traces of Indian customs survive and are transformed. Take the example of *la ispa*—the old tradition of drinking the urine of a newborn baby to celebrate its birth. They substitute liquor now. Then there is the *yacucheo,* a second baptismal ceremony to scare away evil spirits when an infant is one or two years of age. And people still dance and sing in front of a child getting his first haircut—the *lanta tipina* ceremony. But these are all just traces. Pure Indian culture was stamped out in Iquitos many years ago. Outside of a few neighborhoods, you won't even hear Indian dialects spoken. The younger people refuse to speak them at all. Deep in the jungles, some tribes still remain. And there are a few tourist lodges up the Amazon River where Indians are paid to dress up in native costumes and dance and sing for visitors."

The demise of the Indians and their culture, which began with the appearance of the Iberian conquistadores four hundred years ago, took its most brutal form during the heyday of the rubber era at the turn of the century. The rubber trade was an unmitigated disaster for the Amazon natives. They were pressed into slave-labor gangs to gather latex from trees in the remote rain forest. Ravaged by disease and severely underfed, they died in droves. Attempts to escape were punished by flogging and execution. The rubber traders, tiring of their own slave-hunting forays, learned that they could bribe rival tribes with liquor and guns to round up their enemies and sell them to the rubber estates.

In a recent issue of his magazine, Father García had published a scathing interview with the German director Werner Herzog, who had brought a crew to Iquitos to film the story of Fitzcarrald, a rubber baron who operated in the jungle around Iquitos during the late nineteenth century. The priest took Herzog to task for portraying

Fitzcarrald as an eccentric romantic whose greatest ambition was to build an opera house in Iquitos.

"Fitzcarrald was a craven killer," said Father García. "He massacred hundreds of Indians who refused to gather rubber for him. Back then, the Indians were considered no better than animals. They had no protectors, not even the church."

Rummaging through Father García's library, I came across an account written in 1897 by a priest, Father Gabriel Sala, who had been commissioned by the Peruvian president to investigate the rubber-growing regions south of Iquitos and report on the status of the Indians and whites living there. The priest was a guest of Fitzcarrald's aboard the rubber baron's river steamboat and was evidently deeply impressed by his host and his splendid vessel.

"Everything was so clean, elegant and orderly that we had nothing to envy from even the best of the European steamers," he wrote. "A half hour before dinner, we were invited for a drink, and when we approached the dining table after a second ring of a bell, we were struck by both admiration and satisfaction at the luxury of it all, as well as by the good service and the varied and exquisite delicacies and liquor."

Clearly seduced by Fitzcarrald, Father Sala saw that a fortuitous alliance might be forged between the church and the rubber barons.

> Through terror and moderate punishment, [the Indians] will feel obliged to throw themselves at the mercy of the missionary father, and he in turn will be able, with great charity and prudence, to exercise his divine ministrations on those unfortunate creatures. . . . Once a rubber boss has subjugated the ferocious Indian at gunpoint, the time will be opportune for the missionary father to immediately step in and offer him the services and consolations of our Holy Religion. . . . By colonizing the lands [of the Indians], surrounding and absorbing them, we can obligate them either by force or shame to accept the customs of civilized people.

Among the Peruvian rubber barons, no man achieved more grotesque notoriety for the mistreatment of Indians than did Julio Cesar Arana, a contemporary of Fitzcarrald. Born in the mountainous jungles southwest of Iquitos, Arana began his career as a barefoot peddler of Panama hats throughout the upper Amazon basin, where Peru, Colombia and Brazil join together. He soon expanded his line of wares and became an important supplier of food, merchandise and credit to rubber bosses north of the Putumayo River, a zone about two hundred miles north of Iquitos that was then claimed by both Peru and Colombia. Using loans he had extended to rubber traders as leverage, he forced them to pay off their debts by turning over their jungle estates to him. Eventually, Arana owned an expanse of rubber-rich rain forest in the Putumayo region as large as Belgium. And in the first two decades of this century, he was the undisputed political and economic czar of a vast Peruvian territory, including Iquitos and its giant province of Loreto, all the way to the contested borders with Colombia.

Seeking capital for his growing empire, Arana registered his rubber enterprise as a British company in London and issued stocks there. His method of keeping labor costs to a minimum was hideously simple: his labor foremen enslaved the Indians, worked them until they dropped dead of exhaustion, illness and starvation, and then scoured the jungles for new slaves. Many of the foremen were British subjects, blacks from Barbados, whose earnings were based on a percentage of the rubber loads they could extract from their Indian gangs.

Stories of the brutal treatment of the Indians began to surface in Peruvian articles in the early 1900's, but they were ignored by the government. Finally, an account written by an American engineer who had stumbled into Arana's rubber camps while exploring the region was published in a British magazine and caused an uproar in Parliament. Because Arana's company was registered in Britain and had hired Barbadian foremen, the British government commissioned an investigation headed by Roger Casement, its consul general in Rio de Janeiro, Brazil.

Casement had already distinguished himself for an earlier probe into cruelties of the rubber trade in the African Congo. He visited Arana's operations in the Putumayo, interviewed Indian laborers and Barbadian foremen and, in December 1910, he delivered a report that confirmed the worst charges of atrocities.

According to Casement's investigation, Arana's agents descended on Indian villages, ransacked and burned them and carried off all able-bodied natives in chains. Indian children, too young to work, were killed in front of their parents, either by drowning or by having their skulls smashed against trees. Women were routinely raped and given over as prostitutes to the foremen. The Indian laborers were kept in stocks overnight after milking the rubber trees for latex from the early-morning hours until dusk. Weakened by malnutrition, they easily succumbed to white men's diseases like smallpox and influenza. Whiplashings were so common that almost every Indian interviewed by Casement bore permanent scars. The beatings were meted out most often when a laborer failed to match his daily quota of latex. Many died under the whip and their corpses were fed to the dogs. Others survived in agony for days or weeks, their flayed skins infested with maggots and bloated with infections. Witnesses reported that fugitives, most of whom were recaptured, were beaten and burned to death as gruesome warnings to their colleagues.

By conservative estimates, about half of the thirty thousand Indians in the Putumayo region died in Arana's camps, victims of disease and maltreatment. A Peruvian government investigation that followed Casement's probe backed his findings and uncovered even more abuses.

In Britain, the scandal that erupted in the wake of Casement's report led to the withdrawal of British participation in Arana's rubber venture. But in a bitterly ironical turnabout, Arana fared much better than Casement. Even without British stockholders, he was able to continue his rubber operations. In the jungles, the Peruvian was far too politically and financially powerful to be brought to justice. He denied all the charges against him and asserted that Casement was a paid agent of the Colombian government, which was pressing territorial claims to the Putumayo region under Arana's control. Mobs loyal to Arana demonstrated in the streets of Iquitos until a judge agreed to quash an indictment against him, and a few years later, the rubber baron won election as senator from his province, thus making himself even less vulnerable to prosecution.

Meanwhile, Casement was arrested in England as a German agent. In 1916, he was tried, convicted of high treason and sentenced to be executed. Diaries found in his possession indicated that he was a homosexual, and entries in his private journals even detailed his liaisons with some of Arana's foremen, whose testimony he had used against the Peruvian rubber baron.

A gleeful and cynical Arana dashed off a cablegram to Casement, who waited in a London prison for his trial and hanging:

> Am informed you will be tried for High Treason on 26th June. Want of time unables me to write you asking you to be fully just confessing before the human tribunal your guilts only known by Divine Justice regarding your dealings in the Putumayo busi-

ness.... You tried by all means to appear a humanizer in order to obtain titles fortune, not caring for the consequences of your calumnies and defamation against Peru and myself doing me enormous damage. I pardon you, but it is necessary that you should be just and declare now fully and truly all the true facts that nobody knows better than yourself.*

It was only the disastrous decline in rubber prices after World War I, with the emerging supremacy of the Asian plantations, that finally brought the downfall of Arana and the rest of the Amazon rubber barons. Arana lost his vast jungle estates in 1935 when the Peruvian government upheld the terms of a treaty turning over the disputed Putumayo region to the Colombians. And some years later, the notorious rubber baron died almost penniless.

To this day, however, Arana is hailed as a hero in Iquitos for his role in the rubber boom that brought this jungle capital to its economic high tide, and for his staunch defense of Peru's frontier lands against the claims of the country's neighbors. The overwhelming evidence of his crimes against the Indians is dismissed as foreign-inspired slander.

* Quoted in *The Amazon: The Story of a Great River* by Robin Furneaux. London: Hamish Hamilton, 1919.

6

rana left no lasting monuments. What remains of his legacy—
the heritage of the Amazon's rubber era—I would have to discover in the neighboring jungles of Brazil. And before I could
even begin to trace the present remnants of this legacy, I would have
to flesh out the brief, turbulent history of the Amazon rubber trade
in Brazil.

It was Brazil that provided by far the largest stage for the South
American rubber saga. For all his notoriety, Arana was a relatively
small character in this drama. Perhaps he played the most malevo-
lent role, but it was a minor one nonetheless. How could it have
been otherwise? More than half of the 2.7 million square miles of
the Amazon basin lies in Brazilian territory. Brazil spawned the
most prevalent and valuable variety of rubber tree, Hevea brasil-
iensis. The country's rain forests accounted for seventy percent of
latex production in the heyday of South America's rubber boom before World War I. And most of the rest of the smoked latex—from
Peru and Bolivia—had to be shipped down the Amazon River
across Brazil in order to reach markets in the United States and Europe.

Manaus, a Brazilian Amazon port, became the great entrepôt of
the rubber trade. Located fourteen hundred winding miles down the
Amazon River from Iquitos, it was far more important and imposing than the Peruvian city. Before rubber, Manaus was just a tawdry
jungle town of a few thousand souls. But by the turn of this century,
its population had swelled to seventy-five thousand, and, for a city
that size, it flaunted more luxury than Paris. With the advent of
steamships in the late 1800's, travel time over the eight hundred
miles that separated Manaus from the Atlantic was reduced to less

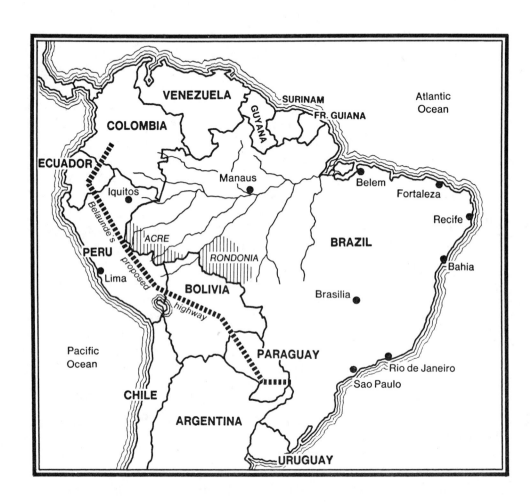

than a week, instead of the six to twelve weeks it took the old wind-jammers to ply the Amazon River against the current. The Brazilian government declared Manaus a federal port of entry, with its own customhouse, and welcomed ocean liners and freighters that carried rubber directly from this jungle outpost to the docks of the eastern United States and Europe. It was a profitable two-way journey for the ships because Manaus became a world market for wine and food delicacies, haute couture and precious stones, furniture and lavish construction material.

The city was adorned with granite and marble government buildings and private villas, some of them twenty- and thirty-room mansions designed like the huge sugar plantation houses on Brazil's Atlantic coast. Manaus boasted electricity, piped water supplies, a sewage system and tram service that were the envy of Brazil. There were public gardens, a library and museum. But the crowning jewel, the ultimate symbol of the extravagance of the Amazon rubber era, was the opera house. Like the boom towns of the American Old West, it provided an improbable setting for theatrical and opera companies from Europe. But the Manaus opera house was in a distinctly higher category than the wooden "cow palaces" of California, Montana and Texas. Its dome of imported European tile cast the silhouette of a sumptuous Istanbul mosque. Italian paintings graced its lobby, and Venetian chandeliers hung from its ceiling. Velvet-sheathed mahogany chairs could seat an audience of two thousand silk-bedecked patrons scraping their diamonds as they applauded a performance of *Tosca* or *Madame Butterfly*.

At the very pinnacle of this glittering jungle society were the king-makers of the rubber trade, the heads of the large import-export establishments. Usually Europeans representing big financial houses in London and Paris, they advanced credit and supplies to the owners of rubber estates deep in the Amazon rain forest in exchange for the smoked, coagulated latex which was then shipped abroad for processing into finished rubber products. The rubber-estate owners, who visited Manaus only once or twice a year, in turn advanced credit and supplies to the rubber tappers, who lived as virtual serfs in remote estates which they never left.

The whole rubber commerce was thus built on credit. But it was a grotesquely unequal system with risks and burdens that grew as the organizational ladder reached its base. The owners of the import-export houses might complain that all supplies had to be shipped from the Brazilian coast and Europe at prices three and four times higher than they fetched in New York. But they managed to maintain their European aristocratic life-style in Manaus. The rubber-estate owners bemoaned the isolation of the wilderness. But they thought it their right to profit twice from their tappers, obliging them to accept a low price for the rubber they gathered and a vastly inflated price for the foodstuffs and supplies which they could buy only at the rubber estate's general store.

At the bottom of the ladder were the lowly tappers, the *seringueiros.* In their vast majority, they came from the impoverished northeast of Brazil, particularly the state of Ceará. During the periods of drought when the northeast was swept with famine, the agents of the rubber estates would recruit the half-starved peasants who huddled in the slums of the Atlantic coastal cities waiting desperately for any jobs. Even before arriving in the rubber estates thousands of miles from their hometowns, the new tappers had already piled up debts for their passages and supplies. There was no need to pay them money because the rubber they collected rarely exceeded in value the prices for goods they acquired from the estate owner's store.

Their status fell somewhere between the Indian tappers of Peru and the indentured servants who came to the American colonies from Britain in the period before independence. The Brazilian tappers were not subjected to the wholesale torture and massacres that befell the Indians who were pressed into slavery in the Peruvian rubber estates. But while indentured laborers in North America— who accepted their servitude to repay their passage across the ocean or in lieu of prison terms—usually regained their freedom after five to seven years, the Brazilian rubber tapper was likely to remain for life in a jungle estate, prevented from leaving because he sank ever deeper into debt.

For these tappers from the northeast, Manaus was only a mirage, a sparkling apparition that loomed beyond the Amazon harbor where they were herded from their Atlantic steamship to a smaller flat-bottom boat which could navigate the shallower tributaries. The last leg of their one-way voyages was made by canoe to the clearings where the rubber-estate owner built his house and general store. There were no highways in the entire Amazon. The only roads in the rubber estates where the footpaths, or *estradas,* that guided the tapper to his rubber trees and circled back to his shack.

The great Brazilian writer Euclydes da Cunha, who visited the Amazon rubber estates in the early part of this century and was appalled by the constantly growing indebtedness of the work force, coined a cruel phrase that has haunted the tapper for decades: "A man who labors to enslave himself."

Da Cunha drew a telling distinction between the treatment accorded to European immigrants who settled in Brazil's Atlantic coastal states and to the miserable northeast peasants who flocked to the Amazon. "While an Italian colonist transplants himself from Genoa to the remotest ranch of São Paulo, paternally assisted by our public authorities," wrote Da Cunha, "the man from Ceará makes a more difficult journey at his own expense and altogether bereft of aid. . . . [These] exiles had the sole and painful mission of disappearing from the face of the earth."

According to Da Cunha, it was politically convenient for the government to disperse the multitude of disgruntled, jobless northeast peasants into the deepest recesses of the Amazon, to send them to isolated rubber estates where their protests would never be heard. But instead of simply disappearing, these peasants-turned-tappers populated the farthest reaches of the jungles and claimed for Brazil huge expanses of contested land that brought the country to its present geographical limits. They crossed into Bolivia's Acre province, a territory the size of Georgia that was the richest rubber zone of the Amazon, and soon overwhelmed the sparse Bolivian population. In the war of 1902–03, a conflict ignited by the Brazilian rubber tappers, Brazil then wrested control of Acre from Bolivia and became an even more dominant force in the world rubber market.

But the victory brought no special benefits to the tappers. Their meager pay continued to lag far behind their debts. The Brazilian government spent none of its millions of dollars in rubber tax revenues to improve the primitive, disease-ridden backwaters where the tappers dwelled. No attempt was ever made to drain the malaria-infested jungle estates, or to subsidize crops and cattle ranches that might have lowered the crushingly heavy prices that the rubber workers had to pay for food. No research was undertaken to determine whether rubber plantations could replace the widely spaced, wild rubber trees, or to supplant the crude, arduous process by which the tappers coagulated their latex over smoky fires with more scientific, manageable techniques.

Instead, the government was absorbed with grandiose geopolitical visions. Brazil already controlled much of the Amazon River and most of its navigable tributaries, and so the bulk of the rubber commerce. To this fluvial network it now sought to add railway and telegraph links that would further impose the country's predominance over the neglected heart of South America and draw an even greater portion of the continent's trade through the Brazilian interior.

Between 1907 and 1915, the so-called Strategic Telegraph Line was strung 835 miles through virgin rain forest and savanna. It ran from Cuiabá in the giant state of Mato Grosso, at that time the edge of Brazilian civilization, westward to the outskirts of Pôrto Velho, the capital of the present-day state of Rondônia, which was then a rubber zone. Before the telegraph, Brazilian businessmen back in Rio de Janeiro, São Paulo and Belém had to wait several weeks or even months to communicate with the rubber-rich Amazon. The telegraph was able to inform them within hours, a couple of days at most, about the movement of boats and rubber shipments in the heart of the jungles.

At almost precisely the same time, between 1908 and 1912, a railway, called the Madeira-Mamoré, was built connecting the Bolivian border with Pôrto Velho 228 miles to the north, and from there permitting access by ship along a tributary into the Amazon River down to the Atlantic Ocean. Like the telegraph line, the railway's main economic impulse was rubber. In return for the rubber lands of Acre that it had won from Bolivia in the 1902–03 war, Brazil agreed to construct the railway. It would circumvent a series of nineteen dangerous rapids and falls on the Mamoré and Madeira rivers as they flowed from Bolivia into Brazil and then into the Amazon waterway. For landlocked Bolivia, the Madeira-Mamoré represented a lifeline to world trade. Until then, Bolivia's only other outlet for external commerce was a railway line from its Andean mines and cities to Chilean ports on the Pacific Ocean.

Both the Madeira-Mamoré Railway and the Strategic Telegraph Line were hailed in Brazil and abroad as magnificent technological achievements that would unlock a new El Dorado in the Amazon, perhaps all the way to the edge of the Peruvian and Bolivian Andes. Theodore Roosevelt, who led a hunting and exploratory expedition through the Brazilian Amazon on the eve of World War I after leaving the White House, compared the two projects to the Panama Canal, which he considered the crowning achievement of his presidency.

In terms of lives and investment, the Madeira-Mamoré was indeed comparable to the Panama Canal. The Brazilian government contracted out the construction work to a leading American railway engineering company which at its peak employed five thousand men—Americans, Germans, Italians, Arabs, Barbadians, English, Portuguese and Brazilians. Cutting a path through the dense jungle took on the average six times as long as chopping down trees in the North American forests. At sundown, the base camps were ravaged by clouds of mosquitoes, while at night the workers' bedding was invaded by armies of fierce red fire ants. Occasionally, there were Indian attacks. But the worst threat was malaria, afflicting more than half the labor force at any one time.

In Pôrto Velho, the northern terminus of the Madeira-Mamoré, I once met an elderly man, Orlando Evangelista, who had worked during the railway's construction as an assistant to his father, a cook for the labor crews. Father and son had come to Pôrto Velho in 1910 from their native state of Ceará on the northeast Atlantic coast of Brazil. It took me a moment to grasp the enormity of the distance they had traveled. The month-long journey, made entirely by boat westward up the Amazon River and then southward up its tributary, the Madeira, covered as many miles as separate Boston from San Diego. Orlando Evangelista stayed on at Pôrto Velho after the Madeira-Mamoré was completed, first as a railroad station clerk for several decades, then as a grocer and part-time farmer. When we talked he was eighty-two years old, with snowy wisps of hair, faded eyes deeply set in an ocher, heavily creased face and the bent back and gnarled fingers of advanced arthritis. But his memories of the railroad crusade more than six decades before were still vivid:

> Never did men perform more hellish work. They were brought from far away, and none of them knew what they were getting into. My father and I probably had the easiest jobs—we cooked for the Brazilian crews—if you can call that easy. Sometimes weeks would go by before we got fresh supplies, and we would have only dried fish and manioc to cook. But it was the construction crews that got the worst of it. They would come back to camp bitten raw. Their hands were so swollen they couldn't make a fist, and they were bleeding even through their calluses. At night, it was impossible to sleep with the mosquitoes—the small ones could get through any net. Everybody had malaria. I got it six times in two years, and many more times years later. But God forbid you got so sick you

had to be sent to the hospital. You were more likely to catch some other disease there than to be cured. There was drinking and fighting all the time. A lot of people died that way also. Sometimes the company didn't have the money to pay salaries on time, and there would be uprisings among the workers. Many times people wanted to leave—usually as soon as they got here and saw what the jungle was about. But there was no way to leave quickly. Who was going to pay the boat out of here? Who was going to give them the money to live on while they waited for a boat to take them away? So they stayed, for a year or two, and if they didn't die, most of them left for good. How many must have died! They say that the Madeira-Mamoré cost a life for every railway tie and I can believe it.

Evangelista's death estimate was far too high. But as many as six thousand men did, in fact, perish during the railroad's constructon. It was a pointless sacrifice. Only a few years after its completion, the railway was rendered obsolete. The rise of cheap Asian rubber brought a swift collapse in the Amazon trade, and made the Madeira-Mamoré an uneconomical enterprise by 1913, its second year of operation. It continued its weekly runs for almost six more decades as a money-losing, government-subsidized venture carrying relatively few passengers and mostly contraband cargo between Bolivia and Brazil. In 1971, it was finally abandoned. Almost no trace of the railway remains today. Its tracks have been virtually reclaimed by the rain forest. Two ancient locomotives draped in jungle foliage lie outside Pôrto Velho as rarely visited museum relics.

The Strategic Telegraph Line met a similar fate. With the advent of radiotelegraphy in the early 1920's, the telegraph line was reduced to obsolescence less than a decade after its completion. In 1938, Claude Lévi-Strauss, the French anthropologist who followed the telegraph line while doing research on Brazilian Indians in the western Amazon, described it in these terms:

> Nobody quite dared to shut the line down; but nobody thought of using it, either. The poles were left to tumble down, the wire to go rusty; as for the last survivors of the staff, they had neither the courage nor the means to leave [the telegraph stations]; and so, slowly, one after another, eaten away by sickness, hunger, and solitude, they were dying off. . . . As has often happened in the history of Brazil, a handful of adventurers, madmen, and starvelings had swept into the interior on an impulse of high enthusiasm, only to be abandoned, forgotten, and cut off from all contact with civilization. Each little

"station" consisted of a group of straw huts, fifty or seventy-five miles from its nearest neighbor—a distance which could in any case be covered only on foot—their isolation was complete, and each individual wretch had to adapt himself to it by devising his own particular brand of insanity. . . . The tale is retold, with grim humor, of the missionaries who were massacred in 1933, or the telegraphist who was found buried up to his waist, with his chest riddled with arrows and his automatic sender perched on his head. For the Indians have a morbid fascination for the servants of the line.

Like the Madeira-Mamoré Railway, virtually no physical traces remain today of the Strategic Telegraph Line either. But as a legacy, it did leave behind a path and a legend. The path was the primitive route traced by the telegraph line, 835 miles long and about 120 feet in width—wide enough to prevent the line from being damaged by falling trees. The path was rarely used, except by ox-drawn carts that supplied the telegraph stations. But many years later, in the late 1960's, a road was bulldozed into the western Brazilian Amazon frontier roughly following the telegraph's axis and often taking advantage of the path it had cleared.

The legend that grew out of the telegraph belonged to Colonel—later Marshal—Cândido Mariano da Silva Rondon, the army officer who headed the commission that built the line. He was a taciturn, almost mystical man, short and narrow-shouldered, with a dark complexion and piercing gaze that strongly hinted at his part-Indian ancestry. He was modern Brazil's greatest explorer. For many of his compatriots, he embodied the best qualities of the seventeenth- and eighteenth-century *bandeirantes,* the adventurers whose continuous expeditions into the wild backlands in search of fortune expanded the country's domains almost to its present continental limits. Besides leading the telegraph teams through virgin savanna and rain forest, Rondon mapped out unknown stretches of the gigantic state of Mato Grosso in the center of Brazil and plunged forward into other Amazon regions farther north and west. On one of his expeditions, he was accompanied by Teddy Roosevelt, who hailed him as a trailblazer and frontiersman in the American western mold.

But Rondon was motivated by more humane and progressive notions than either the *bandeirantes,* who amassed their wealth by enslaving Indians, or the American frontiersmen, whose heroic reputation often rested on killing Indians. Rondon was well aware that his Strategic Telegraph Line was supposed to chiefly benefit the rubber barons. But he envisioned the project as the spearhead for a new Brazilian frontier society that would draw vast numbers of settlers from the established eastern coastal regions into a peaceful coexistence with the Amazon Indian tribes, who would be integrated into the national mainstream. Even while he directed the Strategic Telegraph Line Commission, Rondon founded the Indian Protection Service. In fact, at times the two organizations seemed to merge. The telegraph stations often served as Indian posts and were sometimes manned by Indians, despite attacks from hostile tribes.

When Rondon penetrated the rain forests of the western Brazilian Amazon, he found that bands of rubber tappers who had preceded him were intent on expelling Indians from lands where rubber trees proliferated. Rondon graphically described the massacre of one tribe he encountered in 1911 while laying telegraph line in what was later to become Rondônia:

> Many of [the Indian villages] had been destroyed by fire; the plantations and the barns had been sacked and robbed; the women kidnapped and raped; the children had been stolen and carried away; sickness hitherto unknown had appeared and was causing a mortality never before seen. In fact, the tribe, which at the moment of entry into relations with the rubber tappers was at six hundred in number, could now scarcely muster more than sixty.

Rondon remarked that he found tribes whose members were so accustomed to the violence of the rubber tappers that they flinched in the presence of any white man:

> This gesture or tic consists in a quick and wide oscillating movement of the body as would be made by an individual attacked by an enemy who was endeavoring to sight him in order to strike him a death blow; and in order to elude the aim [he] bobs incessantly from one side to the other.... [The Indians] act in this way on all occasions when they get into the presence of a civilized man; their attitude is always that of men who are awaiting a sudden and treacherous blow.

Rondon developed the techniques still used by Indian agents today to contact Amazon tribes who never before dealt peacefuly with white men. He laid simple gifts—a machete, pots and pans, small mirrors, a long length of rope—in a clearing where Indians had been sighted. Each day the offerings were placed closer to the base camp where Rondon and his men were temporarily located.

When the Indians first stepped out of the shadows of the forest, Rondon would fearlessly and gently greet them, communicating as best he could by gestures, rudimentary sign language, tension-relieving laughter or songs.

Rondon would occasionally emerge from his lengthy sojourns in the Amazon to give accounts of his work in lectures delivered to admirers at Rio de Janeiro's baroquely ornate Phoenix Theater. For the most part, these speeches were bland but informative. Only when Rondon spoke of the Indians did he give his audience a glimpse of his emotional side, his personal courage and intuitive insights into Indian behavior.

"Close to me many Indians sat," recounted Rondon about his first contacts with the Nambiquara, then a feared tribe in western Mato Grosso. "In order to give them a further proof of confidence, I stretched myself out on my bed of leaves, resting my head on the knee of one of them. I did not err in doing this, for the fellow was so content at having been chosen for this sign of affection and abandonment that he took the greatest care to avoid the slightest movement that might be taken as a sign of uneasiness or of fatigue. . . . I went off to sleep and did not awake until daybreak. My uncle, a true representative of the old prejudices of our people with regard to the Indians, kept awake during the entire night."

During his long tenure as head of the Indian Protection Service, Rondon managed to enforce his slogan, "Die if need be, but never kill." In the first five decades of this century, there were no reported slayings of Indians by Rondon's agents, even when they themselves were wounded or killed by hostile tribes. Indians were guaranteed protection within their own territory, and were assured equal citizenship rights with other Brazilians, wherever tribes came under Rondon's jurisdiction.

Rondon died at the age of ninety-two in 1958. He had been promoted to the rank of marshal for his jungle exploits, and shortly before his death the western chunk of Mato Grosso—an expanse of rain forest as large as West Germany—was renamed the Federal Territory of Rondônia in his honor. Nowadays, anthropologists tend to view his ideas on the Indians as outmoded, paternalistic and hopelessly optimistic about the speed and ease with which Amazon tribes could be peacefully integrated into Brazilian society.

But for all their shortcomings, Rondon's policies seem to have produced a brief golden age by comparison to what came before and what followed. Only a decade after his death, the Indian Protection

Service which he had created was accused of wholesale atrocities against its wards. In a five-thousand-page report issued in 1968, a government investigative committee charged that the Protection Service had collaborated with land speculators in the massacre of entire Amazon tribes. Witnesses gave testimony of the machine-gunning and bombing of Indian villages from the air and ground, the use of poisoned candy to kill infants, the deliberate spreading of epidemics among tribes through gifts of blankets and clothing infected with smallpox virus, the enforced prostitution of surviving Indian women—all in an effort to clear whole territories of the Indians and steal their lands.

At the end of the investigation, more than half of the seven hundred employees of the Indian Protection Service were dismissed and many of them charged with homicide and complicity to murder. The Protection Service was abolished and replaced by the National Indian Foundation. FUNAI, as this new organization is known by its Brazilian acronym, has never been accused of large-scale corruption or atrocities. But it has barely a fraction of the power and prestige that Rondon was able to exercise on behalf of his Indian trustees in the early decades of this century.

Claudio Villas Boas, who along with his brother, Orlando, gained fame in Brazilian anthropology after being drawn into work with the Indians by a personal appeal from Rondon decades ago, once gave this double-edged assessment of his mentor to a French journalist, Lucien Bodard:

> I even ask myself if Rondon understood everything. Wasn't he duped too? He ended his long and noble life in 1958, covered in glory, without realizing that all his work on behalf of the Indians had been turned against them. He had given them land: it was the signature of their death sentence.... Poor, proud Rondon. He showed that it was easy for whites to seduce the Indians with gifts and fair words.... Once the Indians were tamed by a man of noble spirit, they were then defenseless in the face of the adventurers who arrived hotfoot after him. These hordes did what they wanted with the Indians, which usually meant killing them.... Rondon and his lieutenants, when they pacified the Indians, assumed terrible responsibilities without knowing it. They were in fact delivering their charges to evil.

Of course, Rondon, with his unbounded energy and confidence, saw no essential contradiction between the welfare of Indians and whites. His solution was to hold a tight reign over both the organization designed to protect and tutor the aboriginal tribes and the Strategic Telegraph Line that was supposed to lead the penetration of Brazil's vast western wilderness by non-Indian society. He undoubtedly believed that other men of enormous talent and good faith would succeed him. But Rondon's optimistic vision was never put to a strenuous test in his lifetime. With the collapse of the rubber boom by 1920, the migration of whites into the western Amazon sank to a low point and the Indians gained a temporary reprieve. If Rondon was bitterly disappointed at the quick obsolescence of the Strategic Telegraph Line he had spent so many years constructing, he never so indicated in public speeches or his writings. In any case, during his last decades he took greatest pride in his efforts to aid the Indians.

Both the Strategic Telegraph Line and the Madeira-Mamoré Railway were projects of immense cost, imagination and technological prowess carried out primarily to accommodate what was viewed in Brazil as an endlessly growing bonanza of rubber. The myriad uses of rubber were still in their infancy at the beginning of this century. The mass assembly of motor vehicles was just getting started, and the automobile industry's appetite for rubber tires was voracious. Factories and homes were daily discovering new ways to adapt rubber products for insulation and waterproofing.

But with hindsight, it seems incredible that the Brazilians and other South Americans made no attempt to modernize the primitive methods by which rubber was collected. Indeed, they studiously ignored efforts elsewhere in the world to produce natural rubber more efficiently. These efforts got underway decades before the Strategic Telegraph Line and the Madeira-Mamoré Railway were conceived, and doomed these great pioneering enterprises as soon as they were completed.

Great Britain was among the earliest and most prolific consumers of rubber. By 1870, well before the heyday of the Amazon rubber boom, the British were already seeking ways to break the South American monopoly over latex. At about that time, a British subject, Henry A. Wickham, arrived in the Brazilian Amazon in the hopes of starting a rubber plantation. Until then, rubber was gathered from wild trees spread out across huge tracts of virgin rain forest.

Wickham was more an adventurer than a planter. He soon abandoned his attempts to domesticate the wild rubber varieties in Brazil. Instead, in 1876, for a handsome commission from the British government, he smuggled more than seventy thousand rubber seeds on a ship down the Amazon River, past the Brazilian customs authorities in the Atlantic port of Belém and then across the ocean to Kew Gardens in England. Like Drake and Raleigh, pirates who plundered South American riches in another era, Wickham was also rewarded for his daring with a knighthood from the British Crown.

It took many more years before British botanists managed to produce a hardy enough strain of rubber and then grow it in commercial quantities on colonial plantations in Ceylon and Malaya. In 1900, the Amazon was harvesting forty-four thousand tons of rubber, while the new Asian estates exported only fifty tons. But by 1913, Asian output had surpassed the Amazon by fifty-three thousand tons to thirty-six thousand tons. And in 1934, Amazon rubber accounted for a pathetic 1.4 percent of a world output that had burgeoned to more than one million tons. Moreover, the price of rubber had tumbled from its peak of almost three dollars a pound in 1910 to twenty-five cents a pound in 1934.

Asian rubber had every conceivable advantage over the Amazon strain. The Ceylonese and Malayan trees were grown densely together in rows, enabling tappers to work them far more quickly than Amazon laborers whose wild rubber trees were spaced a hundred yards or more apart and hidden among scores of other arboreal species. The Asian strains produced more latex, which eventually was coagulated with chemicals rather than by the slower smoking process used in Brazil. The Asian plantations were closer to ports than the Amazon estates. Asian workers suffered less from disease, and while paid as poorly as the Amazon tappers, they at least bought cheaper food and supplies. Then also, the huge British market preferred its colonial rubber supplies and deliberately undercut Amazon exports elsewhere. Following the British lead, the Dutch and French soon were harvesting rubber in their own Asian colonies.

There is no doubt that for decades the Brazilians were aware of the British attempts to hybridize and domesticate wild rubber into plantation varieties. But still, the Brazilians made no effort to meet this threat by undertaking serious plantation experiments of their own. Even as Asian rubber began to capture an increasing share of the world market, the Brazilians confidently predicted there was no cause for alarm. Typical of this ostrichlike mentality was an article that appeared in 1910 in the *Album do Estado do Pará,* published by the governor of the most important Brazilian Amazon state, which informed its readers that

> We have nothing to worry about the rubber plantations that have been created in Asia. The exceptionally favorable climate of the Amazon, our methods of extraction . . . the enormity of our production . . . the importance of our trade outlets, all permit us not to pay too much attention to what the other producers are doing.

Within three years, the Brazilian and other South American rubber traders were scrambling desperately and hopelessly to survive against the Asian onslaught. By 1913, world rubber prices plummeted to one-third their levels in 1910. South American producers at first sought to stabilize prices by withholding large quantities of their rubber from the market. Ironically, when the Madeira-Mamoré Railway opened to great fanfare in 1912, its cargo trains were virtually empty becaue Bolivian producers refused to ship their rubber with world prices at such low levels. But prices continued their plunge as the Asian plantations stepped up their exports. The Brazilian rubber trade was already precariously built on debt even before Asian producers appeared on the world scene. Now, the Brazilian import houses were forced to gouge the rubber-estate owners by cutting credits to them and demanding lower prices for their latex. And the estate owners passed on these burdens to their already destitute rubber tappers, who received even less money for their latex and became even more indebted to the estate general store. The Amazon rubber trade tottered and then crashed. Tappers fled the estates and settled in slums ringing the villages and towns that had grown up as service centers for the jungle rubber commerce. Estates went bankrupt and were abandoned.

The glorious jungle capital of Manaus saw its fortunes collapse as quickly as they had climbed only decades before. The aristocrats pawned their diamonds and silks and boarded up their mansions. The big import-export merchants pulled up their stakes and moved back to the Brazilian coast or Europe. Ocean liners stopped calling. By the late 1920's, the lights literally went out in Manaus because the municipality was no longer able to foot the electricity bills. The opera house, darkened and unused, stood silent like a mausoleum.

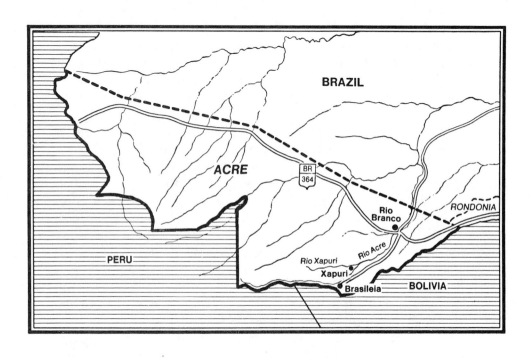

7

The only region in South America where natural rubber survives as an essential economic activity is in the western Brazilian Amazon state of Acre, adjoining Peru and Bolivia.

From Iquitos, in the Peruvian jungles, I decided to travel to Acre to seek out the remnants of the rubber saga as I continued my journey through the continent's frontier lands, roughly following a northwest-to-southeast axis parallel to Belaúnde's imaginary highway.

In a straight line, Rio Branco, the capital of Acre, is only 580 miles southeast of Iquitos, no farther than Atlanta to Miami. But, as is often the case in the frontier lands straddling South American nations, the only straight lines are made by rulers placed across paper maps. Because commercial and political links between neighboring countries tend to be weakest along their borders, passengers and cargo are forced to make lengthy detours to reach their destinations.

Only a decade ago, to get from Iquitos to Rio Branco, I would have had to fly a circuitous route totaling 4,300 miles—the distance separating New York from Rome. It would have meant flying 650 miles from Iquitos back to Lima on the Pacific coast, from there 2,100 miles east across the continent to São Paulo near the Atlantic Ocean, and then back over Brazil 1,550 miles in a western direction, making several stops until I reached Rio Branco. Today, there is still no direct flight between Iquitos and the capital of Acre. But I could consider myself fortunate to fly the weekly jet from Iquitos nine hundred miles east to the old Brazilian rubber entrepôt of Manaus, and then from there, take another flight eight hundred miles southwest to Rio Branco. It was still a switchback route of seventeen hundred miles, almost three times the straight-line distance between Iquitos and Rio Branco.

Back at the height of the rubber era, Acre's sole link to the outside world was by boat. The rubber estates sent their latex by canoe and flat-bottom vessels along the streams and rivers that led to Rio Branco. From there, larger boats plied the Acre River and the Purus River eighteen hundred jagged miles northeast to the Amazon port of Manaus, and then eventually to the Atlantic Ocean. This is still the route for much of the rubber that comes out of Acre.

Rubber continues to account for thirty-five percent of the gross economic product of Acre. Two thirds of the active population is engaged in the gathering, smoking and shipping of latex. But the statistics hide an otherwise stagnant economic life, for rubber has only a flicker of its former vitality. The Brazilian government has long subsidized the state's rubber industry in the absence of any other meaningful economic activity that could support Acre's three hundred thousand inhabitants. In fact, Brazil could easily meet its entire rubber requirements more cheaply from synthetic rubber or imports of natural rubber from the plantations of Southeast Asia.

Even with government subsidies, latex prices have remained low for so long that many of the old jungle estates in Acre have been forsaken by their owners for decades. Only in the remotest corners of Acre's rain forests does the old pattern of serfdom persist, with tappers spending their lives in a futile effort to pay off their growing debts to the estate owners. It is far more usual to see tappers virtually in business for themselves. They have carved out small plots on the old rubber estates to grow corn, manioc and vegetables. They continue to milk the trees for latex and coagulate it over smoky fires. They sell the hardened black balls or flat slabs of elastic to the estate owners, if they are still around, or, more often, to merchants arriving periodically at the estates in boats and pickup trucks laden with simple, essential goods like kerosene, cloth, sugar, salt and batteries that the tappers cannot provide for themselves.

This life of bare subsistence would probably have continued on its own inertia until the older tappers died out or retired and their children drifted away from the jungle. But in the 1970's, a dirt highway was built for the first time connecting Rio Branco overland with the bulk of Brazil to the east. The road meanders deep into the Acre jungles, splits into several branches and reaches all the way to the borders of Peru and Bolivia. The road system was completed by 1975, anticipating the day when Belaúnde's proposed highway is constructed. If that ever happens, Brazil will have an overland route through Peru to the Pacific Ocean, a dream that has fired the Brazilian imagination for a century.

The Brazilian military government certainly did not bulldoze its roads through Acre to benefit the nearly moribund rubber industry. No improvements in the transportation system could ever make natural rubber a profitable business again. Instead, the government hoped that the old rubber estates would be replaced by cattle ranches that eventually would create new jobs and investment capital for Acre, and find market outlets in Peru and the rest of Brazil.

But the web of new jungle roads unexpectedly sparked a bitter struggle for land between the rubber tappers, the estate owners and the cattle ranchers. The heart of the problem was the very ambiguous land tenure system that has existed for so long in much of the Brazilian Amazon. In the hundred years since the advent of the rubber industry, Acre and the rest of the Amazon had developed a peculiar attitude toward land ownership. The land itself was of little value. What counted were the number of rubber trees that grew on a property—usually no more than one per acre—and access to the rivers and streams that fed into the Amazon's tributary system. The original estate owners of the nineteenth century bought "concessions" or "exploitation rights" to large tracts, not titles to the land itself. Complicating matters today is the fact that concessions may have been granted by several different governments over a century's time.

In Acre, for example, some estate owners claimed rights to their properties dating back to the era when the territory was still part of Bolivia. But in 1903, as a result of the successful war fought by the Brazilians against the Bolivians, Acre was declared an independent republic and shortly afterward annexed by Brazil. It then became successively a part of the Brazilian territory of Amazonas, a federal territory in its own right and finally a state. At each new stage, new rights to the same land might have been granted by the different local governments, so that by the 1970's, an exasperated governor of Acre complained that if all land claims were honored, his state would have to be five times its actual size. And in almost all these cases, the question remained whether a claim was based on land or the rubber trees on it.

This question became explosive when the new road system began to be constructed through Acre's rain forests in the early 1970's. The old estate owners had no illusions that the rubber business would revive. But they were ecstatic at the prospect that a fortune could be made by selling their huge tracts of land, which they had always considered worthless, to cattle ranchers. And what a fortune it was! Between 1971 and 1976, the price of land in Acre multiplied one hundredfold, from twenty-five and fifty cents an acre to twenty-five and fifty dollars an acre.

The new landlords were mostly wealthy businessmen from the Atlantic coastal state of São Paulo, fifteen hundred miles to the east. They were risking very little of their own capital because the military government, seeking to encourage the development of Acre, was granting them tax write-offs and long-term loans at interest levels set far below the inflation rate. Cattle raising was the most attractive venture to put these generous credits to use. Once a tract was cleared and replaced with capim—a sturdy, weedlike grass that resists the encroachment of jungle undergrowth and trees—a ranch had low maintenance costs. The whole operation could remain dormant for years while the ranchers waited for the herds to multiply and for road improvements to facilitate access to markets.

The only problem was what to do with the rubber tappers. For generations before any thought was given to cattle ranching, the jungle estates had often changed hands, and the succeeding owners had taken charge of the indebted tappers much like landlords in Czarist Russia had inherited serfs. But these new entrepreneurs from São Paulo were proposing to raze the rubber trees that provided the tappers with their meager livelihood. The new ranches, which needed only a limited labor force, were hiring only small numbers of displaced tappers.

Suddenly, the tappers, who had spent their whole lives on an estate and may even have been born there, were considered illegal squatters. When they refused to leave willingly, thugs hired by the new property owners burned their huts and drove them off at gunpoint. Since 1970, about fifty thousand rubber tappers and their families have been pushed across Acre's borders into Bolivia and Peru. Perhaps an equal number have crowded into slums ringing Rio Branco, Acre's only real city. There, in a diabolical turn of events, they are often recruited by the ranchers as peons to clear the jungle from the old rubber estates. And the ranchers, while posing as progressive agents of development, have resuscitated the old feudal, rubber labor methods of saddling the peons with debts that they can never hope to match with their feeble salaries.

I was arriving in Rio Branco at a particularly tense period in the land struggles between the rubber tappers and the cattle ranchers. The dramatic physical transformation of Acre could be sensed from the plane as it circled for a landing. Below me, the rain forest around Rio Branco had been stripped away and carpeted with capim grass for cattle. On either side of the roads leading north, south, east and west from the city, wide swathes also had been cleared.

Despite the real-estate boom in the nearby jungles, Rio Branco itself showed few hints of prosperity. On one side, the city sagged into the brown, fetid Acre River. Once a famed rubber route, the river had steadily declined in importance as latex exports dropped and airplanes replaced boat traffic. A dozen small flat-bottom vessels were loading grain and hardware goods in the harbor, apparently preparing for journeys south into the rubber country. Two larger barges laden with yellow-and-black slabs of smoked latex were also about to cast off and head north along the river's squiggly course to Manaus. But the overpowering stench of raw sewage funneled into the harbor revealed the river's true present purpose and eclipsed any visual sensations.

The city's center of gravity has shifted away from the river toward the main plaza, an unkempt grove of tropical trees bounded on one side by a cumbrous brick fort that houses the military police. A few large hotels recently opened to accommodate the São Paulo entrepreneurs who are buying up the rubber estates. The cattle business has at least improved the restaurants, which now serve fresh beef as well as the usual catfish.

Not far from the plaza, I paid a visit to a yellowish, two-story building with small windows that seemed to squint in the sun. It served as the headquarters of the Confederation of Agrarian Workers, a union that was founded in 1975 to organize rubber tappers and ranch peons. This was the first successful attempt to form a pressure group on behalf of rubber workers in Acre. The chief delegate of the confederation, João Maia, acknowledged the bitter irony that the union was seventy years too late, coming into existence at a time when the value of latex was too insignificant to give the tappers any political or economic leverage.

"Back in the days when rubber was king, the idea of a labor union was inconceivable," said Maia, a forty-year-old former tapper with slick black hair, heavily calloused hands and a middleweight boxer's frame and bobbing moves. "It was perfectly acceptable that a man had to work off his debts before leaving a rubber estate, and if he dared to complain, he was told that he should have had more sense than to sign up for this type of work in the first place. Any attempt to change the system was considered subversive. Nobody, not even a politician, could visit workers at a rubber estate without the owner's permission or he would be considered a trespasser on private property. The police were in the pay of the estate owners. The few times that a workers' revolt took place, the police would descend on the estate and beat them unmercifully."

According to Maia, the steep drop in rubber prices had undermined the economic and political clout of the estate owners to such a point that police no longer found it profitable to rally behind them in every labor emergency. With little money to be made in rubber, the owners allowed the tappers to milk the latex trees at their own pace and carry on subsistence farming. But when in the 1970's the estate owners began to sell their rubber groves and drive the tappers from the jungle, the union movement was born.

"We are arguing that the estate owners were never given titles to their properties, only to the rubber trees," said Maia. "The tappers have at least as much right to the land as the estate owners. They have lived there all their lives. They were already given the right to build homes and own plots for their small farms. For generations, they accepted all the rules, no matter how unjust: they worked for less than the minimum wage; they never left until they paid their debts; they agreed to buy goods only at the estate stores at usurious prices. And now, suddenly, they are told that all these sacrifices amount to nothing and they have to move on like animals."

In its seven years of existence, Maia's labor union had swelled its ranks with fifty thousand members. It was strong enough to confront the enfeebled rubber-estate owners. But the new cattle ranchers from São Paulo were more formidable opponents. They had money, police support and the sympathy of politicians, including the governor, who hailed their arrival as an economic godsend for Acre. Maia and his colleagues were trying to publicize a series of ugly cases of forced labor perpetrated by the ranchers. But the union had neither the resources nor the official backing to investigate abuses on properties that were being cleared of rain forest and rubber tappers in the more remote tracts along the new roads.

"Just to get the judges and police to carry out an investigation is a victory of sorts," said Maia, adding that he could not recall a single case of a rancher being brought to court on charges of forced labor.

Maia referred me to a young, stocky mulatto, Francisco Correia, whose case the union had taken up. Correia was born on a rubber estate deep in Acre, near the Bolivian border, and had been expelled when the property was bought up by a São Paulo rancher. He drifted toward Rio Branco and eventually found lodging at a run-down flophouse on the edge of the Acre River, where he had heard that ranchers were recruiting peons to slash and burn old rubber estates. Lingering at the hotel for almost two weeks, he and several other tappers finally signed up with a labor contractor who paid their hotel bills and promised them three dollars a day and free housing at a ranch being built about a hundred miles west of Rio Branco. Arriving at the property, Correia discovered that the "housing" consisted of a crude lean-to strung with hammocks. He chopped trees and slashed the underbrush from dawn to dusk, and was forced to pay exorbitant prices on credit for food and supplies at the estate store. Then, after a month, he asked for his wages. He was told that he was deeply in debt and would have to remain at the property until he had worked off what he owed the rancher.

One day while chopping wood, Correia mutilated a hand. He was given only a painkiller by his foreman. Early the next morning, he fled the estate hidden on the back of a truck carrying latex to Rio Branco. In town, he checked into a hospital to have his hand treated. Later, he visited the new trade union's offices and was introduced to Maia, who sued the rancher on Correia's behalf. But the following day, Correia was kidnapped by the rancher and two local policemen, who drove him in handcuffs back to the estate. As punishment, he was forced to carry buckets of water until his stitches burst. A few days later, he escaped again and made his way back to Rio Branco on foot, hiding in the jungle until dusk and walking along the road at night. He was not recaptured. But he was unable to find employment, and lived on the union's charity.

Maia gave me the name of the flophouse in Rio Branco where Correia had been hired into peonage. It was the Panamericano, a crumbling, pink, wood-frame hotel overlooking the muddy banks of the Acre River. The manager, a small, cocky youth named Vilson Vale de Melo, welcomed me with a smirk that never once left his face during the next few hours. He explained that his guests were almost exclusively jobless tappers and farmhands who received room and board until they obtained employment.

"A peon eats and sleeps here for [about five dollars] a day," said Vilson. "Then a foreman shows up within a week or so, pays the bill and takes the peons away. If a peon declines a job offer, he has to pay his own bill or go to jail. I've had up to twenty people staying here at a time. They were never here more than two weeks. Somebody always comes by for them. It's not that easy on me. Sometimes these guys get drunk and pull knives and bust up the place. I put the damage on their bills."

Vilson was expecting an employer that afternoon to take away a dozen people who had enjoyed his hospitality for the last ten days. Shortly after lunch, the man arrived. He was deeply tanned, of medium height, built like a weight lifter and with a long, white, angry scar on the right side of his scowling face. His name was Roberval Rodrigues and he was a labor contractor for an estate that was being converted into a cattle ranch. The workers he had come to hire would hack the jungle to make way for grazing land.

Rodrigues insisted that the laborers were being given a valid contract and working papers, with wages and free room and board. He would take care of their hotel bills and subtract it from their salaries, he said. In his five years as a labor contractor, he estimated he had hired more than a hundred fifty peons to work on four different jungle tracts.

"They're low class—people without the least bit of education," said Rodrigues, not minding at all that the peons were in earshot. "Very few of them better their lives. Sometimes, a rancher will pay them off with a small plot of land, and then maybe they improve themselves. But many of them just quit their jobs and stake out land without asking permission from the boss."

These squatters, said Rodrigues, were his biggest headache. He lifted his sleeve to show me a muscular forearm pockmarked by shotgun pellets, the result of a recent skirmish with squatters on a jungle estate. "I took care of them," he said with a weird smile. "The problem with these peons is that they start drinking and end up creating a lot of confusion. When they sober up, they feel sorry, real sorry."

I left the Panamericano and headed over to the imposing, red-brick police garrison at the edge of Rio Branco's central square, where I had arranged to meet with Geraldo Almeida, the federal police chief in Rio Branco. He was a short, beer-bellied man with a smooth, round race that reeked of after-shave. Sweeping an arm over a large wall map of Acre—a state larger than Florida—he said his three hundred policemen had neither the manpower nor the money to scour the jungle in search of labor-law violations. "Besides, the military government may not like it to be said, but the labor legislation in Brazil is socialist," asserted Almeida, sounding even more right wing than the conservative generals who have ruled the country since 1964.

I told him he probably would not have to range too far afield to come across cases of forced labor, and I recounted my visit earlier in the day to the Panamericano. Almeida said he was sure his men would pick up Rodrigues if it turned out he had no legal working papers for the people he had hired. One of his aides walked in, Almeida excused himself and bid me good-bye.

The next morning over breakfast in my hotel room, I read the local newspaper. According to a front-page article, Roberval Rodrigues and a dozen workers in his charge had been stopped by the federal police as their truck pulled out of Rio Branco. The article said Rodrigues had failed to produce any valid working papers for his peons and was being detained on suspicion of hiring slave labor.

I made an appointment with Edson Martins, the journalist who wrote the article. A short, bearded, blue-eyed and brown-maned fellow in his early forties, Martins had a soft voice that belied the forceful way he expressed his political convictions in his newspaper writing. He had gained a reputation of almost reckless courage for an unending series of articles on slave labor, hired gunmen and militant trade unionists. Besides reporting for a local commercial newspaper, he edited and financed from his own meager resources a more radical publication that appeared sporadically.

I remarked to him that I was impressed by the police's quick arrest of Rodrigues. But Edson pointed out that what probably caught the eyes of most readers was a passage mentioning that Rodrigues had offered the police too paltry a bribe in an attempt to extricate himself.

"He has been picked up before," said the journalist. "He probably was caught short of cash. But he'll be out of jail in a few days."

Edson was a man who had turned down every opportunity to leave the Amazon jungle, which he held in almost perverse fascination. He insisted that the writer Euclydes da Cunha had gotten it all wrong when he wrote that people in the Amazon were "overwhelmingly dominated by an incurable nostalgia for their native lands."

And Edson mentioned his own father as an example to the contrary. The elder Martins had come to Acre from his native northeast to work first as a rubber tapper, then as a cook in a remote jungle estate. Upon his retirement, Edson, his youngest son, had arranged for him to spend his final years in his hometown back in northeastern Brazil. It was an act of generosity that the father never forgave.

"He lived to be a hundred yeard old," said Edson. "But he blamed me for cutting his life short by coaxing him out of the jungles."

Edson himself had been one of fifteen brothers and sisters born on the rubber estate where his father was employed. He had lived there for his first twelve years, and was then sent to school in Rio Branco. He attended university in Belém, on the Atlantic coast near the mouth of the Amazon River, and worked there briefly as a chemist for a dairy company. Later he became a journalist in several jungle cities before returning to Acre. In all his life, he had visited São Paulo only twice and Rio de Janeiro once in what amounted to a deliberate rejection of coastal "civilization"—an attitude that is rare among Brazilian professionals and the middle class. Edson's friends—including his wife, a sociologist from São Paulo—were mostly younger journalists and social scientists who had also willfully turned their backs on the cities of eastern and southern Brazil.

According to Edson, the inhabitants of the Amazon, even the lowly tappers, might want to improve their livelihoods, but few of them really hoped to flee the jungles. The turmoil that Acre was undergoing recently, he suggested, was probably more than anything a response to the arrival of powerful outsiders, the cattlemen, who were bringing about too sudden a change.

"The trouble with Amazon intellectuals—and we really do exist—is that we want to keep the jungle as it is," he said. "It's a romantic hope that the old rubber estates can be run better and more justly, that somehow there can be prosperity here and yet we'll still be able to visit the rubber tappers on weekends, the way people elsewhere drive out to country houses. But changes are happening so quickly, and we have no realistic response. We often talk about it among ourselves—journalists, professionals, university researchers—and we don't come up with any answers. Maybe we have this idea that the jungle can produce a different, fairer type of civilization than the savage, industrial capitalism of Rio and São Paulo. Maybe we are just deceiving ourselves. I mean, can Acre really sustain an economy based on rubber? Is there really a world market out there for natural rubber? Aren't the new roads going to transform this place in ways nobody ever imagined?"

Edson suggested we travel down one of the new jungle roads leading out of Rio Branco to glimpse some of the unsettling changes he was talking about. The cattle ranchers had bought most of their rubber estates along these roads because they offered easy access between their properties and potential markets. But they were encountering stiff resistance from rubber tappers and squatters who staked their own claims to these lands. With state elections scheduled in the months ahead, local politicians were courting votes among the tappers, and the police were temporarily declining to interfere in land struggles. Rubber tappers and squatters were brazenly firing back at gunmen hired by ranchers to clear them from newly purchased estates.

Edson and I drove in a Jeep south from Rio Branco toward a contested zone about three quarters of the 110 miles separating Acre's capital from the Bolivian border, where the road comes to an abrupt stop. The highway had been paved recently, and it took us less than three hours to reach our destination, a rubber forest that had been the scene of some of the bitterest land disputes between ranchers and tappers.

At first sight, it seemed that the ranchers had overwhelmingly won the battle. On either side of the route, the land was bare of jungle. Cattle grazed amid the charred carcasses of once majestic nut trees. The rain forest was only faintly visible in the far horizon. But off the main road, and closer to the rivers and streams that had always been the focal points of the rubber estates, there were much larger tracts of virgin jungle where the tappers held sway.

Clouds swelled blackly ahead of us. A strong gust swirled the red jungle dirt, and we could smell the approaching rain. The brief downpour revived the wilting, dust-covered bushes at the roadside. In its wake, the hot, wet asphalt produced clouds of steam, and we drove almost blindly through a heavy fog. But as soon as we turned off the paved road, about thirty miles from the Bolivian border, the mist was miraculously replaced by brilliant sunshine.

We were on a boggy lane that became narrower as it pressed into the jungle and finally turned into a footpath. We abandoned the Jeep and walked along the thin track past an orange grove. Edson said the land was part of an old rubber estate called Santa Fé which had been taken over by its tappers two years before when a cattle rancher bought the property and tried to clear it. We were heading toward the shack of one of the oldest tappers, Antonio Osterno, who had recently received a title for his 250-acre claim.

The house was set on thick wood stilts two feet above the ground. There were eight people in the family, living in three rooms criss-crossed with hammocks. A long table and a few stools and wicker chairs were the only furniture. In the kitchen in back, Antonio's wife hovered over a blackened pot that was bubbling with a thick stew of paca, a beaver-sized rodent whose meat was prized most by the tappers.

Antonio was tall and thin. He had a chalky-brown complexion, the result of spending the daylight hours in the constant shade of the jungle. Though sixty-five, he looked and moved like a man twenty years younger. His hair was jet-black, his face almost uncreased and cleanly shaven except for a pencil-line mustache. He deftly peeled oranges, cutting the skin in one long strand, and offered us the slices as Edson explained that we wanted to hear about his life on the rubber estates.

Like almost all the tappers, Antonio compensated for his illiteracy with a remarkable verbal agility. He had an aural memory that allowed him to dredge up entire conversations, mimicking the language and accents of the characters who populated his anecdotes. He sat on his haunches, placed a thick, hand-rolled cigarette in the corner of his mouth, closed his eyes and repeated several times, "I can tell the whole story." Then, without a pause, he picked up the strands of his life forty years before. I felt like Coleridge's wedding guest, who "stood still, And listens like a three years' child: The Mariner hath his will."

Back in 1943, Antonio left his family's parched farm in the interior of Ceará and moved in search of employment to a cousin's house in Fortaleza, the state's capital and main Atlantic port. The Japanese had overrun the rubber plantations of Southeast Asia, and the United States, deeply concerned over shortages, had struck a deal with Brazil to revive the old Amazon rubber industry. The Brazilian government announced a "War of Rubber" and encouraged estate owners to send their agents to the drought-stricken Northeast, to the slums of cities like Fortaleza, to recruit "soldiers of rubber" who would tap the jungle latex. Antonio recalled meeting an agent resplendent in a white linen suit, who promised him housing and salary in Acre and a "war pension" when the battle for rubber had been won.

"There was a band in the port playing music, and we were sent off like patriots to fight for America and Brazil," said Antonio. "But the ship's engine failed and we were afraid we would sink and drown there in the harbor of Fortaleza."

The damage was repaired, and the boat, still listing heavily, headed northwest along the Atlantic coast past Belém, then up the Amazon River to Manaus. There, the tappers transferred to a smaller vessel that made its way south to Rio Branco, then to Xapuri, about forty miles from the Bolivian border, and finally by canoe to a rubber estate not far from Antonio's present home. The entire journey took almost two months. There was little food on the boats and hardly space enough to sleep.

"We were supposed to find working estates here, with homes and paths between the rubber trees," said Antonio. "Well, there was nothing. We were cheated, vilely cheated. We spent months just cutting paths through the jungle. Everything was three times as expensive as in Ceará. We were not allowed to leave the estate to buy cheaper food and supplies in Xapuri. If we tried to sell our rubber outside the estate to make a bit more money, we were considered thieves and sent to jail. There were no schools for the children, no doctors, sometimes no pills for malaria. Everybody got malaria, not once but many times. And no one paid you if you were sick. The only thing that counted was how much rubber you collected. Once I was bitten by a snake, and I was told to wait for a boat to take me to the doctor in Xapuri. It never came, and I just lay in a sweat, fighting the poison until I won."

Antonio worked two *estradas,* or rubber trails, each about ten miles long, beginning near his shack and circling back to it. He would trek into the jungle on the first *estrada* at four A.M. when the cool, early-morning air was supposed to make the latex run more easily. On his head, he wore a crude kerosene lamp, called a *poronga,* that looked like an Indian ceremonial helmet. He carried a shotgun in case he was lucky enough to spy a deer or paca, or so unfortunate as to encounter a jaguar. The only time a jaguar crossed his path, his gun jammed and he had to scare the beast away by throwing his poncho at it and screaming loudly. Antonio's only tool was a short, flat-tipped sharp knife to make the incisions on the rubber trees from which the milky latex oozed out. The trees were spaced about a hundred yards apart. Antonio claimed that an experienced tapper could judge by the way a tree leaned where the next rubber tree would be found, and then clear a path between them.

At the beginning of the collecting season in June, Antonio placed his first incision as far up a tree trunk as he could reach. He made subsequent cuts beneath it, until at the season's end in January, he had almost struck the tree's base. He preferred the so-called *bandeira,* or flag cut, which supposedly caused the least harm to the rubber tree. He made a two-foot-long horizontal incision, followed by a short vertical slash, and then another smaller horizontal cut. At the end of the incision, he stuck a wooden spigot into the bark and beneath it a small metal cup. As the white, viscous sap began to dribble into the cup, Antonio walked to the next tree.

It took him five hours to complete his journey through the first *estrada.* When he returned home at nine A.M., his wife had prepared a large lunch of rice, beans, manioc and, with luck, dried beef, or possibly an animal he had shot the previous day. After a siesta, Antonio returned to the jungle, this time to collect the latex from the trees he had cut in the morning, pouring the sticky sap from the individual cups into a large wooden gourd. He worked only one *estrada* a day, allowing the trees along the other rubber trail to regenerate their latex.

By four P.M., he was back home again, with his most unpleasant task still ahead. In a small hut next to his shack, he fired up a clay oven, using green wood or large palm nuts to produce as much smoke as possible. Over the oven's narrow mouth, he poured the thick latex on a wooden paddle, revolving it slowly so that the heavy smoke coagulated the white sap into a harder yellow-and-black consistency. The heat was debilitating. The smoke burned his eyes and nostrils and left him coughing. Sometimes the fire at the base of the oven singed his legs, eyebrows and hair.

When the latex reached a layer of about an inch thick, he slipped it off the paddle and wrapped it around a wooden pole. After a couple of weeks, the blackened latex formed a heavy ball weighing a hundred pounds or more. Once a month, Antonio and his sons would carry two of these balls, balancing the poles on their shoulders, to the estate's warehouse.

Antonio always suspected that the warehouse scale was rigged to cheat the tappers on the true weight of their latex. As it was, the accountant automatically subtracted ten percent of the scale's readings, claiming that the latex would shrink in weight as its moisture evaporated on its way to markets in Manaus and Belém. The market value of the latex, which fluctuated weekly, was the privileged information of the estate owner. Antonio had no cash reserves that would enable him to withhold the latex until the estate owner announced that rubber prices had risen. And the tapper was prohibited from selling his latex elsewhere. In all, Antonio was required to turn over one half of the market value of his latex to the estate owner, who justified his exorbitant share with several arguments. In part, it was supposed to meet the cost of transporting the latex to Manaus and Belém. It also covered a commission charged on the tapper for use of the trees. And it amounted to rent for the privilege of living on the estate and keeping a private food garden during the seven months of the work season and the remaining five months when the rains prevented latex collection.

Even after these machinations, Antonio rarely received cash for his latex. Instead, the accountant marked him down for credit on one side of the estate's ledger, and on the other side he subtracted Antonio's food and supply purchases in the general store, which, of course, were priced far higher than goods available at shops in nearby Xapuri.

"I couldn't read or figure out numbers," said Antonio. "So I was at the mercy of the boss. And his figures showed we were all in debt most of the time."

In the quarter century following Antonio's arrival in Acre, rubber prices were mostly on a downward trend. Antonio heard about workers' revolts in nearby estates, all of them violently repressed by the police. No uprising ever took place in his corner of the jungle. But many of the younger tappers, heavily in debt, fled the estate. They never found jobs in other rubber groves because an understanding existed between estate owners not to hire anybody unless they agreed to pay off his debts to the previous employer. Sometimes, to set an example for the other tappers, an estate owner called upon the other rubber bosses and the police to track down and return a fugitive who allegedly owed a substantial sum. His punishment varied from beatings to incarceration in a windowless back room of the estate's warehouse, or a "fine" that would limit his credit at the general store and impose a near-starvation diet on his family for weeks on end.

"They say that slavery ended in Brazil a long time ago," said Antonio. "But somebody forgot to tell the bosses."

By the late 1960's, the natural rubber trade was so unprofitable that many of the remaining estate owners began to abandon their properties. A new law allowed the tappers to sell their latex to anybody they wished. Only in the most isolated estates, on the small rivers deep in the Acre jungle, does the old feudal pattern persist even today. For most of the tappers, a brief period of economic independence began about 1970.

It was cut short by the arrival of the cattle ranchers. All around Antonio, rubber estates were being razed and their tappers expelled. In 1976, at almost sixty years of age, he decided to join the new Confederation of Agrarian Workers. He began proselytizing for the union among rubber workers in his estate. When the tract was sold to a rancher, Antonio urged the tappers not to accept any promises from the new owner to give them indemnities and relocate them on land elsewhere because similar agreements were being violated by ranchers throughout the valley.

"One day, the rancher arrived unannounced to my house," said Antonio. "He had a lawyer with him and two *jagunços* [gunmen]. The rancher put a gun on the table and next to it a paper, and told me I better put my thumbprint on it. I did as he asked. But I never had any intention of keeping the agreement. No sir, the law doesn't recognize an agreement made that way. When the rancher sent his peons to clear the land, we were all there, all the tappers, with our shotguns and machetes, and we chased them away. The police came and arrested many of us and beat us in jail. But the rancher never was able to expel us, and his peons were too scared of us to enter the estate."

In the years that followed, Antonio and his sons traveled often to nearby estates and participated in *empates*—prolonged occupations to ward off ranchers' peons and gunmen. Tensions reached a climax in 1980. During a gathering sponsored by the government to air differences between estate owners and tappers in nearby Xapuri, and broadcast on a local radio station, a choleric estate owner brazenly called for the assassination of the leaders of the rural workers' union. "From now on," he said, "there are going to be many widows in Acre."

A month later, in Brasileia, a rubber-gathering center on the Bolivian border about forty miles from Xapuri, a trade-union leader, Wilson Pinheiro, was fatally shot in the back as he watched a television detective drama. The assassin, aiming from the porch of Pinheiro's shack, had timed his bullets to coincide with a shooting episode on the television program. The gunman easily escaped before Pinheiro's neighbors realized what had happened.

Antonio remembered hearing about the murder on the radio that night when a group of excited rubber tappers seized the local station and asked workers in the valley to converge on Brasileia for a demonstration of protest. Antonio traveled there the next day and joined a thousand other tappers, squatters and settlers who filed past Pinheiro's coffin. After the funeral, a group of tappers surrounded a Jeep driven by a ranch foreman who had once allegedly threatened to kill Pinheiro. They dragged the man from his vehicle and lynched him.

Several of the assailants were arrested by the police. But they were all released within a few months, apparently because the local government decided to reduce the potential for violence. Already, many of the ranchers, who had profitable businesses back in São Paulo and Rio, were growing disenchanted with the drawn-out conflicts in this southern corner of Acre. When the ranchers withdrew their claims, the local courts gave a number of tappers deeds to plots on their rubber estates. In 1981, the property on which Antonio had worked for thirty-eight years was legally divided by a court order among its tappers.

From a chest in his shack, Antonio retrieved his prized deed, a white document which he had pressed between two strips of cardboard for protection. At the bottom of the paper, his name had been typed in, and above it was his thick, black thumbprint. The document granted him 250 acres covering the two oval-shaped paths that guided him past his rubber trees.

Besides becoming a landowner, Antonio had lived through several other important changes in recent years. He no longer had to endure the odious smoking process. Instead, he used an acetate chemical to coagulate his latex, or sent it for treatment to a small, nearby plant owned by a cooperative of rubber tappers. He sold most of his latex to merchants who drove their pickup trucks to the edge of his property and offered their goods and cash in exchange. He no longer had any debts, and for the first time he had opened a bank account, which now held an equivalent of sixty dollars, his life's savings.

Antonio said he had no desire to leave the jungle. Like other tappers, he embraced a crude ideology of sorts that exalted the role of rubber gatherers in Brazilian history down to the present day. Acre, they insisted, was won over to Brazil from Bolivia not by soldiers but by an army of tappers. Sir Henry Wickham and the British government were symbols of perfidy for having stolen rubber seeds out of Brazil a hundred years before. The War of Rubber in the early 1940's was a crucial battle that turned the tide against the Germans and Japanese. And even today, the tappers seem to fervently believe that rubber is their country's main product.

"Rubber is the lifeblood of Brazil," said Antonio, apparently oblivious to the dominant role of synthetic rubber. "And we the tappers produce it, and even so, for the government, we have always been worthless. That's what doesn't make sense. Without rubber where would Brazil be?"

I didn't have the heart to tell him that natural rubber would continue to have a bleak future no matter who owned the rubber groves. I could only hope that perhaps his 250-acre plot would someday turn out to be fertile enough for agriculture and that Antonio would then make the difficult transition from rubber tapper to full-time farmer. If not, his hard-fought struggle would inevitably become a hollow victory.

Having spun out his long tale, Antonio rose to his feet and offered to show me his rubber trees. The jungle began twenty yards from his shack, beyond a small brook that gurgled and hissed as it wound toward the vegetable garden in back of the house. Antonio glided down the rubber trail, skipping over rotten logs and large puddles. On all sides, the chirping of a hundred different birds merged into a loud warble. We were in a world of dusk where shadows surrounded small cataracts of light pouring down from the cracks in the rain forest's canopy. In the sun, the temperature was in the mid-eighties Fahrenheit, but under the trees it was at least ten degrees cooler. We were nearing the end of the wet season, the five months when most of Acre's 120 inches of annual rainfall (double the usual precipitation in New York State) poured over the rubber forest. Antonio said that work stopped during this January-to-May period because the trails turned too soggy and the rain filled the collection cups, causing the latex to overflow.

Fifty yards into the jungle, Antonio halted in front of the first rubber tree. It was at least eighty feet high with a trunk more than ten feet in circumference. Its branches began about twelve feet from its base. Its trifoliate leaves were long and narrow and tapering at each end, almost shaped like elm leaves, only larger and thicker. The tree's bark was slashed with innumerable, surgically thin scars. In a rapierlike motion, Antonio cut it once again. The white fluid dripped down the path of the incision into the small collection cup.

One of Antonio's daughters called from the shack that lunch was ready.

Plates were heaped high with beans, rice, manioc powdered to a sawdust consistency and chunks of paca, which tasted like rabbit. There were no women at the table. Occasionally, Antonio's youngest daughter would peek from the kitchen and hide herself with a nervous giggle when I looked up from my plate. His wife never joined us.

It was late in the afternoon when Edson and I climbed back in our Jeep and began the hour-long drive to Xapuri, back north in the direction of Rio Branco. I had hoped to meet up with some rubber estate owners in Xapuri, but we stalled several times in deep puddles and gazed with envy at the rubber tappers trotting by on horseback.

The light of day faded to a cerise glow as we reached Xapuri, wedged between a river with the same name and the broader, murkier Acre, which flowed north to Rio Branco and then far beyond into the Amazon River. A large brick-and-alabaster church dwarfed the rest of the town like a cathedral in a medieval European village. Xapuri's treeless, empty square reverberated with the angelic, high-pitched strains of a girls' chorus inside the church.

Seven decades ago, Xapuri had been a small, prosperous rubber center of eight thousand inhabitants. There are now three times as many people. But the rising population curve long ago crossed the declining vector of prosperity. The town has swelled with tappers and their families who abandoned the foundering rubber estates and now subsist on part-time construction jobs and crude farm plots. There is a smell of mustiness and decomposition everywhere. The banks of the Xapuri River rise steeply and crumble as the muddy waters relentlessly eat away at vegetation, exposing roots and stones and clay. An abandoned social club, with rusty wrought-iron grill-work, juts over the river on the town's highest bluff. In its small courtyard stands Xapuri's only monument, a stone bust of Placido de Castro, the man who led the Brazilian rubber tappers' revolt against Bolivia, which ended in 1903 with Acre's incorporation into Brazil.

The largest buildings, except for the church, are the warehouses and general stores that face the river. The proprietors are simple shopkeepers, shipwrecked survivors in a forgotten backwater. But their names—Abad, Zaire, Zahle, written in big, faded letters above their stores—were once synonymous with intrepid adventurers and rubber barons. These forebears arrived in Amazonia in the nineteenth century from the Middle East with passports issued by the Ottoman empire, a bureaucratic accident that earned them the sobriquet of *Turcos* (Turks) instead of Arabs. Like their ancient Phoenician ancestors, they were sailors and merchants in their very souls. Only instead of commanding galleys on the Mediterranean, they plied the streams and tributaries of the Amazon in canoes and flat-bottom boats brimming with cloth, tools, alcohol, medicine and preserved foods. They followed the rubber-estate owners and the hordes of northeastern peasants-turned-tappers into the remotest corners of the jungles. These traveling Arab salesmen would spend four or five months a year visiting the numerous rubber camps, haggling and bartering their wares for rubber and nuts and animal skins. Then, their boats laden with booty, they returned to their starting points in Manaus and Belém. Their profits were enormous, usually several hundred percent, but their risks—from armed thieves, disease and river accidents—were great as well. The more successful of these Syrio-Lebanese merchants eventually established supply depots and general stores in river ports like Xapuri, exchanging their goods for bulk shipments of latex from the rubber estates. And sometimes, when the estate owners went bankrupt, they paid off their huge debts to the merchants by turning over to them their rubber lands and tappers.

At Edson's suggestion, we stopped by the largest of the riverside general stores. It was owned by Guilherme Zaire, who had once been a prominent politician and rubber baron in Acre. Zaire, almost seventy years of age, is old enough to remember the waning days of the rubber boom, or at least the stories of flowing champagne and flaunted diamonds that his parents passed on to him. They were traders born in the Middle East who arrived in the 1890's and established themselves in Xapuri. After Acre seceded from Bolivia—a revolt which the Zaires like other Arab merchants helped to finance—they acquired the rights to a fifty-thousand-acre rubber estate. Of their three sons, only Guilherme, the bachelor, was disposed to live and work in the jungles. But twenty years ago, even he relented. He served a term as governor of Acre and afterward moved permanently to Xapuri to take over the family's general store and warehouse. He still owns the rubber estate, about seventy miles west of town, along the Xapuri River. But he rents the property, with its sixty thousand rubber trees and forty tappers, to another, younger estate owner.

Zaire's cavernous store had windows only in front. Two naked light bulbs dangled from the high ceiling, but the back recesses were dark and humid. The floor was made of hard, packed earth and was piled high with hardware supplies, canned food and bags of grain. In the adjoining warehouse, there were stacks of blackened latex slabs that smelled like smoked pork.

Zaire is white-maned, with pale, parchment skin, and he wore thick-lensed, wire rimmed glasses. His tall frame was hunched over an Atlas-sized account book. Next to him was Chico, a chunky thirty-five-year-old former rubber tapper and now the local leader of the rural workers' union. There is no ill will between these two men, one of them once a boss and the other once an indebted laborer. Zaire long ago gave up hope in the rubber trade, and his estate was too far removed from any roads to attract the interest of a cattle rancher. When he became governor of Acre, Zaire made his peace with the tappers and courted their support. Now he exudes the good cheer of a Rotarian and neighborhood grocer.

"I lived for more than twenty years in the jungle," said Zaire. "One has to have a certain strength of character for that kind of life. One had to learn to live alone. For me, it was often unbearably lonely. There was nobody to talk to except the foremen and the tappers, and they didn't have much to say. There was no radio back then, not in the jungle anyway. We got our news from the river merchants who brought us month-old newspapers. I suppose it was harder still for the tappers. The smoking process, especially, was terrible work. They often developed respiratory ailments, pneumonia, tuberculosis, terrible illnesses. But I respect those who triumph in life despite adversities, men who consider their jobs a badge of honor. Like Chico, here, he didn't let the jungle keep him down. He started out as the lowliest rubber tapper, and now he's got a political career ahead of him."

Chico, the pudgy labor leader, fidgeted uncomfortably, but didn't say a word.

"I spent my time at my estate walking a different trail every day to see that work was being done properly, that the trees weren't being mistreated," continued Zaire. "Sometimes the newer tappers cut the bark too deep, and then if they did it often enough, the trees would die. I always picked out two or three tappers who were good workers, the kind who brought in a hundred kilos [220 pounds] of latex every couple of weeks. I rewarded them with a rifle, a sewing machine or a cow so that the other workers would look up to them and follow their example.

"What gave spice to my life was coming out of the jungle every three weeks and spending a few days partying in Xapuri," said Zaire, smiling as a pleasant memory flickered by. "Xapuri wasn't anything like what you see now. It had three cabarets with jazz bands and samba groups and women who came from France to sing and dance the cancan. There was one of them, a redhead. She was really something. Anyway, I would scrub off the mud and mildew from the jungle, and I would put on a white linen suit, a bright tie and a broad-brimmed hat, and I would go to the clubs with the other estate owners. Those were classy cabarets. They wouldn't let anybody in without a suit and tie, even if it was hotter than a smokehouse. This place was even livelier in my father's time. That was the golden era. Everybody had money, and traveled—all the way to Europe. There were three newspapers in this little town back then, with news from around the world. Parents would send their children to school in Rio and Lisbon and Paris, and they would come back and take over the family business."

Only once, after he stepped down as governor, did Zaire himself travel abroad. He visited Los Angeles, San Francisco, Las Vegas and New York. "But I felt like a fool," he said. "I can't speak anything but Portuguese, Amazon Portuguese, and I would just nod and grin. To be a rubber-estate owner, even governor of Acre, means nothing over there."

"You can say what you want about the estate owner, but he was quite a man," asserted Zaire. "He set the laws. He made sure the supplies got through the jungle. He brought civilization to this frontier. Those stories about cruelty and punishment of workers were very exaggerated. Hell, he didn't want to lose a worker. There were never enough of them. Sure there were some colleagues who were sadists. They had no souls. They hunted down their workers with the police. Well, I never went to the police. If a man owed me and wanted to leave, I'd let him go. Otherwise, he would just create problems and destroy morale. But before he went away, he would have to give me back his tools and gun, that's for damn sure. And if he owed me money, he wasn't going to get a job with my friends until they paid off his debts."

"I left the jungle twenty years ago," said Zaire, "because this store was making more money than my rubber estate. It's even worse out there nowadays. Rubber isn't worth a damn, and labor is too expensive. The mentality of the workers has changed. They're more militant. I guess some people call that progress. All that union propaganda. Well, maybe it was good for them, but it was certainly bad for any estate owner. Right, Chico?"

But Chico still wouldn't rise to the bait.

Zaire has even less use for the new ranchers than for the trade unionists. To him, they are speculators, people looking for tax shelters while living in the coastal cities far away.

"The government has made it easy for the cattle people to buy land from rubber-estate owners who were going bankrupt," he said. "When I was governor, you know, I fought the land deals. I didn't steal a cent. What you see here is all I have. I ride a bicycle instead of a car. But then they built those jungle roads, and the Peruvians were supposed to build us a road to the Pacific, and everybody was just hypnotized into thinking that we would have another boom in Acre just like the best of the rubber days. It was those damned roads that changed everything."

8

For Zaire and Edson and the rubber tappers and cattle ranch-ers, the new roads through the Acre jungles are significant above all because they are cracking a feudal social and eco-nomic system rooted in the century-old rubber trade.

But the roads into Acre are only the last segments of a much larger frontier highway network that is meant to spearhead the final conquest and settlement of Brazil's vast Amazon wilderness. This effort got underway a few years after the Brazilian military regime gained power in 1964. By the early 1980's, a 6,700-mile Transama-zon highway system was completed from Belém on the Atlantic coast westward, circling around and through the heart of Brazil, and on to the borders of Peru and Bolivia, awaiting eventual links with Belaúnde's proposed road.

What makes this Brazilian crusade so profoundly different from any other attempt to penetrate the jungle frontier lands is its deter-mination to carry out the economic development of the Amazon through intensive agriculture in new settlement projects connected by the new roads.

Before the Transamazon highway system—throughout the 450 years that followed the arrival of the Europeans in Brazil—almost all efforts to exploit the Amazon rain forest were extractive, remov-ing far more resources from the jungles than were ever invested back into them. The conquistadores and *bandeirantes* searched for gold, precious stones and Indian slaves. The missionary settlements for Indians, with their riverside agricultural plots, came closest to breaking the extractive mold. But they depended for their economic survival on hunting and fishing, and a modest commerce in wild an-imal hides, nuts, cinnamon and medicinal herbs—all extractive enterprises. The rubber trade, entirely linked to the milking of wild trees, was the extractive industry par excellence. The oil fields that I encountered in my own travels through Peru were yet another, more modern form of extractivism in the jungles.

The fledgling cattle ranches I had seen in Acre hinted at the beginnings of a widespread agricultural approach to the Amazon. But ranching, the replacement of rain forest tracts with capim grass for livestock, is a simpler, less demanding process than coaxing annual harvests from the jungle soils. If the new Transamazon highway system is to be economically successful, it will have to prove that large portions of the red jungle earth can render agricultural produce year after year without suffering erosion, and that a much greater population can be sustained in the Amazon without destroying the rain forest's ecology.

For hundreds of years after the European discovery of Amazonia, there was a common conviction that the luxuriant vegetation of the jungles offered irrefutable evidence of their boundlessly fertile soils. The belief remained unchallenged for so long because there was no interest in extending agriculture into the continent's interior. Farming was relegated mainly to the coastal zones where the European colonists were concentrated.

The first Spanish expeditionaries to sail down the Amazon River in 1541 had seen plentiful examples of native agriculture. Father Gaspar de Carvajal, who chronicled Orellana's voyage, asserted that Indian settlements along the river were so numerous that they were often separated by no more than a crossbow shot. And in many of these villages, the Spaniards came across manioc, sweet potatoes and other vegetables in well-tended patches on riverbanks, which were encrusted with layers of fertile silt carried by the Amazon from its sources in the Andean slopes. The early Jesuit missionaries also established agricultural settlements for their Indian wards along the streams and rivers. But they never tested the fertility of soils farther inland, beyond the reach of the Andean silt borne by the Amazon and its tributaries. Portuguese colonists, who first discovered Indian villages deep in the Brazilian jungles, were puzzled at why the natives practiced a rotational form of agriculture different from the sedentary farming they had seen along the rivers. They noticed that the Indians worked their small farm plots for only one or two years before abandoning them and starting new ones in forest patches that had to be chopped, burned and cleared anew. The process consumed so much time and energy that only superstition seemed to explain the reluctance of the natives to remain rooted to one site. It never occurred to these early Portuguese observers that the Indians were aware that the jungle soils eroded after a few years. By rotating their farm plots, the Amazon natives were practicing a crude but effective soil conservation.

The first scientists to encounter the abundance of plant life in the jungles were so dazzled that they declared the Amazon a Garden of Eden. "I fearlessly assert," wrote Alfred Russel Wallace, the famous British naturalist who spent four years in the northern Amazon in the mid-nineteenth century, "that here the primeval forest can be converted into rich pastureland, into cultivated gardens and orchards, containing every variety of produce, with half the labor, and, what is more important, in less than half the time that would be required at home."

But it was not until 1924 that a serious attempt was finally begun to cultivate the Amazon and move away from a purely extractive economic model in the jungles. In that year, Henry Ford, the American automobile magnate, decided to buy a huge expanse of rain forest in Brazil and carve out a rubber plantation along the lines of the Southeast Asian groves. The plantation, the size of Connecticut, was named, aptly enough, Fordlandia. It was located south of the Amazon River, along one of its main tributaries, the Tapajós, precisely on the site where fifty years before Sir Henry Wickham had collected the rubber seeds that he smuggled to Kew Gardens. Ford intended to ensure his own cheaper source of rubber and thus reduce the cost of tires for his automobiles.

It was not poetic justice or irony that led Ford to choose Henry Wickham's old territory for his rubber plantation. Ford's botanists were making what seemed to be an astute genetic bet that Wickham's rubber seeds would proliferate at least as well in their native soil as they did when transplanted to Ceylon and Malaya.

Ford spared no expense to ensure the success of his jungle venture. By Brazilian standards, his three thousand workers were well paid. Housing, hospitals, sanitation and recreation facilities were built; diesel-powered generators provided electricity. Bulldozers were brought in to flatten the jungle, and a sawmill was erected to produce a constant supply of lumber. A private railway linked the plantation to Fordlandia's harbor on the Tapajós River one hundred miles south of the point at which it flowed into the Amazon. And from there, Ford's rubber boats could proceed east 450 miles to the Atlantic Ocean.

By 1928, a million rubber seedlings were planted, and two years later the rubber trees began to blossom. The price of rubber on the London Exchange started to plummet, falling from more than a dollar a pound in 1928 to only twenty-five cents in 1932. But shortly thereafter, Fordlandia's rubber production showed its first signs of decline. Many of the saplings, with no protective jungle canopy overhead, either withered in the sun or drowned in the tropical rains. The trees that survived were attacked by insects and leaf-rust fungus. The soil itself seemed to lose its nutrients and become barren.

In 1938, Ford exchanged his lands in Fordlandia for another, smaller concession in Belterra, located on what were supposed to be more fertile soils on the banks of the Tapajós only twenty-five miles south of the Amazon River. This time, Ford's botanists brought over saplings from the Southeast Asian plantations. They even grafted the Asian variety onto the trunks of Amazon rubber trees. But again, the same symptoms of catastrophe appeared. The rubber trees, planted close to each other, were vulnerable to pests and disease. The soil turned sterile. In 1946, after spending about $30 million in his Amazon rubber venture, Ford gave up his jungle dream and accepted only $250,000 from the Brazilian government for his holdings in Belterra.

A generation later, another American titan attempted to create a plantation empire out of the Brazilian rain forests. In 1967, in the northeastern corner of the Amazon, not far from the river's mouth, the shipping magnate and financier Daniel K. Ludwig bought a 2.5-million-acre tract of jungle as big as Fordlandia. On this property, called Jari, he planted almost three hundred thousand acres of commercial trees imported from the Caribbean and West Africa. He bulldozed a network of roads and railway. He constructed a deep-water port and installed there a $200 million pulp mill seventeen stories high and three city blocks long that was built in Japan and towed on a barge for seventeen thousand miles, across the Indian and Atlantic oceans and up the Amazon to Jari. But by 1982, Ludwig, eighty-four years old and ailing, had to abandon his billion-dollar Amazon project as costs continued to mushroom without producing a fraction of the expected returned.

* * *

The Transamazon highway system was far more grandiose in concepton and costs than Fordlandia and Jari. Yet curiously, for a project of such magnitude, it lacked the careful research and preparation that preceded the two failed American ventures. Before beginning construction of the new roads, the Brazilian government did not make any extensive topographic surveys or soil analyses, nor did it train a large cadre of agronomists to instruct the expected wave of colonists and pioneers. Rather, the decision to build the Transamazon highway system was the result of emotional factors.

One of these emotional considerations was the fear among Brazilian military officials that as long as their country's Amazon lands remained undeveloped they would tempt foreigners who coveted the supposed riches of the rain forest. This nationalist anxiety often reached almost paranoid levels. Every pronouncement by foreigners on the subject of Amazonia caused Brazilians to bridle. When American oil firms expressed doubt that petroleum existed in the Amazon basin after their own surveys in the jungles during the 1930's and 1940's proved unsuccessful, their statements were denounced by Brazilian nationalists as a foreign conspiracy to keep secret the true dimensions of Brazil's oil deposits and to discourage Brazilians from exploiting these energy resources. When an American research foundation, the Hudson Institute, produced a farfetched plan in the 1960's calling for the inundation of the Amazon valley by building dams along its main rivers in order to generate electricity, control flooding and increase navigation, some Brazilian commentators saw an attempt from abroad to wrest control of their wilderness from them.

Another emotional factor behind the proposal to build the Transamazon highway system was the fervent desire of the Brazilian military regime to leave a tangible legacy of its own for the nation. Military officials were keenly aware that Juscelino Kubitschek, president from 1955 to 1960, was the country's most popular political leader, in part because of his daring decision to construct the futuristic capital of Brasília during his term in office. Brasília, located six hundred miles inland from the former capital, Rio de Janeiro, had captured the public imagination and forcibly shifted the gaze of Brazilians toward their country's vast, undeveloped interior. The Transamazon highway system seemed to be the logical next giant step in further drawing Brazil's population and resources away from the old colonial strongholds on the Atlantic coast and into the hinterlands.

But perhaps nothing emphasized the emotional underpinnings of the jungle highway project more than the incident that finally provoked the decision to begin the road's construction. In 1970, General Emilio Médici, then president of Brazil, paid a visit to the drought-stricken Northeast, inland from the colonial Atlantic port cities of Salvador and Recife. The general was so stunned by the human misery there that he impulsively announced a plan to settle the Amazon with a million impoverished Northeast peasant families. In dramatic, authoritarian fashion, he traced a straight line on a map paralleling the southern flank of the Amazon River not far from its mouth on the Atlantic, and ordered his minister of transport to build the first segment of the Transamazon Highway along that axis. Cities and towns would be established on the route, and rain forest would be cleared to provide free land and timber for the pioneers.

But when construction of the highway began, the Brazilian engineers were horrified to discover that most of the terrain was hilly, often rising and falling 120 feet over a quarter mile, rather than the flat basins General Médici had expected. Much of this Amazon region—located not far to the east of Ford's hapless rubber estates in Fordlandia and Belterra—proved unfertile, with no more than a two-inch layer of rich earth giving way to red dust once the jungle canopy was cleared. Many northeastern peasants, who had little financial or technical assistance and no agrarian experience in the jungles, saw their farming efforts collapse. The rising cost of petroleum, from which asphalt is produced, forced the government to leave long expanses of the Transamazon Highway unpaved and vulnerable to heavy rains and fast-growing underbrush. Almost half of the road crossed lowland jungles which were inundated during the long rainy season. As disease-ridden, defeated settlers straggled back home to the traditional eastern coastal zones with tales of hardship, the expected tide of pioneers failed to materialize. Fewer than nine thousand northeastern families have installed themselves along the northern segment of the highway.

The failure of this initial settlement effort unleashed a torrent of criticism against the Brazilian military government. Domestic opponents denounced the Amazon crusade as a crude and costly attempt by the military to divert attention away from the country's endemic poverty, inequality and political injustices in the heavily populated cities and coastal plains. Abroad, environmentalists warned that the assault on the wilderness was endangering the very existence of the

Amazon rain forest, with dire consequences to global ecology. Dubbing Amazonia "the lungs of the world," some environmentalists suggested that the wholesale destruction of the jungle would sharply reduce oxygen in the atmosphere. Others predicted that it would increase carbon dioxide, creating a hothouse effect that would raise temperatures around the world with devastating impact on plant and animal life.

The Brazilian government and its supporters reacted with scorn to the criticism of the Amazonian development program, particularly when it came from abroad. Brazilian nationalists claimed to see a revival of past attempts by foreigners to allegedly foil Brazil's ambitious plans for tapping its Amazon riches. Typifying this viewpoint was a now-famous article by Murilo Melo Filho, a conservative journalist writing in the magazine *Manchete* in February 1973:

> Precisely as the hour of the Amazon has arrived, with the sound of trumpets heralding our coming victory over the so-called Green Hell, intricate maneuvers and campaigns have begun inside and outside the country against the construction of the [Transamazon] highway. They started with suspicious rumors that the highway and the clearing of the rain forest would deprive humanity of oxygen and thus endanger the ecological balance of the earth. . . . But we do not intend to surrender one millimeter of our rights over a fabulous region that is exclusively ours.

To a visitor journeying through Amazonia for the first time, the notion that its soils are infertile and its flora fragile seems outlandish. From the air, the thick jungle canopy stretches endlessly without a visible patch of ground. It often obscures hundreds of rivers and streams that snake their way through the huge basin, covering more than half of Brazil and equivalent in area to almost two thirds of the continental United States. So dense is this rain forest that airborne explorers using radar mapping equipment discovered a three-hundred-mile-long river in the western Brazilian Amazon only a decade ago.

Yet, aside from the riverbanks and deltas that are perpetually enriched by Andean silt, most of Amazonia is indeed infertile. A combination of ancient geological formations, constant rainfall and heat have rendered much of its soils poorer than many deserts. The upper crusts of earth on the Amazon date back millions of years before the soils of the northern hemisphere, and have remained undisturbed and unreplenished by volcanic activity and glacial drifts. The continuous pounding of heavy rains has long ago eroded most of the topsoil to deposits of sand, granite and sterile iron and aluminum oxides. The heat and water continue to further leach the soil of soluble minerals and organic substances, except for a thin layer formed by dead plant and animal matter which is cyclically deposited, washed away and replaced.

The secret of the luxurious vegetation blanketing Amazonia is the extraordinary ability of plants to store and recycle as much as seventy-five percent of their nutrient requirements within their own bulk. Plants in temperate zones like Europe and North America largely depend on nutrients stored in the soil. But Amazon trees must use their leaves to block much of the sunlight and rainwater that would destroy the delicate topsoil at their roots. The nutrients of dead foliage dropping to the ground are then quickly reabsorbed by the trees.

The enormous variety of Amazonian plant life has been another important adaptation for survival. Amazonia has at least twenty times as many tree species as Europe. A few acres of jungle may sustain several hundred tree varieties, each with slightly different nutrient needs that allow them all to profit from the weak soil rather than having to compete for its meager resources. If vast numbers of only a few species—most of them with similar nutrient requirements—sought to grow on the same Amazon tract, they would quickly deplete the soil and perish. The proliferation of species in the same plot of land also provides a natural protection against jungle pests that could ravage a homogeneous plantation—as happened to the rubber estates of Fordlandia and Belterra.

The pattern holds for animal life as well. Louis Agassiz, the nineteenth-century Swiss-American naturalist, claimed to have discovered over twelve hundred distinct species of fish in the Amazon River—far more than the varieties then known to inhabit the Atlantic, yet obviously far fewer in total population than the ocean's fish. Henry Bates, a nineteenth-century English naturalist who spent eleven years exploring the northern Amazon, was also puzzled by the contradiction of a relatively small number of animals divided into a myriad species. "The region is so extensive and uniform in the forest clothing of its surface that it is only at long intervals that animals are seen in abundance when some particular spot is found which is more attractive than others," wrote Bates. "The huntsman would be disappointed who expected to find here flocks of animals similar to the buffalo herds of North America, or the swarms of antelopes and herds of ponderous pachyderms of South Africa."

Betty J. Meggers, an American archaeologist and anthropologist whose book *Amazonia: Man and Culture in a Counterfeit Paradise* has become a classic on the region's ecology, explained the effect of the vegetation on the evolution of animal life. In temperate zones, she noted, "the existence of plentiful and wholesome plant food has favored the evolution of herbivores with large body size (bears, moose, deer) and gregarious habits (bison, caribou, horse)." But in the Amazon, "conditions of high average temperature and rainfall are coupled with low inorganic fertility to produce vegetation with large bulk and limited protein content. . . . Leaves and grass developed under these conditions are luxuriant in appearance, but their limited food value is reflected in a fauna that is sparsely distributed and small in body size in comparison to that of temperate regions."

Brazilian scientists have recently confirmed Meggers's observations. In the last decade, they have surveyed small plots of Amazon rain forest and discovered that their animal mass—mammals, birds, reptiles, amphibians and insects—is far less in total weight than one would find in similar experiments carried out in Asian and African tropical lands.

This paradox of a jungle growing from a desert, or a surface variety masking an underlying scarcity, was quickly brought home to the hapless Northeast peasants who settled the edges of General Médici's Transamazon Highway in the early 1970's. By slashing and burning the forest cover, and then allowing the rains to drench the soils with the ash of plant and animal matter, the pioneers were able to produce bountiful harvests in their first year of cultivation. But with the combined action of unobstructed rain and sunlight, there were smaller and fewer crops growing out of the leached earth the second year. By the third year, the thin soils were eroded to a red desert consistency. What remained of the harvests was attacked by insects and fungus, which proved far more devastating against monocultural vegetation than against the multiple plant species of the natural jungle. Even attempts to extract timber were thwarted because the settlers were unable to find more than a few trees of economic value in a terrain where so many different varieties proliferated. The optimistic predictions of a trillion-dollar wood bonanza in the Amazon disintegrated when lumberjacks had to pick their way hundreds of feet between each commercially exploitable tree.

In 1973, the Brazilian military government shifted the focus of its Amazon program. It decided that large chunks of the rain forest would be cleared for pastureland to support huge cattle ranches rather than smaller plots for paupered, inexperienced settlers. Firms as diverse as automobile manufacturers, steelmakers and food packagers were encouraged to invest profits in lands near the Transamazon Highway in exchange for tax rebates and low-interest loans. The government's logic was that only big private capital, backed by state aid, could afford the risks and costs of developing the Amazon.

The change in direction infuriated domestic critics who claimed that the inequality of land tenure so prevalent in the traditional coastal agricultural regions was being extended to the Amazon frontier, with political support and economic subsidies from the government. Among ecologists, the fears of Amazon devastation were magnified by the new specter of large cattle ranches.

But the initial pace at which the jungle was being slashed and burned began to slow. Satellite photographs taken in the early 1980's indicated that less than three percent of the rain forest had been cleared—well short of the rate which pessimists had asserted was leading to the death of the jungle by the end of this century. The slowdown has been partly attributable to growing concern for environmentalism in government circles. Probably more important has been the failure of Amazon cattle-ranching operations to approximate the profitable levels that investors had anticipated. Despite all the subsidies and tax rebates, livestock production in the jungle has been too costly to compete with cattle raising in southern and central Brazil. The pasturelands and ranches in the northern Amazon frontier exist more on paper than in reality. Often they are relatively small patches of cleared forest intended to stake a large landholder's claim against squatters.

By 1975, the military government's scheme to settle the northern Amazon along the first segments of its jungle highway system had reached an impasse bordering on fiasco. It appeared that this would be the most short-lived of all the attempts to conquer the rain forest, and would leave a briefer legacy than the conquistadores, missionaries and rubber barons.

But the well-publicized failures and controversies swirling about the colonization efforts in the northern Amazon jungles largely obscured a much more important and massive pioneer drive taking place almost simultaneously far to the west, in Rondônia. Roughly

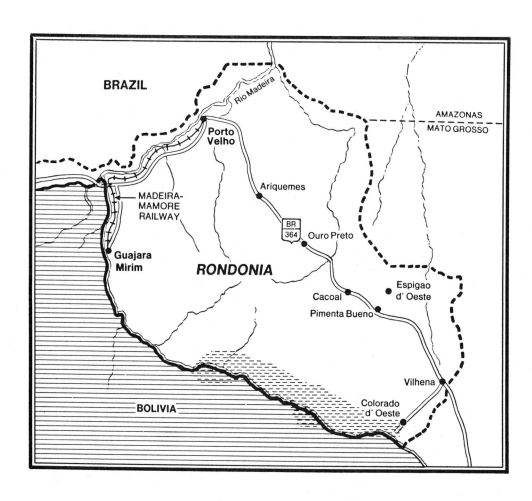

BRAZIL

Rio Madeira

AMAZONAS
MATO GROSSO

Porto
Velho

Ariquemes

MADEIRA-
MAMORE
RAILWAY

BR
364

Ouro Preto

Guajara
Mirim

RONDONIA

Espigao
d' Oeste

Cacoal

Pimenta Bueno

Vilhena

BOLIVIA

Colorado
d' Oeste

following the 835-mile-long path that Colonel Rondon had cleared earlier this century for his Strategic Telegraph Line, the military government in the late 1960's ploughed a dirt highway from Cuiabá, in the state of Mato Grosso, westward to Pôrto Velho, the capital of Rondônia. At Pôrto Velho, the road eventually was joined from the north by the much larger Transamazon highway system, and then continued its western course into Acre, branching into the roads I had seen during my visit there.

The road through Rondônia is known as BR-364. It differs from the Transamazon highway system in two very important respects: the quality of the land it crosses and the spontaneous nature of the pioneer movement it has attracted.

By an incredible stroke of luck, the lands which the BR-364 highway slices through are far more fertile than soils elsewhere in Amazonia. A volcanic terra roxa, or red earth, extending in large swathes over Rondônia, makes about half of the huge state—larger than New York and Pennsylvania combined—suitable for agriculture, particularly perennial crops like coffee, cocoa and fruit trees that provide a continuous cover for the soil from excess sunlight and rain. There is less volcanic terra roxa in Acre. But in that state, the government claims to have recently discovered an equally fertile expanse of thick, loamy topsoil spreading over forty thousand square miles, or about the size of Ohio.

BR-364 has sparked a land rush into Rondônia unmatched in speed and ferocity by any rural migration since the settling of the nineteenth-century American West. Nowhere else in the world are people moving into virgin territories on the scale witnessed in Rondônia. Between 1968 and 1982, the population of Rondônia increased ninefold to almost one million inhabitants, and the pace shows no sign of slowing.

The first waves of pioneers into Rondônia in the late 1960's and early 1970's were not beckoned by the kind of government colonization projects attempted in the northern Amazon. The Rondônian settlers were initially a more independent, spontaneous phenomenon. They either bought plots from private developers or squatters, or heard that BR-364 had opened lands that were available to anybody who staked a claim.

Many of the settlers are mulattoes and mestizos who originally had their roots in the drought-stricken northeast of Brazil, inland from the old colonial Atlantic port cities of Salvador and Recife and

Fortaleza. To escape the cyclical dry periods that killed their crops and livestock, they moved two and three decades ago to the thriving agricultural south of Brazil. But they were forced to move again, this time to Rondônia, because they were displaced by the growing mechanization of agriculture in the prosperous, modern coffee and soybean plantations of southern Brazilian states like São Paulo, Paraná, Santa Catarina and Rio Grande do Sul. Other pioneers flooding into Rondônia, almost as numerous as these dark former northeasterners, are the blond or pale-skinned descendants of nineteenth-century German and Italian immigrants to southern Brazil. Their families' farms were too small to accommodate them, so they migrated to Rondônia in search of plots of their own.

All of them are riding into Rondônia through the red dust and mud of BR-364. Entire families crowd into trucks or buses or even ox-drawn carts that set out from the eastern third of Brazil to the western Amazon frontier. They have been joined by armies of laborers deployed by real-estate speculators and big ranchers to raze the jungles. And in their wake have come the hired gunmen, con artists and other criminals who flourish in the inevitable disputes over possession of land.

By the time the government realized the scope of this migration, Rondônia had become the scene of the most violent, confused and widespread struggles over land anywhere in Brazil. The land wars have pitted white man against aboriginal Indian, peasant against large property owner, legal settler against squatter and private developer against government land agent.

These conflicts continue to this day. But they had their genesis in a giant land grab by a large clan known as the Melhoranças, whose sudden appearance in Rondônia sparked one of the strangest episodes in modern South American frontier history.

9

In 1967, the Melhorança brothers, land speculators from the Atlantic coastal state of São Paulo, arrived in Rondônia following the government bulldozers that were gouging out the BR-364 highway. There were four brothers and thirty-six other family members—wives, cousins, children, nephews and nieces. The head of the clan, Nilo Melhorança, was a fleshy man of middle height in his late forties, with a soft double chin, thinning black hair and wet, mournful eyes. He had been a topographer in the southern state of Paraná, where booming coffee and soybean plantations sprouted on former jungle land. Rondônia, he believed, was destined for a similar bonanza, and this time he would possess a massive share of frontier land rather than just survey it for other investors.

At Pimenta Bueno, a settlement about a hundred fifty miles into Rondônia from the western border of Mato Grosso, the Melhorانças turned off BR-364 and ploughed their own primitive dirt road some twenty miles north. There they founded Espigão d'Oeste —the Ridge of the West—and claimed 3.5 million acres of land around it, an expanse of rain forest half the size of Belgium.

Holding on to large reserves for themselves, the Melhordanças then formed the Itaporanga Real Estate Company. The firm, which had absolutely no legal basis, partitioned and sold off hundreds of plots ranging up to five thousand acres in size to potential settlers who were contacted in the adjoining state of Mato Grosso and the southern states of São Paulo and Paraná.

The Melhor 안ças—the name roughly translates as "those who make things better" or "those who provide relief"—rented out tractors and bulldozers to the new arrivals, and advanced them loans. Soon Espigão d'Oeste became a full-fledged frontier community with an administrative building, where Nilo Melhorança kept his head-quarters, a general store, saloons, an elementary school, a chapel and a doctor's office.

The Melhoranças were not ordinary land-grabbers. Nilo claimed to be a "spiritualist." According to settlers who flocked to Espigão d'Oeste, he was a fine, often hypnotic orator, who advocated a fraternity of small and large pioneers, banded together, ignoring their racial and economic differences, against a hostile outside world. Here in this wilderness, they would create a new society and achieve the financial and emotional security that had eluded them in the east.

The Melhoranças always asserted that they had bought part of their huge property from a rubber-estate owner whose family had acquired title to the land back at the turn of the century. But Brazilian law—designed to counter real-estate speculation—allots frontier lands within sixty miles of a federal road to the national government, which can then decide to sell at whatever price it deems fair. Moreover, much of the land that the Melhoranças claimed already belonged to the Surui Indian tribe.

At first, there were no conflicts with the Suruis. Curious about the settlements and the road, the Indians wandered into Espigão d'Oeste. The Melhoranças skillfully used pacification techniques, giving small gifts to the Suruis, offering them free truck rides along the roads, trading knives and mirrors for their fish and game, occasionally even hiring the Indians to help slash and burn the rain forest and introducing them to paper money.

But as hundreds of pioneer families moved into the land they had bought from the Melhoranças, problems began. The expansion of farmland encroached on Indian hunting preserves and chased wild game away. Hungry Suruis stole crops from the settlers' fields. Other Indians were reduced to begging and prostitution. Surui girls as young as twelve and thirteen were infected with syphilis and gonorrhea. Severe alcoholism became widespread among tribe members. Unequal battles erupted between Indians, armed with bows and arrows, clubs and spears, and settlers with shotguns and revolvers. But the Suruis were mostly wiped out by simple colds that quickly precipitated fatal pneumonia and bronchitis among a people who had never developed immunity to white men's diseases. Brazilian government officials estimated that there were as many as seven hundred Suruis when the Melhoranças arrived, and of these only about three hundred survived.

It was not the decimation of the Indians that finally impelled the government into action. Rather it was the success of the Melhoranças in attracting settlers into Rondônia. Other land speculators were also arriving in the territory, selling off huge expanses of rain forest to big ranchers and partitioning, for publicity purposes, some smaller properties for settlers. The military regime was at a crossroads in Rondônia. Would this frontier be developed by private entrepreneurs selling mainly to big landlords, or would it be handled by government agents encouraging the establishment of small farms for land-starved pioneers?

Tentatively, the government decided to favor the small pioneers. In 1970, three years after the arrival of the Melhoranças, the government established the National Institute for Colonization and Agrarian Reform, or INCRA as it is known by its Brazilian acronym, and created a branch of this new agency in Rondônia. INCRA's chief purpose was to distribute 250-acre plots of Amazon land to peasants and small farmers arriving to the frontier. But this decision did not immediately resolve the dispute over land development. The military regime, which ruled the cities and rural areas of the eastern half of the country with such iron-fisted resolve, was a good deal weaker and vacillating on the frontier. This was not only because the security forces were too small to impose a semblance of law and order in these backlands. Just as important was a lack of consensus at the highest levels of government.

Those who advocated an Amazonia dominated by hordes of small pioneers asserted it would be an ideal way to tackle the country's land problems without resorting to a costly, politically explosive agrarian reform program in the traditional farm zones. There are ten million landless peasants in Brazil. The vast majority of the forty-five million agrarian Brazilians live in poverty as sharecroppers, seasonal laborers or subsistence farmers. Hadn't the government already decreed the Amazon "a land without people for a people without land"?

Opposing this line of thought were government officials, some of them in the cabinet, who took the view that the Amazon frontiers, including Rondônia, were big enough to accommodate both small and large farmers. Wasn't the military government committed to the free enterprise system? Couldn't private entrepreneurs bring to the western backlands the same economic boom that the industrial cities and southern agricultural zones were experiencing? Undoubtedly, a few of these government officials were secretly collaborating with big land speculators for a percentage of profits or gifts of land. The Melhoranças always claimed that they were encouraged to plunge into Rondônia by the local authorities and officials in the Ministry of Interior, even some who dealt with Indian affairs.

The creation of INCRA alone would not settle the debate. Much would depend on the land colonization agency's leaders—how they interpreted their mandate, how adept they were in finding their way through the bureaucratic maze of Brasília to rally support from high government officials, how successful they were in administrating and staffing their organization with underpaid but motivated people, and how willing they were to confront big landowners and determined squatters.

To head INCRA in Rondônia, the government selected a retired army officer, Captain Silvio Gonçalves de Faria. It is doubtful that the officials in Brasília considered him an exceptional candidate. He himself would often say that the only qualities that attracted the government were his long experience in the jungle and his desire to remain there.

Captain Silvio, as everybody called him, was a big, husky mulatto with a booming voice. Born into rural poverty in the northeastern state of Minas Gerais, he was one of eleven brothers and sisters. He never got past elementary school and enlisted in the army as a teenager. Throughout most of his military career, he was a sergeant, having probably spoiled his chances of advancement by participating several times in politically activist groups of noncommissioned officers. For more than twenty years, he was stationed in the Amazon, assigned to contingents of the army engineering corps who surveyed Brazil's borders with neighboring countries and built roads and airports in the jungle. He was promoted to captain only upon retirement, and was forty-five years old when he was chosen to head INCRA's Rondônia office in 1970.

Captain Silvio carried out a two-pronged strategy. Under his orders, INCRA filed lawsuits against the big real-estate speculators and landowners, accusing them of illegally appropriating federal property. At the same time, in 1971, he hurriedly launched INCRA's first land colonization scheme in Rondônia, distributing 250-acre plots to one thousand settler families at a development project known as Ouro Preto, straddling BR-364 at its midway point through the territory.

The large landholders and the press organs they controlled virulently denounced Captain Silvio, suggesting he was enriching himself through bribes and by secret land deals, that he was a Communist, even a sexual pervert. In a lawsuit brought by INCRA against one of the newspapers that had published the most scurrilous charges, the editor responsible for their dissemination confessed that he had been bribed by a large real-estate corporation. But irate editorials against Captain Silvio continued, and soon there were anonymous letters and phone calls threatening to kill him.

"He was absolutely fearless," recalled Amir Francisco Lando, a lawyer for INCRA during those early years before going into his own private practice. "He would walk and drive around without a gun or bodyguards. He would brush off the threats by saying that the big landlords knew that if he got killed, the person who replaced him would probably be even worse for them. And you know, the funny thing is that he was right: some of those landlords and speculators would provide their own *jagunços* [hired gunmen] to protect him because they really were afraid all hell would break loose if he were murdered."

I briefly interviewed Captain Silvio once in his INCRA headquarters, a small, two-story stucco building in Pôrto Velho. He was twice the age of most of his subordinates and was dressed in khaki shirt and pants—civilian clothes that gave him a military aura. His staff always addressed him as captain, and scurried about as he barked out orders like an officer.

"When we began the first colonization project at Ouro Preto, we didn't have even the most rudimentary plans," he recounted. "I just flew over the zone and picked it because it was in the middle of the territory, and I figured that we would then establish other projects spaced evenly on either side of Ouro Preto along BR-364. We didn't carry out any soil tests. We didn't have more than a couple of agronomists to advise the settlers coming into Ouro Preto. We had barely marked off the plots before we started distributing them. And we didn't even have standardized documentation procedures to give out titles. But I felt we had to move quickly because settlers were pouring into Rondônia and some order had to be imposed. Also, I felt we had to prove as quickly as possible that INCRA could do a better job than the big real-estate companies and that, given a chance, the small pioneers could succeed.

"Given the choice between distributing ten thousand hectares [twenty-five thousand acres] to one big rancher and giving a hundred [two hundred fifty acres] apiece to a hundred settlers, I'll always choose the small guys. And why not? The big rancher comes from São Paulo, where he already owns a lot of property. He risks very little of his own capital out here. He can always find cheap loans to pay for his land, and if he fails, he gets a tax write-off. The pioneers come here with nothing. This is the end of the line for them.

"And another thing: those big land companies feel no responsibility to anyone. What right do they have to grab federal lands without paying for them? They bring settlers into lands that belong to Indians, and a situation develops that nobody can resolve. They don't even provide their settlers with the most minimal services. Sure, INCRA is understaffed and underfinanced. But we have had to become much more than a simple land distribution agency. We provide agricultural extension services. We show settlers how to apply for lands. We have had to supply them with health services. Sometimes, the schools are built right in the INCRA grounds. We lend out bulldozers to open and maintain feeder roads. We're not supposed to be providing these services, and we do them badly. But no one else is there. The government agencies responsible for all these services haven't arrived yet in the frontier."

For years, a confrontation seemed inevitable between Captain Silvio, representing an orderly, government-controlled colonization of Rondônia, and the Melhoranças, symbols of an unfettered private enterprise in the frontier. But in spite of his bluster, Captain Silvio moved cautiously against the Melhorança clan. Even after the courts ruled that the Melhoranças had no right to their lands, INCRA hesitated to call upon the security forces to oust them. The seven hundred settlers and their families in Espigão d'Oeste were well organized, heavily armed and loyal to Nilo Melhorança, who convinced them that INCRA was plotting to steal their lands and imbued them with an almost fanatic zeal.

It was this pseudoreligious aura about the Melhoranças that most troubled INCRA and military officials. Over the centuries, the backlands of Brazil have spawned numerous messianic movements. Desperate peasants would rally behind a mystical leader who called upon them to withdraw from a corrupt Brazilian society and establish their own paradise on earth. Usually these movements withered and burned themselves out. But occasionally, they would assume fanatic proportions, posing a separatist challenge that the national authorities felt compelled to bloodily repress.

The worst such incident occurred at the end of the nineteenth century, in the arid backlands of the Northeast known as the *sertão*. There, a deranged mystic, Antonio Conselheiro, traveled about on foot preaching the imminent end of the world. His fiery speeches gathered thousands of converts, and he led them to an abandoned town, Canudos, which he claimed would be the only outpost on earth to survive the coming Armageddon. In Canudos, the zealots built a large stone church and maintained a rigorously ascetic, orderly existence in accordance with the religious precepts laid down by Conselheiro. But when the droughts swept the Northeast, destroying crops and livestock, Conselheiro's followers would storm out of Canudos and plunder the countryside to sustain their holy city.

The national government sent troops to put down the fanatics. But by the time the soldiers had exhausted themselves trekking through the scorched, dusty hinterland, they were easily crushed by the rebels. A second and third expedition were also wiped out. Finally, the government sent a force of six thousand troops who besieged Canudos, exterminated every one of its inhabitants, including Conselheiro, and demolished every building in the city. Accompanying this expedition was a young army engineer, Euclydes de Cunha, not yet renowned as a writer. At first repelled by the Canudos movement, he grew sympathetic to its followers' fervor and wrote *Os sertões—Rebellion in the Backlands—*a nonfiction book of Tolstoyan dimensions about the massacre.

"The last thing we wanted was to have people consider the Melhoranças and their followers as martyrs," said Lando, the ex-INCRA lawyer. "We really allowed them to get away with a lot. I handled the lawsuit against the Melhoranças. Even when the courts ruled against them, they refused to surrender. They had the equivalent of a feudal barony, and had built an almost impregnable fortress. They were well armed. They had lookout posts along the only road into Espigão d'Oeste, and they communicated by walkie-talkie. When INCRA sent its topographical teams to survey their land, the Melhoranças and their followers stripped them of their equipment, threatened to kill them and finally sent them packing on foot. The Melhoranças really had declared themselves in a state of war against INCRA, the territorial government, even the police.

"What finally did them in was their decision to blow up a federal bridge on the road to Espigão d'Oeste. The government just could not tolerate a blatant act of subversion like that. So in 1976, we went into Espigão d'Oeste with a lot of military police, armed with machine guns, even helicopters. We arrested Nilo Melhorança—the other brothers went into hiding—and we impounded all the documents we found in his administrative building. It was only then that we had a true notion of how large the project was. We had to tell the settlers that they were victims of a land hoax of gigantic proportions. Most of them really had no idea what they had gotten themselves into. They had paid money, received deeds, cleared and worked their lands. Some of them had never heard of INCRA. After all, in Brazil in 1970, there was very little government involvement in the distribution of lands. It was far more usual for private developers, like the Melhoranças, to carry out that task. The Melhoranças had really created a tremendous paranoia among their settlers against the government. They told them we were on the payroll of other land-grabbers who wanted to steal their farms. You know, there is a terrible loneliness and isolation here on the frontier. You see no police, no authority. So it was quite natural that people would fall back on a man like Nilo Melhorança. He was strong, confident, convincing. He opened up a wilderness for people who had always been losers, and he even gave them a sense of religion."

After his arrest, Nilo was sent to prison for several months in Belém. Both his hold over his settlers and the influence he wielded among government officials dwindled rapidly. Upon his release, he went back briefly to Rondônia, saw that his empire had collapsed and returned to São Paulo, stripped of all his frontier lands and reduced once again to anonymity. It was to take INCRA another four years, until 1980, to unravel the chaos over land titles he had created in Espigão d'Oeste. Some of the smaller settlers were allowed to stay. The larger ones had their properties reduced to 250 acres. Other pioneers, particularly those who arrived after 1973, either were given land elsewhere or wandered about aimlessly, hiring out as peons or squatting on somebody else's property. The Surui Indians, of course, were the biggest losers. No one ever thought to transform Espigão d'Oeste back into an Indian preserve. Instead, they were placed on smaller lands farther to the west, and soon found themselves again under encroachment by other settlers.

With the perspective of several years, Lando and other officials associated with INCRA have a more nuanced view of Nilo Melhorança. They now believe that he was a catalyst for the development of Rondônia, the man who forced the government to come up with a serious plan of its own to open the frontier to small settlers.

"I would never have admitted it back then," confessed Lando, "but Nilo was a courageous person. He was a real *bandeirante,* a man of the frontier. He was doing something important by opening new lands, bringing people out here. Maybe if the Melhoranças had not acted, INCRA would not have been pushed into action. You know, a lot of people around here don't think he was so evil. In the end, he made no money in Rondônia. His Itaporanga Real Estate Company went bankrupt. He came here to become rich, but he wanted so much more. He saw a territory without law, without values—and he imposed his own. He probably even convinced himself along with his followers that he was acting out of selfless motives."

Captain Silvio, the head of INCRA in Rondônia, emerged from his victory over the Melhoranças in a far stronger political position. His first project at Ouro Preto was widely deemed a success, and he quickly launched dozens of other settlements along BR-364, the dirt highway slicing through Rondônia. The territory was deluged by pioneers, more than ten thousand arriving every month. By the mid-1970's, there was no longer any question that they had gained the upper hand against the big estate owners. With little hope of expanding their holdings, the landlords sought to guard the perimeters of their properties against squatters.

Battles continuously blazed between the ranchers' hired gunmen and hordes of squatters. INCRA was overwhelmed by the massive numbers of migrants seeking land and was able to accommodate only a fraction of these supplicants. The violence and disorder provided the big landholders with the ammunition they needed to eventually undermine Captain Silvio. He was vulnerable also because Rondônia was growing so fast that it would soon become a state, and that prospect aroused the political ambitions of people who feared that the captain might easily become a candidate for governor.

At the beginning of 1977, Captain Silvio was relieved as head of INCRA. A year later, at the age of fifty-three, he died in Rio de Janeiro, following his eighth or ninth bout of malaria. The newspapers and radio stations in Rondônia rarely evoked his memory.

Local government officials never mentioned his name. The ranchers and big landholders congratulated themselves on his departure from the frontier. But Captain Silvio had correctly surmised that even his removal would not reverse the direction of Rondônia's development. No politician would dare to suggest that the frontier be turned over to the private land developers.

"Eventually, Captain Silvio stepped on too many toes—landlords, military officers, high-ranking bureaucrats," said Lando, recalling his former boss. "A lot of generals and colonels resented the fact that this former sergeant had become the lord of Rondônia. But there is just no question that he and Rondon were the two greatest figures in Rondônia's history. He really created a mystique about the settling of the Amazon the same way Rondon had done before him. He really inspired INCRA people who were young and inexperienced. And he had a huge following among the settlers, even those who were frustrated because they hadn't yet received lands. Whenever he would show up at one of those settlements, everybody, and I mean everybody, would turn out to see him. And now the powers that be here in Rondônia and in Brasília pretend he never existed. All his enemies who spread all those lies about how he had secretly enriched himself didn't have the guts to admit that he died penniless. He was so poor that his widow, who brought his remains back to Rondônia, didn't have enough money to bury him. He always said he wanted to be buried here on the frontier, in Ariquemes [one of the settlements he founded alongside BR-364]. Can you believe it, his bones are in a sack in Ariquemes still waiting for somebody to pay for a decent monument."

The rivalries between Captain Silvio and the big land speculators like Nilo Melhorança may have determined the political battle lines in the conquest of Rondônia during the 1970's. But for thousands of small, anonymous pioneers, those battle lines were very blurred. More often than not, they were caught up by a maelstrom that left them disoriented and bewildered, and finally deposited them either on a plot of their own or back on the road, landless and destitute.

Typical of the simple people who got caught in the crossfire between the Melhoranças and Captain Silvio's INCRA were Jesuino da Silva and his wife, Durvalina. He is a tall, sturdy mulatto in his fifties, with a lantern jaw, close-cropped gray hair and a bass voice. Perhaps ten years younger, Durvalina is much shorter and thinner, with cream-and-coffee skin and a high-pitched, singsong voice. They have ended up on the Rondônia frontier after an odyssey that has spanned thousands of miles and three decades in search for land of their own.

Jesuino was born in the state of Minas Gerais, part of Brazil's overpopulated Northeast, a region of stultifying rural poverty. Cyclical dry spells every few years shrivel the corn and manioc and sugar cane plantings. When the livestock die of hunger and thirst, riots erupt and peasants ransack food warehouses. Then the frenzy subsides. Most of the inhabitants resume their lives of quiet desperation. But others, in the millions, move elsewhere in Brazil in search of a livelihood.

Jesuino was twenty-two years old when he joined this exodus in 1951. He faced a choice back then between heading to the expanding factories of São Paulo, or moving even farther south, six hundred miles from his hometown, to the new agricultural frontier in Paraná, where virgin forests were being cleared for coffee and soybean plantations. Because his father had been a coffee sharecropper in Minas Gerais, Jesuino wanted to remain a farmer. His plan was to work as a coffee picker for a few years, and eventually save enough money to buy a plot of his own. But the coffee boom in Paraná had sent the price of land soaring. No farmer could make a profit with fewer than two hundred acres. Try as he might, Jesuino could not save enough money to afford even a few acres. The years turned into one, then two decades. In the meantime, he married Durvalina, the teenage daughter of another Northeast migrant. When their eighth child was born, Jesuino was still a coffee picker.

In 1971, a frost killed the coffee trees on the plantation where he was employed. He remembers that day well. A cold wind sweeping up from the South Atlantic blanketed the land with a fine spray the night before. In the early dawn, the plantation was enveloped in a cottony fog so thick that Jesuino could not see the trees in his backyard. His heart thumping, he rushed out to the coffee bushes, hoping against the odds that the pale disk in the slate sky would quickly swell into a warm, bright tropical sun before the freezing temperatures could wreak their irreparable damage. But the leaden morning light had penetrated the mist only enough to unveil the fearsome beauty of the frost. The gentle rain had congealed on the trees, the ground, the telephone poles and wires, forming a thin, transparent shell on everything it touched. The green coffee beans and every leaf on every bush were plated with ice, like candy dipped in a sugary glaze.

"It was the second straight harvest that was lost to the freeze," said Jesuino. "Only this time, I really felt as if it were my own coffee because I knew the boss was losing too much money to keep his workers."

For some time, the owner had been investing heavily in mechanization to cut down labor costs and partially shield himself from the losses caused by periodic frosts. The new machines looked like squat, miniature bulldozers. They swept down the rows of coffee trees ripping off the beans faster than a dozen experienced pickers could manage, even working at a forced pace. Scores of laborers had already been fired. Jesuino had been reduced to a scavenger, following in the wake of a puttering machine to pick up the odd beans that had eluded its blind grasp and scattered on the ground. A few months after the terrible frost, the plantation owner informed Jesuino that he also would lose his job.

"I came to Paraná to escape the drought in Minas, and I had to leave Paraná to escape the frost," said Jesuino, with humorless irony.

He was a strong man in good health. But at forty-two years of age, black and barely literate, with a wife and eight children to care for, Jesuino was hardly a candidate anymore for an industrial job in the metropolis of São Paulo. Even if a factory owner overlooked his age, he would never find the housing to accommodate his family in the crowded city.

It was at that point that a man he had never met came around to Jesuino's shack and told him that the opportunity of a lifetime was available fifteen hundred miles northwest, in the wild Amazon frontier of Rondônia. Big real-estate developers, the Melhoranças, were selling countless acres of virgin land there at rock-bottom prices. With a two-hundred-dollar down payment, the stranger asserted, Jesuino could own one hundred fertile acres and pay the remaining eight hundred dollars in low-interest installments over five years.

Jesuino was relieved that the fat man in a grease-stained beige suit was not a debt collector or an emissary carrying an eviction notice from the plantation owner. Jesuino listened politely to the smooth sales pitch, barely asking a question. He didn't jump at the offer on the spot, and the stranger was not insistent. But within a week, the whole plantation was shaking with land fever, and a dozen jobless pickers had spent their savings to purchase plots from the Melhoranças. When the fat man came around again, Jesuino da

Silva gave him two hundred dollars for a very official-looking land deed.

That spring of 1972, all ten Da Silvas and a neighboring peasant family of six, the Ribeiros, set out for the Rondônia frontier in an old flatbed truck called a *pau-de-arara,* or parrot's perch, its back sheltered from the elements by a flimsy tarpaulin cover. It cost the pioneers a few hundred dollars to rent the vehicle and its driver. The passengers squeezed themselves between their boxes of clothes, food, kitchen utensils, bedding, farm implements, water cans, a dozen caged chickens, a collared sow and her brood of piglets.

They barreled past the coffee and soybean farms of Paraná and São Paulo. Then, in the huge state of Mato Grosso, an area as large as France, Italy and West Germany combined, the asphalt petered into gravel as the road led past sprawling cattle estates carved out of hot plains and scrub forests.

At Cuiabá, the capital of Mato Grosso, the truck reached roughly the halfway mark. From then on, the highway became the famous BR-364 that carried hundreds of thousands of other pioneers into Rondônia. Gravel and asphalt turned to red dirt. As the vehicle lumbered on at a much slower pace, the ocher dust clung to the hair and clothes of the passengers and caked on their sweaty faces. When the rains splashed down, BR-364 became an impassable bog, and the migrants had to pull up on the roadside for a day or two until the sun baked the mud enough to continue. On either side of the high-way, the terrain had become thick jungle, with blackened patches where trees and underbrush had been slashed and burned away. There were no longer any real towns or stone buildings, only ram-shackle communities of flimsy wood homes. At night, the truck would park on the outskirts of these settlements next to dozens of other pioneer vehicles circled like a wagon train. The travelers would sleep in and under the trucks. Occasionally, they found nearby creeks to bathe in, or else they doused themselves with water buckets drawn from wells.

"There were so many people marching to the west," recalled Durvalina. "It seemed like the whole country was searching for land in Rondônia. At first I had this terrible doubt that there would not be enough land for all of us, that we would get there and have to turn back. There were many people who were worse off than we were. There were people who begged for food. There were people whose trucks were broken down beyond repair, and they would have to split up their families and hitch rides the rest of the way hoping to meet up again soon. But most people were very kind also. Some youngsters would play guitars and beat drums to radio music, and pretty soon there was a party going. Then I would stop worrying whether there would be enough land out there and I would think that maybe it wasn't such a crazy idea to go to Rondônia because all these people couldn't be wrong."

Everybody except for Jesuino and Durvalina came down with dysentery just before they reached Rondônia. All of the Da Silvas survived. But the youngest child of the Ribeiro family, a two-year-old boy, died after four days of violent fever and was buried in a shallow roadside grave marked by a crude wooden cross.

Two weeks after setting out from Paraná, the truck arrived at its destination, disgorging its weak and exhausted passengers in Espigão d'Oeste. The Melhoranças' stronghold was a small clearing in the rain forest, no more impressive than the ragged communities Jesuino and his companions had passed during the last stages of their harrowing journey. There were about fifty wooden buildings, including a dirty flophouse where the travelers stayed for almost a week.

On the first evening, Jesuino and his family were greeted by Nilo Melhorança. He took out a copy of Jesuino's deed and a map marking off his hundred acres about two miles west of the settlement.

"Welcome home," Jesuino recalled Nilo saying to him. "You have much work ahead, but your worst troubles are behind you."

The Melhoranças had used a bulldozer to gouge a primitive path to Jesuino's property. During the next two months, Jesuino and his family built a large dirt-floor cabin and cleared almost a dozen acres of jungle. The two oldest Da Silva boys hired out as peons to the larger settlers. As payment, they received credits for the general store and the occasional loan of a chain saw for use on their own property. But Jesuino and his other children who were big enough to work used mostly machetes and long-handled scythes and axes to hack away at the trees and bushes on their land.

It was backbreaking, sometimes dangerous labor. One of Jesuino's children, a fourteen-year-old boy, broke an arm and suffered a concussion when a tree he was cutting fell on top of him. At the end of every day all of them emerged from the jungle covered with mosquito and ant bites, and with painfully swollen and bloody hands. Several times they narrowly escaped being bitten by poisonous snakes.

When the dry season arrived in late June, the acres of slashed rain forest were set afire. There were blazes all around Espigão d'Oeste and in settlements throughout Rondônia. The smoke billowed densely, sometimes blocking out the sun. For weeks on end, a haze lingered that made eyes smart and left throats raspy. Then the rains would come, fertilizing the soil with the ashes. The Da Silvas planted manioc and rice in their small clearing.

While they waited for their first harvest, the family rarely ate anything more than manioc, rice and beans, bought on credit at the general store. Prices were two or three times what Jesuino had paid back in Paraná. But he had no choice. Food costs were high throughout the frontier, and the general store at Espigão d'Oeste was the only one within twenty miles.

Jesuino saw a lot of the Melhoranças. They encouraged the settlers to discuss anything on their minds. They held meetings, usually on Sundays after services at the chapel in Espigão d'Oeste. Nilo delivered stirring speeches, blending religious sermons with exhortations to work and help each other. He compared the settlers to the *bandeirantes* who had thrust into the Brazilian wilderness centuries before. He told them that the nation would be grateful for their pioneering efforts, and that someday in the not-so-distant future Rondônia and its farmers would be as wealthy as the Paraná, with its coffee and soybean plantations.

But problems began to surface, problems for which Nilo had only vague answers, or no solutions at all. The heavy rains destroyed many of the rice plantings and turned the paths to Espigão d'Oeste and the road back to BR-364 into muddy quagmires. Much of the surviving rice harvest rotted in the fields before the routes dried enough for trucks to finally bull their way through.

Nilo had urged the settlers to show kindness to the Indians, whom he asserted were as docile as children. He had said it was the settlers' duty to slowly integrate them into the economy of Espigão d'Oeste, and he had always scorned the idea that the lands around the settlement were part of an Indian reservation. But some of the settlers were reporting that the Indians were becoming angry, and demanding that settlers leave what they asserted was Indian land. A few of the pioneers had been wounded by arrows and had shot back at the Suruis.

Worse still, strangers were appearing throughout Espigão d'Oeste. Some of them could obviously be dismissed as squatters. But others claimed to have titles, given to them by a government organization with the name of INCRA. A family had staked out a plot on the far side of Jesuino's farm and told him that his land had been deeded to them by this mysterious INCRA.

When Jesuino and other settlers complained to Nilo Melhorança, Melhorança told them that the strangers were common land thieves and that they should be expelled by vigilante action. He warned his followers that there was no law and order in this wilderness, and that they should not be fooled by corrupt government officials who hoped to steal their hard-won farms.

"Sometimes, visitors would come to Espigão, well-dressed men who looked very educated," recalled Jesuino. "And when they left, Nilo would say they were important government officials who had come to give us support against the land thieves. But many of us had doubts. We could hear and see roads being built on the edges of Espigão, and there were so many settlers coming in that we would wonder if we were just facing bandits or people who had the legitimate backing of the government. Then I heard that the Melhoranças had stopped a government survey team along the road into Espigão and had almost shot them. I was not a man of violence and I was very concerned."

One day, Jesuino and Nelson Ribeiro, the head of the family who had accompanied the Da Silvas from Paraná to Rondônia, decided to visit the nearest town, Pimenta Bueno, and investigate for themselves just what this organization called INCRA was about. They met with a young official who explained to them that INCRA was the government land colonization agency. He introduced them to another young man, who said he represented the National Indian Foundation, FUNAI, another name that Jesuino and Nelson had barely heard. The FUNAI man told them that his organization was designed to protect the rights of Indians and that Espigão d'Oeste was land stolen from the Surui tribe. The INCRA official asserted that the Melhoranças were outlaws and that their Itaporanga Real Estate Company was not legally registered and had no rights to distribute land titles.

"My heart sank," said Jesuino. "I told them I had given over my life's savings to the Melhoranças, that my family and I had worked ourselves near to death and that there were hundreds of people like us in Espigão who had deeds. The INCRA man said that all of us would get land if we cooperated. Maybe not right away, but eventually, yes. But if we resisted, we would get nothing and maybe we would be sent to jail or even killed because it was only a matter of time before the government sent in the army to deal with the Melhoranças."

Shaken and confused, Jesuino and Nelson returned to Espigão d'Oeste. They told neighbors about their visit to Pimenta Bueno, and at the next Sunday meeting, they publicly asked Nilo what the real truth was about Espigão d'Oeste, Itaporanga Real Estate, INCRA and the Indians. Nilo repeated his assertions that the lands legally belonged to his followers. Then, in a more ominous tone, according to Jesuino, he warned that paid agents of the land thieves were infiltrating themselves among Espigão d'Oeste's settlers.

"After that, I kept my mouth shut," said Jesuino. "But I would not join any vigilante groups. I reached an understanding with the other family on my property that we would both clear our own patches of land and plant our crops until the issue was settled. Whenever the Melhoranças or their people would visit me and ask for my backing, I would stall or do nothing. Then one day I heard that they blew up the bridge on the road into Espigão. It seemed so stupid because now there was no way to receive supplies from the outside or to get our crops to market. Then early one morning I heard sirens and helicopters and shots, and I knew the end was at hand."

Scores of military policemen had invaded Espigão d'Oeste that morning in 1976. Along with a dozen of his followers, Nilo Melhorança was arrested and taken away. Several officials of INCRA installed themselves in the administrative building and took over management of the settlement. But there was no sudden end to the affair as Jesuino had foreseen. Instead, it took several years to sort out the confusion over land ownership in Espigão d'Oeste.

They were bitter times for Jesuino and his family. Not knowing the status of their plot, they could not clear more than a few additional acres. Without title to their land, they could not apply for bank loans and pay for seeds and fertilizers to raise cash crops like coffee and cocoa. Instead, they continued to subsist on manioc, rice and beans. Jesuino's sons still hired themselves out as underpaid peons for farmers who had received legal deeds from INCRA. There were terrible tensions between the original pioneers of Espigão d'Oeste and the INCRA settlers. Each group accused the other of being squatters. Gunfights erupted. Some of the families who had followed the Melhoranças left the settlement, resuming their desperate search for land elsewhere on the frontier.

It was only a year later, in 1977, that Jesuino was informed by

INCRA that he was being moved to Cacoal, fifty miles to the west. There he would be given 250 acres. The money he had paid to the Melhoranças would be credited to his account with INCRA. For the first two years, he would not have to make any payments for his new land. Then he would have four additional years to pay INCRA the equivalent of fifteen hundred dollars.

Jesuino was astounded by his good luck. At six dollars an acre, he was being offered land even more cheaply than in Espigão d'Oeste. Under the terms of his contract, he agreed to take sole responsibility for razing trees and undergrowth from his property, and INCRA promised him technical assistance, advice on crops and aid in applying for bank loans.

Although 250 acres—the normal size of plots granted by INCRA to settlers in Amazonia—seems like an unusually large expanse, the Brazilian government requires the pioneers to permanently maintain half of this land in its virgin state for environmental reasons.

When I met Jesuino and Durvalina after they had settled on their property in Cacoal, they had cleared fifty acres and planted coffee and cocoa. Their home was a simple two-room wooden structure with a high roof of palm leaves for ventilation and a smooth, hard dirt floor. They still had no electricity or running water. They had dug a well and built a crude stone mill to grind manioc and corn, which they grew in their garden. A ninth child was born to the Da Silvas in Cacoal, and they named him Salvador—"the Savior."

"I remember thinking just after we arrived here that this was really a paradise compared to what we lived through," said Durvalina. "Here there were stores and churches and trucks coming and going all the time. And there was no uncertainty over our land titles. Everything grows here—coffee, corn, rice, cocoa. You just plant the seeds and they sprout. And you can get two crops a year."

Paradise was the last word that would come to mind to describe Cacoal when I first saw it in 1977. It was a disease-ridden place, with one of the highest infant-mortality rates in the country and a level of violence that recalled Dodge City a hundred years before. Raw sewage poured into open ditches, its smell barely disguised by mounds of burning garbage. There was almost no electricity, and the only running water was supplied by vats collecting rain on the roofs of the one-story wood-frame buildings.

Yet neither pestilence nor savagery could stem Cacoal's explosive growth. In 1972, it had started as no more than a rectangular jungle clearing with a dozen shacks off BR-364. Five years later, there were fifteen thousand people in the town, and another forty thousand spread in an ever-expanding arc through the rich red farmlands.

I arrived in Cacoal in 1977 with a Brazilian friend, Elio Gaspari, a huge, bearish, affable young journalist who lived in Rio de Janeiro. He had already traveled to the United States, Europe, Africa and the Orient. But like many Brazilian intellectuals and professionals, it had never occurred to him to visit his country's vast Amazon backlands. After ribbing him often about this large gap, I got him to agree, practically on a dare, to join me for his first foray into the jungle frontier.

It was perhaps a measure of his uneasiness that he had asked his wife, Dorit Harazin, to accompany him to Rio's airport. It was one of the few times she had seen him off on a trip. As we were standing at the exit ramp in those early-morning hours, I couldn't help but think that they were tenderly saying good-bye as if Elio were embarking on an expedition with little probability of his ever returning to civilization.

The quickest way to reach Cacoal from Rio de Janeiro was to first fly 1,700 miles northwest to the old Amazon rubber port of Manaus, then 460 miles south to the Rondônian capital of Pôrto Velho and finally 220 miles southeast to a small landing strip near Cacoal. On this last leg, we hired a one-engine taxi-plane. The pilot, barely out of his teens, startled us by confessing during the flight that we were the first passengers he had ever carried. He then proceeded to ram the plane through the top branches of a jungle tree, losing a wheel just as the aircraft landed in several bounces on the dirt runway.

It took us several hours more to reach Cacoal by car along the rutted highway. When we arrived, we asked several people for the best hotel. We were directed to a dilapidated wood-frame flophouse on the main street, a true monument to filth. The front of the establishment was a restaurant—also, we were assured, the best in town. It had a dirt floor and fly-covered tables. Surveying the scene from the rafters was a rat as large as Alice in Wonderland's Cheshire cat and wearing the same grin. As hungry as I was, I quickly gave up competing with the flies for the food.

We wandered down the main street, a stretch of the famous BR-364 that divided Cacoal as it ran its course across Rondônia. There were horses and oxcarts mingling among the Jeeps and overloaded trucks that were carrying new hordes of pioneers into town. The only movie theater was a large circus tent showing an Italian spaghetti western whose title in Portuguese was *I Kill Everybody and Save Myself*. Gun-toting settlers staggered drunkenly through muddy alleys. The wife of one of them, her children in tow, was screaming at her husband, trying to cajole him back home.

We walked into a general store that doubled as a saloon and ordered a couple of tepid beers. A forty-year-old man approached the counter and blurted out to no one in particular that he had just arrived with his family from the east and had his wallet stolen. Every penny he had, gone. The look of helplessness and horror on his face was devastating. He was among total strangers and could not count on anybody for help. More than the stories of violence and disease, more than anything else, this small incident was seared in our memories of Rondônia: the unrelieved shock on that man's face when he suddenly realized how alone, vulnerable and destitute he was in this wilderness.

Two young women approached us and asked where we were from. They were both from the suburbs of Rio de Janeiro. They had children, but no husbands, and now they lived in Rondônia, where they were seamstresses. Just why they had come to Cacoal was a mystery they were not about to clarify. Every question brought a vague answer or shrug. They didn't have a look of burning ambition, an obvious get-rich-quick aura. If they were running away from their husbands, why not seek refuge with family or friends? Had they committed some hideous crime and escaped to the anonymity of the frontier like so many other people?

"Look, one of them has to be a mass murderess and the other did something worse," Elio whispered in an aside to me. "Why else would they come to a place like this?"

They were in their late twenties and attractive. There was a sadness, a depression about them, a feeling that they had endured such hardships that to laugh, smile or banter was no longer possible. But the idea of returning right away to our sinister hotel was so unappealing that we accepted their invitation for a drink.

They lived in a two-room wooden house a short walk off the main street. Cachaça, a crude rum, was all they could offer. They said their business was going badly because few people had money to spend. They disliked Cacoal and hoped to return to Rio someday. But they declined to say what was keeping them in Rondônia. The conversation quickly petered out, and a discomfitting silence descended. We felt like strangers groping for small talk in a train compartment or the waiting room of a clinic. At several points, Elio and I were about to excuse ourselves and leave, but the two women were quite insistent that we linger a bit more, I suppose because they were so lonely and eager just to be with people who still lived in a "civilized" part of the country.

Then, the visit ended abruptly when the house was invaded by a huge column of red ants. What struck me most about the incident was the passive, emotionless manner with which they accepted this natural disaster. Moving about almost somnambulantly, the women picked up the two sleeping children from the bedroom and walked out wordlessly to the porch. At the doorway of the bedroom, Elio and I stared in amazement at the winding snake pattern traced by the ants from the windowsill, along the floor, up a bedpost and across the mattress and sheets. We backed off when the column headed to the door and then turned into the kitchen. There, the disciplined legion of inch-long ants split into numerous flanks and then rushed to encircle bread crumbs and tiny shards of food on the table, the shelves and floor. We retreated to the porch where the women were swaying silently in hammocks, holding their children who were still fast asleep.

I asked them if anything could be done to stop the ants. No, they said, no pesticide would keep them at bay. The only thing to do was wait for an hour or so until the ants had satisfied their hunger and moved elsewhere.

We thanked them for their hospitality and said good-night. There was no response besides a nod and an unintelligible murmur. I had been in some hellholes before during my travels through the frontier lands, but never had I witnessed this kind of resigned despair. Was it my imagination, or were many of the inhabitants of Cacoal traumatized, shell-shocked, pummeled into submission by still unconquered natural elements and man-made chaos?

Elio and I walked back to our flophouse. Showering was out of the question. The bathroom—a closetlike enclosure at the end of the corridor with a mud floor and a single faucet that trickled only drops at a time—was infested by a host of animal life, the most apparent being toads which croaked loudly.

"Cheer up, things could be worse," said Elio with unfounded optimism. Then, as he opened up his leather toiletry case, out jumped the biggest cockroaches we had ever seen. Elio screamed and fell back on his cot, which collapsed on the floor. The electricity shut down, leaving us in darkness. Exhausted, I fell asleep despite Elio's hysterical giggling. When I awoke in the morning, he was asleep, still fully clothed, lying on his collapsed cot just as he had fallen, his arms crossed and embracing his sides.

We spent the morning with an Italian priest, Antonino Lazzarin, a short, stubby thirty-nine-year-old with a sad, round face. His wooden church was next to the newer of Cacoal's two cemeteries. The older one was completely occupied only three years after the town began. Nobody had died of old age. They were victims, mostly of malaria, dysentery and a virulent hepatitis that wiped out whole families in less than a week. Many had also died violently. Father Lazzarin spoke about his parish as if he were adding passages to Dante's Inferno.

"You have people who came here for land, and those who came to exploit them," said the priest. "There are a lot of marginal types, people with criminal records behind them. The social and intellectual and economic level here is the lowest in the country. There are so few people who have had a real family life. Mostly, there are irregular situations: men with second women and families, who left their other families behind; lots of prostitutes, even among the housewives, some of them children. There are government officials who have reserved land for themselves. Our local judge has somehow gotten his own ranch and uses prisoners to clear his land. Doesn't pay them a cent.

"Then there are the land thieves. They stuff a forty-four caliber handgun in their belts, and no one has the courage to confront them. There's a gunman, Oswaldo; everybody knows him. He's the leader of six or seven assassins, and acquires chunks of land through threats. And then he sells them to settlers who have been waiting years for land. Naturally, they jump at any chance to buy, even if the titles are fraudulent. The police? There are only three of them. They uncover corpses, not assassins. In the years I've been here, I've seen drunks and thieves in jail, but never a murderer."

The most important person in Cacoal in those days was Edvaldo Santana, the skinny twenty-four-year-old director of INCRA, the government land colonization agency. INCRA was headquartered about a half mile outside of town in a compound of white-stucco one-story buildings enclosed by a wire fence and a guarded gate. We gratefully accepted Santana's offer to stay in one of the INCRA houses. It was as bare as a prison cell, but it seemed palatial compared to our flophouse.

Santana was a very harried man who lived in constant fear for his life. Every morning, scores of pioneers would line up outside the INCRA compound hoping to receive titles to land, or news about impending settlement projects, or just a word of encouragement. In the last year, INCRA had settled two thousand families around Cacoal, but there were five thousand more still waiting for farms.

"It's hell working here," said Santana. "The only thing we can do is take down names and wait for an opening. These people are so land-hungry that they follow our topographer around as he marks off their plots. They all come into my office like angels, with the sweetest, softest voices. Just a while ago, a man came in here, very politely and quietly. I had to explain to him that he had bought his land illegally and the only thing he could do was to go to the police and denounce the man who had defrauded him. He left here calling me a son of a whore and promising me a bullet in the back."

Santana rode around the settlements in his INCRA pickup truck with a gun wrapped in a magazine at his side. Whenever he was stopped on the road by settlers he didn't know or distrusted, he would smile and wave to them with his left hand, but he would slip his right hand under the magazine and curl it around the gun.

"The last time I went into town, I was followed by two gunmen," said Santana. "The only thing that saved me was meeting up with two friends who happened to be walking in my direction. It's the law of the jungle. People hire themselves out as killers for seventy dollars."

He had virtually stopped going into town, he said, because he was relentlessly set upon by people who wanted to bribe him: doctors who offered free treatment, ranchers who offered their Jeeps, shopkeepers who offered their goods and just everybody offering money.

"For the settlers, a corrupt official is the only one who can guarantee them a title to a piece of land," said Santana. "I'm the fifth INCRA head here in three years. Do you know why the turnover rate is so high? It's because the authorities want to keep their officials from being tempted by bribes. So they don't let anybody stay more than six months. I've had to fire three people in my own office for accepting bribes."

The heart of the problem is the migration of settlers into Rondônia on a scale that has exceeded anybody's expectations. During the dry season from July through November, as many as fifteen thousand people pour in every month. INCRA and the police have set up barricades on BR-364, the only road into the territory. They send out hundreds of thousands of propaganda pamphlets to the migrants' hometowns and rural communities back east, explaining that all the available land in Rondônia is already occupied and pleading that they wait until new zones are opened to settlement. But still, multitudes of peasants descend on the territory. They get off their vehicles, walk around the barricades and climb back on their trucks a few miles down the road. Or they ride tourist buses past the barricades and tell the highway policemen that they are visiting relatives in Rondônia. Often, in fact, they come on the invitation of relatives and friends, who hire them to help clear the land. But then they stay, waiting for plots of their own, or squatting on somebody else's land. Only the tropical rains of the long wet season from December through June have any effect on this influx, sometimes cutting it down to five thousand people a month. This is still a remarkably high figure considering the delays of up to three weeks along the mud-clogged BR-364 highway.

Once people squeeze through these transportation bottlenecks and enter Rondônia, the dearth of roads and their poor quality only aggravate conflicts over land. There are fewer than four thousand miles of roads of any kind in all of Rondônia, a state the size of West Germany. Settlers quite naturally concentrate their search for land around these arteries and their feeder lanes. Because none of these routes are paved, they cannot be easily navigated during the long wet season. There is little government money available for granaries to protect produce during the rains. And the widespread mistrust among settlers contesting the land has blocked the formation of co-operative movements to finance storage facilities. So as much as half of the harvests of perishable crops like rice and corn is lost as it rots on farms in the wet season before the settlers can deliver it to market.

No matter how quickly INCRA settles people, it can only accommodate a fraction of the migrants. The vast majority of pioneers to Rondônia were squatters in 1977, and they still are today.

In Cacoal, the squatters tended first to stake their claims on the periphery of an INCRA settlement, hoping that its boundaries would eventually be extended to include their plots. A second wave of squatters would invade property owned by large ranchers or old rubber estates. Then, the newer arrivals would brazenly move into INCRA land already legally occupied by settlers. And still other squatters would encroach on the newly created reservation for the Surui Indians, who had already been chased from their lands during the Melhorança fiasco.

"I confess to you that we cannot control the invasion of Indian lands any more than the United States government could in the last century," said Santana. "It is simply impossible to keep all these people from grabbing any land they can when it is so close at hand. There are people who will carry their belongings 100 kilometers [60 miles] away from any roads, far into the rain forest, to take land that they know isn't theirs. We will pick up the invaders, put them on a bus and three days later, they are back squatting again on Indian land, white man's land, anybody's land."

Before arriving in Cacoal, while we were still back in Rio, Elio and I had read news reports about growing tensions between settlers and the Surui Indians in Rondônia. The newspapers predicted a last great showdown with the allegedly fierce Indians. Sitting at my bureau in Rio, almost two thousand miles away I had filed an article to my newspaper about this momentous impending battle. But now in Rondônia, on the BR-364 road just a few miles outside Cacoal, Elio and I came across a few Suruis. These supposedly warlike Indians were dressed in tatters, fatigued by either disease or hunger and wearing smiles that seemed to plead for mercy. I felt a deep sense of shame, a feeling that I had been duped into writing a romanticized account that recalled a Hollywood version of a great cowboy-and-Indian war in the American West, instead of the one-sided massacre it really was.

Seventy years ago, Rondon, the great frontier trailblazer and protector of Amazon tribes, had complained that Indian lands he was exploring for the first time were being claimed by whites who had never even seen them:

> The backwoods of Brazil where no civilized man ever trod, already appear on the books of the public registries as belonging to such and such citizens; sooner or later, according to the convenience of their personal interests, these proprietors will expel the Indians, who by a monstrous inversion of facts, reason and morality will be from then on considered and treated as intruders, bandits and robbers.

Rondon lived long enough to see his dire predictions come to pass, despite his own very considerable efforts to defend his Indian wards. At the time he explored Rondônia, there were perhaps forty thousand Indians in that territory. Of these, only about four thousand remain today.

The catastrophic toll on the Indians has been psychological as well as physical. Claude Lévi-Strauss, the famed French anthropologist, who in 1938 visited the Nambiquara tribe on the edge of Rondônia and Mato Grosso, described them as a warm people whose poverty had not withered their sense of humor or joy in human contact:

> Their embraces are those of couples possessed by a longing for a lost oneness; their caresses are in no wise disturbed by the footfall of a stranger. In one and all there may be glimpsed a great sweetness of nature, a profound nonchalance, an animal satisfaction as ingenuous as it is charming, and, beneath all this, something that can be recognized as one of the most moving and authentic manifestations of human tenderness.

Yet, another anthropologist, K. Oberg, who visited the same Indians a decade later for the Smithsonian Institution, found them to be a far more morose tribe after violent contacts with whites and submission to the tutelage of Jesuit and Protestant missionaries:

> The Nambiquara are surly and impolite even to rudeness. On many occasions when I went to visit [an Indian] at his camp he was lying down near a fire and, as he saw me approach, he turned his back to me, saying he did not want to talk. . . . One does not have to remain long among the Nambiquara in order to feel this underlying hatred, mistrust and despair, which create in the observer a feeling of depression not unmixed with sympathy.

The decimation of the Indians and the seizure of their territories by whites did not end the battle over lands. Nor did the struggle between Captain Silvio's INCRA and the big private developers like the Melhoranças. Certainly there were instances of settlers like Jesuino and Durvalina da Silva who in the 1970's finally found their promised land in Rondônia. Through Santana, the young INCRA administrator in Cacoal, we also met many other pioneers who arrived on the frontier with nothing and were given 250-acre plots that they had quickly turned into productive farms. But far more typical of the pioneers in Cacoal and throughout Rondônia were the squatters, reckless people with no land titles or security.

One of these squatters was Mario Lino Ferreira Costa, a squat, pale man with thinning reddish hair and a reputation for a violent temper and quick gun. Costa had invaded land in Cacoal that was part of a large farm and had resisted all attempts to dislodge him. The farmer who legally owned the land had called in the police three times. Costa was once placed under arrest, beaten and left in the middle of the night at a desolate clearing off BR-364 about fifty miles away from his home. He made his way back, and in a saloon vowed that if he ever saw policemen or the big farmer or his gunmen on his property again, he would shoot first.

Costa had planted coffee on his stolen land and had just finished harvesting his first crop when Elio and I warily approached his house, shouting from several hundred feet away that we were unarmed and only wanted to ask him a few questions. Mounds of coffee beans were lying on his porch, and Costa was swinging on a hammock above them, celebrating his fifty-fifth birthday with a cup of his own coffee. His brother and two cousins, shotguns in hand, joined the party.

Costa said he had arrived in Cacoal in 1977 after a three-thousand-mile odyssey that took him from his parched village in the Northeast to Mato Grosso in the central part of the country and then to the southern farm regions. All along the way, he had squatted on land and then sold it off, slowly building his capital. In Cacoal, he claimed he had bought his plot from a previous squatter and discovered too late that the transaction was illegal. "I was so desperate I would have bought the churchyard and the altar too," he laughed.

Costa said he had hired a lawyer, and he asserted that he had built a strong case for himself. Brazilian law does, in fact, offer some protection to squatters. Although Costa could be legally evicted from his plot because he had squatted on private land, the owner would be obliged under Brazilian law to indemnify Costa for any improvements he had made on the land. Since Costa had cleared the property and planted coffee, he could at the very least expect compensation far higher than the money he had claimed to have spent in purchasing the land. The judges in Rondônia were so overburdened by cases like these that the owner would probably even be willing to make a generous out-of-court settlement with Costa. He had evidently played this sort of profitable game several times during his journeys through the Brazilian backlands. But this time, Costa told us, he was going for broke.

"I'm too old and I've worked all my life," said Costa. "This is my land. If they come after me, I'm not running anymore. There's no way they are going to get me out of here alive."

Elio and I lingered another week in Rondônia before flying back to Rio de Janeiro. Elio had prepared for the trip to Rondônia by purchasing several volumes on the history and ecology of the Amazon. I chose art history books that were intended to take my mind off the jungle as much as possible. Having finished our respective readings midway through our journey, we exchanged books. Years later, Elio would claim that I not only got him back to civilization alive but that the best part of the jungle odyssey had been learning about the finer points of Italian Renaissance art. On a visit to Paris, where I was living in 1980, he said he wanted to repay me for guiding him through the Amazon, so he proceeded to lead me through the best tour I ever had of the Louvre Museum's Renaissance collection. Elio always said that the trip into Rondônia had been among the most unforgettable ones he ever made. But it also strengthened his conviction that his vacations would be far better spent wandering through the restaurants and museums of New York, Paris, Florence and Rome.

I lived and worked in some of those cities during the five years that passed before I returned to the Brazilian frontier in 1982. During all that time I somehow could not shake the memory of those characters I had met in Rondônia. Again and again, almost compulsively, I would plunge into readings of American and Brazilian history to try to find parallels and precedents for Brazil's Amazon development.

10

At first glance, there are glaring differences between the settling of the American Old West and the modern Brazilian drive into the Amazon frontier.

The American pioneers never had to contend with a terrain as forbidding as Amazonia. The forests, mountains, prairies and deserts of the United States were far more easily penetrated than the jungles. The soils of the North American frontier were more fertile than the rain forest, even the rich volcanic terra roxa of Rondônia. The modern-day Brazilians are equipped with technologies—not least, the airplane, truck, tractor and bulldozer—that American settlers never envisioned. In fact, Amazonia has seen an inversion of the history of transportation on the North American frontier. In Brazil, airplanes were the major source of transportation before roads were built to accommodate trucks and cars. And the railroads, which played such an essential role in the development of the American West, are totally absent in the western Amazon because the Brazilian frontier drive began in the early 1970's, when oil and gasoline prices were still cheap. As Norman Gall, an American journalist, astutely observed in a recent series of articles on Rondônia, Brazil is the first country "attempting to build a continental civilization around the truck and automobile, despite her inability to provide more than one-fifth of her petroleum needs from her own resources." So committed are the Brazilians to the internal-combustion engine that even high petroleum prices are unlikely to lead them to abandon highways in favor of railroads.

But the parallels between the nineteenth-century American frontier drive and the Brazilian conquest of western Amazonia a hundred years later are also quite remarkable. Brazilians never cease to repeat that Rondônia is their version of the American Old West. Usually, they mean it in the most negative sense. Brazil has certainly matched the gruesome American treatment of Indians. The lawlessness and insecurity of the new Brazilian pioneer communities recall the epoch of the gunslinger in the American frontier. Physically, the newer towns of Rondônia bear a startling resemblance to the clapboard houses, churches and saloons that lined the dirt main streets of the mid-nineteenth-century cattle towns in Texas and Kansas.

There is a tendency among many Brazilians to romanticize the American frontier and to believe that the conquest of Rondônia embodies the worst aspects of the American westward expansion. For example, Santana, the youthful director of the government land colonization agency, INCRA, in Cacoal, was certain that in the United States the settling of the West had been a smoother, more orderly process. An avid student of the American frontier, Santana spoke with unquestioning approval about the homestead movement in the nineteenth-century West, which he contended had lessened conflict over land titles and distributed plots more equitably than in modern Rondônia. Other Brazilian officials are convinced that during the last century in the United States there was far more national consensus about the push westward than there is today in Brazil about the development of the Amazon. Then, also, the American western settlements seemed to have grown demographically and reached economic self-sufficiency more quickly than Brazil's Amazon frontier.

A lot of these assumptions do not hold up if my own readings of American frontier history are correct. Much of the optimism that we Americans and others now share about the settling of the West seems traceable to the writing of Frederick Jackson Turner, the late-nineteenth-century American historian. Until Turner, most visions of American development played up the tensions between the industrial northern states and the rural southern states—tensions that finally exploded in the Civil War. The western frontier was viewed as important but peripheral to this great North-South confrontation. So that when, in 1893, Turner spelled out his thesis, it did indeed seem startling at the time. In his famous address to the American Historical Association in Chicago that year he asserted that the constant expansion westward was the most crucial factor in the development of the United States and in the formation of the American character and values.

Today, even Americans who never heard of Turner readily accept his basic contention. It has become as deeply imbedded in the American pantheon of self-evident truths as the Declaration of Independence. Yet in the first half of the nineteenth century, in the very midst of the conquest of the frontier, there were many voices raised to question the wisdom and the economic logic of this westward expansion. In the 1840's, Senator Daniel Webster, that quintessential American statesman, opposed the whole development of the frontier, saying:

> What do we want with this vast and worthless area, this region of savages and wild beasts, of deserts, of shifting sands and whirlwinds, of dust, of cactus and prairie dogs; to what use could we ever hope to put these great deserts, or those endless mountain ranges, impenetrable and covered to their very base with eternal snow? What can we ever hope to do with the western coast . . . rockbound, cheerless, uninviting and not a harbor in it? Mr. President, I will never vote one cent from the public treasury to place the Pacific Coast one inch nearer Boston than it is now.

A similar cynicism often pervades the opinion of Brazilians 130 years later. Many of them argue that Amazonia, with only five percent (about six million inhabitants) of their country's total population, is an area of very marginal interest and a drain on their nation's limited economic resources. They would probably be surprised to learn, as Fred A. Shannon, a noted American historian, has pointed out, that ". . . in 1860 an area which was half of the United States, and which lay between the Pacific Coast settlements and the Western frontier of the Prairie farms, contained only one percent of the nation's population."

Rondônia today does not produce nearly enough crops and revenue to pay for the imports it needs for its survival and growth. But American frontier territories showed a similar, lagging economic performance in their early stages of settlement. As Clarence H. Danhof, another American historian, has noted, some of the most important middle western states now hailed as granaries for the world were buyers of grain during the first half of the nineteenth century. "Detroit in 1817, and for some years thereafter, was an importer of agricultural products from the East, some of its flour coming from northern Pennsylvania," wrote Danhof. "Chicago was likewise dependent upon eastern foodstuffs until about 1839, as was Minneapolis until the middle of the 1850's."

Shannon, also addressing the question of whether the early western frontier was a financial burden to the rest of the country, chose the example of Kansas, that modern-day paragon of grain and cattle riches:

> If one takes into account Senator John J. Ingalls' occasional tendency to overstate his case, there was still some truth in his assertion that the exports of the territory before 1860 were not enough to pay for all the whiskey the settlement drank each month.

Is Rondônia today any less economically promising than these American frontier territories were in the first half of the nineteenth century? Is it not conceivable that despite its backwardness and distance from markets and the high cost of transportation fuel, Rondônia with its huge, relatively fertile lands will produce a coffee and cocoa bonanza in the foreseeable future?

For me, perhaps the most intriguing comparison between the American and Brazilian frontier experiences is over the issue of land ownership. Were the lands of the nineteenth-century American West distributed more equitably and with fewer disputes over titles than in Rondônia a hundred years later?

In the American West, the most violent land conflicts were between settlers and Indians. There followed the struggles between cattlemen and homesteaders over property and access to water. But by and large, one title existed for each plot of land.

In Brazil, there has undoubtedly been far greater confusion over legal titles to frontier land. Huge, often ill-defined chunks of Amazon territory were deeded to rubber barons in the nineteenth and early twentieth centuries, as Rondon noted in his exploration of that region. The situation has become even more complicated seven decades after Rondon's observations. Rondônia only became a state in 1981. Before then, it existed successively as part of the states of Amazonas and Mato Grosso, as the territory of Guaporé and as the territory of Rondônia. The governments of each of these entities gave out titles, so that a profusion of deeds and owners claimed the same properties. Speculators and big ranchers bought these archaic titles and then squared off against INCRA, the land colonization agency, which claimed these same properties for small settlers. Squatters, who are to some degree protected by Brazilian law, have also waded into the morass with their own stakes over the disputed lands.

But, in spite of this chaos and violence, has Rondônia achieved a poorer record for the fair distribution of land than the nineteenth-century American frontier? In the United States, the Homestead Act of 1862 gave out free 160-acre tracts to pioneers in the hopes that the West would become a region of small landowners. In fact, the Homestead Act was quickly subverted. A wealthy speculator would hire homesteaders to stake out claims and then would buy these properties from them as soon as the government had issued them titles and patents. Between 1860 and 1900, homesteads accounted for only a fraction of the new lands brought under cultivation in the United States. As Shannon pointed out:

> ... An astonishing number of homesteaders were merely the hired pawns of land monopolists who took over the land as soon as the final patents were received, thus reducing free farms more nearly to an eighth, or possibly a tenth, of the increase for the forty-year period. Again, the bona fide homesteaders usually got only the least desirable tracts, on poorer lands, far from transportation and society, while the ubiquitous monopolist and speculator held the better tracts for resale at a price too high for the class of persons the Homestead Act had presumably been intended to benefit. ...

Moreover, Shannon noted, even when homesteaders took possession of their properties, the government failed to provide them with transportation to reach their lands, or extend them credits for the difficult, first years of farming, or give them any technical guidance. In western Amazonia today, the same charges are often leveled against Brazilian government agencies, which are too understaffed and underfinanced to cope with the ever-growing wave of pioneers.

The American government a hundred years ago was accused of subsidizing big livestock barons in ways that recall the favoritism that the Brazilian military regime has practiced recently toward cattle ranchers in Amazonia. Referring to the plains of Texas and Kansas in the 1870's, Shannon wrote: "Although nearly all the land belonged to the federal government, the states or the railroad companies, not a cent of rent was paid to the government [by the cattlemen who used these grazing lands]."

Similarly, the Brazilian regime in the 1970's and 1980's has helped finance big cattle ranchers in the jungle frontier by extending them tax rebates and long-term loans at interest rates below inflation.

In view of the serious deficiencies in the Homestead Act, it is fair to ask what happened to all the hundreds of thousands of pioneers who plunged into the American West in the second half of the nineteenth century. They became, in their majority, hired laborers and sharecroppers and tenant farmers. By 1880, wrote Shannon, "three out of each seven persons in agricultural occupations were owners of the enterprises they operated, and in 1900, only three out of each eight or nine."

Paul W. Gates, another eminent historian of the American frontier, arrived at a similar conclusion in a study he made of the prairie states:

> The early appearance of tenancy and agricultural labor in the amount that has been shown in or close to frontier areas, together with their rapid increase, provides convincing evidence that government land policy was not producing the results its defenders claimed. In view of the oft-repeated objective of American land policy—to assure a nation of freeholders—how is it possible to account for the early appearance of farm laborers and tenants in frontier communities. . . ? At the close of the nineteenth century the agricultural laborers and tenants outnumbered full owner-operators of farms in five of the states we have studied, and in all of the Upper Mississippi Valley the numbers of farm laborers and tenants were fast growing. Agrarian reform movements offered nothing to improve their lot. It was not until the twentieth century that the status of the tenant was bettered with his gradual accumulation of livestock, equipment, and investment in improvements, which has made him a substantial farmer with an equity worth thousands of dollars.

The point is that Rondônia, for all its disorder and savagery, has carried out a fairer distribution of land in far less time than the American West was able to accomplish it in the nineteenth century. In the twelve to fifteen years of land conflicts that followed its opening to massive settlement in the late 1960's, Rondônia has gradually emerged as the only Brazilian state where the small- and middle-sized farmer predominates. Elsewhere, even in the new frontier areas, the country is characterized by an unequal distribution of land that dates back to the days of the Portuguese empire. In Rondônia's neighboring state of Mato Grosso, for example, eighty-five percent of the agrarian land is held by ranchers and farmers who have properties larger than five thousand acres. In Rondônia itself, however, about two thirds of the farmland belongs to settlers whose properties range from one hundred to two thousand acres.

There is yet another mark of comparison between Rondônia and the American Old West, an obvious one that eluded me until my return to the Brazilian frontier in 1982 after an absence of five years. And that is the speed with which this Brazilian wilderness is being transformed. The Rondônia settlers are compressing a half century of American frontier history into five or ten years. Certainly, there are still widespread struggles over land, conflicts between pioneers and Indians, primitive new settlements—all of which recall nineteenth-century America west of the Mississippi River. But airplanes, helicopters, trucks, tractors, bulldozers, radio, television, telephones, satellite communications, hybrid seed strains and all the other paraphernalia of the twentieth century are quickly closing the gap between the more established Rondônia settlements and the eastern half of Brazil.

Pôrto Velho, the capital of Rondônia, was almost unrecognizable to me just five years after my last visit. The city's population had doubled to 180,000. Many of its streets were asphalted, and multi-storied buildings rose in the downtown district. A half dozen luxury hotels, five more than existed on my previous trip, were crammed with traveling salesmen, construction contractors and investors from Rio de Janeiro, Paraná and mostly São Paulo. Flights twice a day connected Pôrto Velho with any major city in Brazil.

Rondônia is still dominated by small, struggling settlers. Statistically, it is among the poorest states in Brazil. Half of its population is illiterate, and 120,000 of its children have no schooling available to them. Fully half of the recorded cases of malaria in the country are in Rondônia.

But the economic and demographic growth has also spawned a wave of frontier entrepreneurs. In Pôrto Velho, I met a former TV soap opera star, Suzana Gonçalves, who had come to Rondônia with her husband five years before "to escape that stupid fantasy world." They bought a medium-sized plot of land. In the beginning, she supervised groups of peons in cutting down the jungle and carrying out plantings of capim grass, while her husband wandered from bank to bank in search of credit and financing. Now, they have a seventy-five-hundred-acre ranch near Pôrto Velho, a sawmill, a construction company, forty apartments, a luxury hotel and restaurant.

Luiz Bernardi, a thirty-six-year-old businessman from São Paulo, arrived in Jiparaná, 180 miles southeast of Pôrto Velho, in 1970, when the settlement had fewer than one thousand people. Today,

Jiparaná has two hundred thousand inhabitants, and Bernardi's fortunes have grown proportionately: an eight-room home of his own, nine other houses, a chain of electrical appliance stores, a three-story office building, two real-estate agencies offering twenty-five hundred urban lots in eleven different sites around Rondônia, a five-thousand-acre ranch and a radio station.

Farther down the famous pioneer highway, BR-364, about sixty miles south of Jiparaná, I arrived with some trepidation at Cacoal. I need not have worried. The grotesquely filthy flophouse where Elio and I had stayed was gone, replaced by a comfortable brick hotel and restaurant. The circus tent had come down, and in its place stood a real movie theater, of wood and stone, showing dubbed American detective films instead of Italian spaghetti westerns. Most people stayed home at nights to watch television, beamed from a broadcasting station right in Cacoal. Thanks to satellite communications, I could direct-dial a telephone call to any city in eastern Brazil.

Many of the rowdy saloons had been replaced by airy luncheon-ette-cafés with plastic and Formica tables. The grizzled peasants and squatters no longer carried guns. They were also outnumbered by swaggering adolescents, long-haired kids in gaudy T-shirts who arrived at the cafés in souped-up Jeeps trailing swirls of red dust.

I met the proprietor of the general store and bar Elio and I had visited five years before. His name was Divino Cardoso Campos, and he now owned a chain of small department stores, a cattle ranch, a coffee plantation and real estate in Pôrto Velho and in the neighboring state of Mato Grosso.

Father Lazzarin, the morose priest I had interviewed in 1977, had moved to another parish in the Amazon, and his former church was now a bigger, sturdier stone building. Santana, the young INCRA director, had left the government land colonization agency and was living back in his home state of Pernambuco, in the Northeast. But Costa, the feisty squatter, was still around. He had come to an amicable settlement with the farmer whose land he stole and now, sixty years old, he supervised the harvesting and selling of his coffee beans from the hammock on his porch. In the safe of his bedroom, he had the legal title to a farm that had eluded him for four decades.

There were many peasants like Jesuino and Durvalina da Silva who were prospering on farms of their own for the first time in their lives. But there were also many, many more pioneers who, while waiting for land they might never possess, continued to subsist on the frontier much the same way they had lived back east, as share-croppers, peons, tenant farmers and squatters.

Throughout this trip across Rondônia in 1982, I had been on the lookout for telltale signs of soil erosion. Since the massive settlement of Rondônia began around 1970, ecologists have warned that the land might eventually prove to be every bit as fragile as the northern jungle soils that had caused the collapse of the pioneer movement along the first segment of the Transamazon Highway.

Twentieth-century Brazil, like the United States in an earlier era, has had a poor record in soil conservation. When Claude Lévi-Strauss visited Mato Grosso and the Amazon in the late 1930's, he passed through desolate former plantations in western São Paulo and commented with disgust that there was little hope that the wilderness would survive the carelessness of Brazilian farmers:

> The relationship between Man and the soil has never been marked by that reciprocity of attentions which, in the Old World, had existed for thousands of years and been the basis of our prosperity. Here in Brazil the soil has been first violated, then destroyed. Agriculture has been a matter of looting for quick profits.

A hundred years before, the farmers of the American frontier had demonstrated a similar indifference to the health of their lands. As Shannon, that chronicler of the Old West, has noted:

> If the Prairie farmers, while producing their "bumper" crops, did not wear out the soil as rapidly as did the early Virginia planters, it was only because of greater original fertility and the less exhausting qualities of the crops grown. Certainly, their attitude toward conservation in the early years was little, if any, different. This was a subject that just was not considered. Not much attention was paid to rotation, good plowing, or intensive cultivation. In every instance, the reports from new Western lands showed marvelous wheat crops for a few years, and then a decline as single-crop practices exhausted the soil to the point of unprofitability.

In Rondônia, after five to ten years of tillage, there was not yet any widespread evidence of soil erosion, according to farmers and agronomists I consulted. I knew that few settlers could afford fertilizers, so the reason had to lie elsewhere.

The older plots, those which had been in existence more than three years, were mostly turned over to perennial crops like coffee, cocoa and fruit trees, which provided the year-round cover for the soil from the harsh tropical sun and the direct battering of torrential rains—the main elements responsible for soil erosion in the Amazon. Certainly, these kinds of crops were the most prevalent ones in Cacoal, Jiparaná, Ariquemes, Vilhena and other Rondônia settlements I had visited.

Through advice and bank credits, INCRA and other government agricultural agencies had encouraged the planting of these crops. The farmers may not have been particularly motivated by ecological concerns, but they responded because it made economic sense. Coffee and cocoa offered them a good price per weight and were easy to transport, a major consideration given Rondônia's fifteen-hundred- to seventeen-hundred-mile distance from the Atlantic ports, and from there to markets overseas. Also, coffee and cocoa beans are easy to store during the long rainy season when feeder roads and even BR-364 are churned into mud, leaving farms isolated for months on end.

11

efore leaving Rondônia in 1982, I decided to visit a relatively new settlement and see whether its atmosphere evoked the early days of Cacoal. I chose a community called Colorado d'Oeste, partly because the name had an American frontier ring and also because it had been the scene of violent land quarrels in recent months. Colorado d'Oeste is located in the southeast corner of Rondônia, not far from the Bolivian border. To get there, I had to board a bus at Vilhena, the gateway of Rondônia, where the BR-364 pioneer highway enters the state from Mato Grosso. From Vilhena, I would head south about fifty miles.

I showed up before dawn at the Vilhena bus station, a squat, yellow clapboard building with open sides. Passengers bought meat dumplings, bread cakes, coffee and shots of cheap brandy and rum at food stands whose charcoal-fire stoves wafted smoke through the depot. The hardwood benches were crowded with people who had been waiting overnight and had just started to stir from their slumber. Chickens and pigs scurried around the station's dirt floor, begging like dogs for scraps of food. A heavy night mist still enveloped the countryside, exposing only the eerie skeletons of 120-foot-tall Brazil nut trees that had survived the slashing and burning of the rain forest.

Around me were the faces of Brazil's multiracial peasantry. There were lean mulattoes in tight jeans and broad-brimmed cowboy hats; ocher-skinned mestizos with hatchet faces and the smell of week-old sweat; thin women with long, braided black hair and knotted arm muscles; gnarled and toothless old men with dim, squinting eyes; blond, brutish farmers with blank stares on their square faces who looked like Bruegel figures come to life; old women and little kids squatting on their haunches.

With a teeth-rattling screech of brakes and a loud backfire, our bus pulled into the station. There was an unceremonious scramble to get on board and find seats and spaces for baggage. Two young mulattoes bulled their way down the aisle to claim a place for their aged father. Children screamed in glee or panic. A young mother asked me to hold her infant. She smacked her other unruly child, and then, thanking me and tugging them along, made her way to the back of the bus. There were scattered quarrels for seats, but after hooting and whistling, everybody found a place. With a roar of the engine and a blast of recorded polka music, the bus set out on its journey.

Vilhena is located on a plateau. For several hundred yards on either side of the highway the terrain was bare, its vegetation scraped and scorched so that only the carcasses of trees remained. But as the sun evaporated the morning mist, the rain forest loomed in the distance on either side of us. The bus bounced and honked loudly at scrawny, humpbacked cattle on the road. Inside, the vehicle reeked of brilliantine, harsh tobacco and stale perspiration.

Some fifteen minutes into our journey, we turned off BR-364 and drove south along a narrower, more rutted road through dense jungle. The route rose and fell, climbed and tobogganed again like an unsteady roller coaster. The only wildlife we saw were vultures drifting overhead, curving on the wind, rising with the updrafts until they were specks in the clearing skies. Soon there was a brilliant morning sun. The air pulsed and shimmered with heat waves, and we rode the soaring thermometer.

Despite our slow pace, we began to overtake heavily laden trucks carrying goods to Colorado d'Oeste and other settlements beyond. When the vehicles puffed up an incline, our driver would slow and fall back a discreet distance, apparently fearful that their loads of lumber and brick might slide down on top of us. I asked the man seated next to me how long the trip normally took, and he said two to five hours, depending on how badly the recent rains had damaged the road.

A few minutes later, our bus mired itself in mud. All the passengers got out to lighten the vehicle. The driver pressed the accelerator, but the spinning back wheels only dug themselves deeper into the bog. We waited fifteen minutes, a half hour and longer for a truck to come by and pull us out. With the engine silent, the air began to fill with the chirping of birds. A treetop fluttered as a small band of monkeys leaped from branch to branch. A thick cloud of black butterflies swirled on the roadside, scavenging for unseen particles in the red dirt.

Finally, after almost an hour, a large lumber truck came to our rescue. It hitched a chain to the front axle of our bus and smoothly yanked the vehicle out of its mud trap. We clambered back on board and, to the sound of polka music, resumed our porpoise leaps up and down the hilly jungle.

Seated next to me was a loquacious evangelist minister with a well-thumbed New Testament. He probed cautiously at first, asking where I was from, what I was doing in Rondônia, what my religion was. He explained how he had been reborn only two years before, in his forty-fifth year, following a week of divine visitations in his dreams. And then he launched into long quotes from the scriptures, his voice rising steadily until I told him I had lost interest. He looked at me in obvious pity, but relented and resumed his silent Bible reading, only occasionally turning to quote me passages that might change my mind.

Our bus slowed and then stopped. Just ahead of us was an overturned truck, its wheels in the air and its load of lumber sprawled across the road. Its driver, his right arm bloodied and apparently broken, asked for help. At his feet, a tarpaulin sheet covered the body of his riding companion. The evangelist minister rushed off the bus. Kneeling next to the corpse, he prayed loudly for the young man's soul with an almost unseemly gusto.

The distraught truck driver came aboard and was given a front seat by a passenger. The driver explained that his brakes had failed him on a curve. There were sighs and groans and prayers among the passengers, and then a silence that lasted for the hour that remained of the journey.

Colorado d'Oeste first emerged from the rain forest as a clearing of shacks and sawmills. The settlement thickened into clusters of bright pastel wood houses with white picket fences. Its "downtown" district was a potholed dirt street lined with general stores and other shops. Women strolled with parasols past a herd of cattle heading to pasture. Horses, tied to posts, shut their eyes and drooped their heads away from the tropical sun. Young men pedaled bikes slowly, their balloon tires leaving thick tracks in the red dust.

Our bus pulled in front of a general store that also served as a ticket booth. Cheering relatives were on hand to welcome most of the passengers. A large crowd was gathered nearby around a ventriloquist-magician who ended each act with a fervent pitch for his snake oil—literally, bottles of coiled snakes in viscous fluid. A leper, a man missing his nose and several fingers, made his way through the audience begging for money, causing some people to recoil in fright or disgust.

Slinging my duffel bag across my shoulders, I walked up a hill to the headquarters of INCRA, where I was met by an official, Carlos Almeida, a thin, twenty-six-year-old with blond hair, fair skin and a squeaky, high-pitched voice. He had been informed of my visit by radio-telephone from the INCRA head office in Pôrto Velho, more than four hundred miles to the northwest. The radio-telephone, operated by a diesel generator, was Colorado d'Oeste's only communication link to the outside world. For five months a year, during the height of the rainy season, the community was totally isolated. No trucks could break through, and sometimes, when the diesel fuel ran out, even the radio-telephone ceased to operate.

Almeida had arrived in Colorado d'Oeste two years before on a lark. He had been a schoolteacher in Rio de Janeiro, and decided during his vacation to visit the Amazon frontier. In Colorado d'Oeste, the INCRA director had invited him to join the land colonization agency and stay on. Almeida liked the work. Then he met the daughter of a settler family, descendants of German immigrants to southern Brazil. They married and soon had two children.

"I was bored and frustrated back in Rio," said Almeida. "This place just overwhelmed me. It seemed out of the American West, with real pioneers. I thought I would find illiterate peasants. But I met a lot of motivated, educated people, some of them engineers and agronomists. My family was horrified that I settled here. They thought I had married an Indian or a black. But most of the people here are of German and Italian descent, from southern states like Rio Grande do Sul, Santa Catarina and Paraná. My wife speaks German, even though she's third generation. The town where she lived in the south was all German, and a lot of them ended up here."

From Almeida's remarks, and the comments of pioneers and other INCRA officials, I gathered that this new wave of settlers into Rondônia had been carefully screened by the government land colonization agency. They were not sharecroppers and rural laborers. They were people who had sold their farms in southern Brazil because they were too small to survive in the midst of larger, mechanized agrarian estates.

"Of course, the prerequisite is still farmers who hold no land," Rondônia's INCRA director, Ernani Coutinho Filho, had explained to me a few days before in Pôrto Velho. "But we have a selection process for settlers nowadays. We tend to favor people with experience in managing their own farms, people with some education and a stable family life. Those are the people who tend to succeed on the frontier. They are resourceful and motivated. That's the theory anyway. In practice, the majority of pioneers who come to Rondônia are still totally unprepared people, poor and illiterate. They need much more help than we can provide. It is sad to admit it, but it is true."

When Colorado d'Oeste began in 1975, many of its original settlers were, in fact, former sharecroppers and peons with no experience running farms. Large numbers of them failed. They cleared some of their 250-acre plots and then sold them to the newer wave of more proficient farmers. Then they moved elsewhere in search of new land on the frontier, sometimes repeating the process, sometimes learning enough about farm management to settle down permanently, sometimes spending their profits and drifting back to sharecropping and tenant farming.

There are no figures on the extent of this turnover in land ownership in Rondônia. But INCRA officials said the phenomenon was widespread. The land colonization agency did not attempt to block these turnovers, except to enforce the limit of 250 acres per family in order to prevent a buildup of big landholdings.

Here again, there seemed to be a parallel between Rondônia and the nineteenth-century American frontier. Alexis de Tocqueville, that remarkably keen French observer of American society, found during his travels through the United States in 1831 that "it seldom happens that an American farmer settles for good upon the land which he occupies; especially in the districts of the Far West he brings land into tillage in order to sell it again, and not to farm it."

By the time I arrived in Colorado d'Oeste in 1982, the turnover process seemed to have come to an end. There were fifteen thousand people living within the municipality and another fifty-five thousand in its outlying farmlands. Schools and shops had sprouted. There were enough churches to represent the Catholic majority as well as thirty-two Protestant sects, many of them small evangelist groups. It was a stable community, with none of the violence and disorder I had seen five years before in Cacoal.

Colorado d'Oeste was by no means prosperous. There were few

tractors, and most settlers depended on hand-held or horse-drawn plows. Nobody could afford fertilizers. The universal complaint was the poor condition of roads that brought the economy and social life to a standstill for almost half the year. Otherwise, the feelings of settlers about their farms seemed to range from deep satisfaction to mild disappointment.

At one extreme is a man like Raimundo Pinho, who asserted that "you won't find anyone more content than I am." He is sixty-three years old, paunchy but with muscular arms, olive-skinned, with gray hair and pearly teeth. He has a livid scar on his forehead, where a tree he was cutting had struck him. The injury had left him with an involuntary tic, a sudden shaking of the head.

Pinho was originally from Brazil's Northeast, where he managed and then sold his family farm. He moved south to São Paulo and Paraná and became a gold jeweler. But he was prosecuted for failing to pay his taxes and had to declare bankruptcy. He decided to return to farming and came to Colorado d'Oeste in the late 1970's. He lived with his wife and a teenage daughter; his other four children were married and had stayed in southern Brazil.

Pinho's 250-acre plot was located three miles from town, on a dirt road that passed rolling hills, fruit orchards and cows crowded around water holes. I found him drinking coffee on the porch of his three-room wood-frame house. Graça bushes with big red blossoms dotted his front yard, and above them loomed a large tree with a split in its trunk that was occupied by a gray termite nest that looked like a huge tumor.

"When I first got here," said Pinho, "I planted coffee. It didn't work out because the strain was bad and prices were low and financing didn't exist. But I didn't give up. I planted pasture for the cattle herders and rented it out. I also planted rice and beans and corn, and then banana trees and mangos. And I raised chickens. I wake up every morning at five-thirty and I chuck some corn to the chickens. Then I go into my jungle and cut down some more trees and underbrush until about ten-thirty. It's easier now because I use a chain saw. I've cleared about fifty hectares (125 acres) in five years. I don't have the transportation problems that a lot of other people do because I'm so close to town. I sell all my produce to the town. It's not worth going elsewhere until we get some asphalted roads. Roads are really the only thing we need. The rest will fall into place. I'd also like some electricity so we can get a refrigerator and not have to use batteries for the radio. But this place is going upward. Wherever a lot of people get together, the government starts paying attention. It's just common sense. Take my word for it, in five more years there will be a bus stop in front of my house and this will be as civilized as any place back in Paraná. A lot of my relatives have moved here, so I don't really miss what passes for civilization. The ones I left behind spend their time talking about leaving the big cities. Here you don't pile up debts. It's tranquil. I eat my own chickens the way I like them cooked with green sauce. That's happiness."

A few miles farther up the road, João and Guilhermina Naue are more glum about their prospects. Now in their late forties, they had arrived here with their six children in 1977. But they toy with the idea of returning to Santa Catarina in southern Brazil, where they still keep a farm in their children's names.

"We weren't doing so badly with our farm in Santa Catarina," said João, a tall, lean, leathery third-generation German with pale blue eyes. "But we lost a lot of money with a small hotel we started. A stupid idea. We heard there was good land for coffee here. A lot of other people were able to plant coffee. It was our bad luck that this particular plot won't grow coffee. So instead we have pasture for cattle, and a pineapple orchard, and a small sawmill which my oldest son runs. And we grow some corn and beans and manioc. But coffee is where the money is."

Guilhermina, blond and buxom and heavier set than her husband, claims they are no better off than in Santa Catarina.

"But we'll probably stay," she said. "It's difficult to think of moving again. Things will get better. The first people here were the poorest and most ignorant. The weakest fell by the wayside, and their properties were bought by more solid people like us. We're not going to sell out so easily."

On the wall of the porch hang several shotguns and rifles. João is an avid hunter and finds plenty of deer and wild pigs in the rain forest. But he has been slowed down in recent months by a painful bout of lechmaniasis. A disease common on the Amazon frontier that is transmitted by sand flies, it starts as a festering sore that if untreated produces a type of leprosy which attacks the nose and mouth, and eventually proves fatal. João still has a sore on his right ankle, and the medicine tablets he has been taking for almost two months have left him dizzy and crotchety.

The pioneers of Colorado d'Oeste and the INCRA officials who oversaw the settlement took pride in the cohesiveness and the social tranquility that reigned in their community. Colorado d'Oeste was not a rowdy place. Crime was almost nonexistent. There were no violent land disputes. Social life did not revolve around saloons. Instead, people preferred visiting each other at home, dropping in unannounced for lunch or dinner or drinks.

But the calm extended only to the limits of Colorado d'Oeste. On the periphery, thousands of other migrants who had not qualified for INCRA plots had squatted on lands belonging to large ranchers and rubber-estate owners. There were frequent confrontations, as violent as the ones I had seen elsewhere in Rondônia five years before.

INCRA officials disclaimed any responsibility for the disorders, pointing out that they had no jurisdiction over these lands. But that was only part of the story. The road from Vilhena to Colorado d'Oeste, like roads anywhere on the Amazon frontier, had proved a magnet drawing desperate people in search of land. The growth of Colorado d'Oeste, with its stores and clinics and markets, also had encouraged squatters to install themselves on its outskirts. For much the same reasons, large landowners, whose properties had lain dormant for decades, suddenly saw their real-estate values jump. The new road had made it feasible for them to develop big ranches, and the new town now provided them with the services and outlets essential for growth.

I arrived in Colorado d'Oeste in the midst of a spectacular shoot-out between squatters and a rancher's hired gunmen that left three people dead and several others wounded.

The incident had taken place at the Cabixis ranch, about ten miles south of Colorado d'Oeste. The thirty-thousand-acre property, formerly a rubber estate, was owned by Agapito Lemos, a São Paulo investor. He had built a solid legal case for rights to his ranch, first obtaining from INCRA a waiver from any government claims to his land, and then getting a local judge to rule in his favor and order the expulsion of any squatters from his property.

But in November 1981, police had to be called in from Vilhena, sixty miles away, to dislodge hundreds of squatters from the Cabixis ranch. And the police had to intervene again in February 1982 to chase away another wave of invaders. Some weeks later, when I arrived in the area, Lemos had brought in about three hundred peons to slash and burn a large swathe of rain forest on his property. He had also hired a dozen gunmen, led by Domingos do Oliveira, nicknamed Domingão, a burly veteran of land skirmishes with squatters elsewhere on the frontier.

Besides his monthly salary of about three hundred dollars, Domingão reportedly was paid a bonus for every family of squatters he dislodged. He announced that the clearing of the ranchland would begin in an area of several thousand acres occupied by the squatters. Getting wind of Domingão's plan, about a hundred squatters, armed with pistols and shotguns and machetes, marched into the ranch's main compound. They held the cook and two foremen as prisoners and then obliged them to lead the way to Domingão's house. One of the foremen was forced to call out Domingão, and the moment he appeared at the doorway he was cut down by a hail of gunfire. When Domingão's wife, Maria Carolina, ran toward her husband's body, she also was wounded by a shotgun blast and died later at the hospital in Vilhena. Other hired gunmen appeared on the scene, and in the battle that ensued a squatter was killed and several other people on both sides were wounded before the squatters withdrew.

It was only the next day that the police were able to get to the Cabixis ranch. They arrested a dozen squatters and also two Lutheran ministers from Colorado d'Oeste, who were accused of having instigated the squatters.

With a large contingent of police still camped out at the Cabixis ranch, I left Colorado d'Oeste. Reaching Vilhena, I boarded a flight northwest to Pôrto Velho. From the aircraft, a small, twin-propeller plane, the social chaos of Rondônia receded and was replaced by the simplicity of the state's geography. There below me, like a red shaft through the green carpet of rain forest, lay the famous BR-364 highway. Vilhena, Pimenta Bueno, Cacoal, Jiparaná, Ouro Preto—all the pioneer communities that had burst forth over the last decade—looked like ganglia on this red spinal cord that ran the entire breadth of Rondônia from southeast to northwest. There were dozens of small feeder roads joining the highway. Streams and rivers practically curled back on themselves as they snaked through the jungle and farmland and blackened patches where rain forest was being obliterated. But nothing could detract from the essential reality of BR-364. It had transformed Rondônia. It was the center of gravity, the reference mark for every inhabitant and traveler.

Rondônia has become the heart of South America's new frontier lands. The crude, flimsy towns I had visited in 1977 had become booming cities by 1982. I wondered if I would recognize them in five more years. Their streets will probably be paved, and high-rise condominiums will replace many of the single-story wood shacks. Back in 1938, Lévi-Strauss, the French anthropologist, had recalled with heavy irony that Vilhena—"a few huts in the middle of a lengthy clearing several hundred yards wide" whose only inhabitants "were two families who had not had any supplies of food for the previous eight years"—was being touted as the future Chicago of western Amazonia. The image no longer seems to me so outlandish. Well, maybe not Chicago. But possibly this gateway to Rondônia will five years from now be compared to St. Louis, gateway to the American West.

BR-364, the pioneer road, will be asphalted before the end of the 1980's. To the west of the capital city of Pôrto Velho, BR-364 already stretches into Acre and all the way to the Peruvian and Bolivian borders, where it awaits links with Belaúnde's still-unconstructed highway. I have no doubts that before 1990 Acre will also begin to experience a growth as explosive as Rondônia's.

But my conception of this inner frontier of South America was incomplete. I was viewing it only from east to west, pulled along as I was by the axis created by BR-364. To the south, Rondônia's heady surge was also making itself felt in Bolivia, where a very different kind of frontier development—based on an unlikely combination of cattle and drug smuggling—was underway. The growing ties across the Amazon borders of Brazil and Bolivia were beginning to revive a long-forgotten vision of prosperity in this region, a vision that had led to the construction seven decades ago of that remarkable, ill-fated Madeira-Mamoré Railway through some of the most hideous terrain ever penetrated by human beings.

Built to accommodate the rubber trade from Bolivia into the Amazon waterway system, the railway's economic usefulness had collapsed during World War I, when the Asian plantations cornered the world market and sent rubber prices tumbling. After being little used for decades, the Madeira-Mamoré finally had been abandoned. Its 228 miles of tracks between the Bolivian border and Pôrto Velho were replaced by a dirt highway in the early 1970's, just as Rondônia was beginning its spectacular economic expansion.

It was on this road that I decided to travel south from Pôrto Velho into Bolivia, continuing my journey through the continent's frontier lands.

12

My bus left Pôrto Velho at daybreak. The dirt road was narrower, more rutted and less traveled than the BR-364 highway that has brought almost a million settlers into Rondônia. Most of my fellow passengers were gold miners, who clambered off the bus with their burlap sacks and cardboard suitcases at a tent town alongside the Madeira River about fifty miles south of Pôrto Velho. They would have to wait another month for the dry season when the Madeira's waters receded before they could begin panning the banks for small gold nuggets. But by arriving early at the campsite, they could stake out their claims to the more promising plots along the river's edge. The gold panning had been going on for decades along the Madeira River without producing a major strike. Many of the miners had abandoned Rondônia for a much richer vein that had been discovered a few years before in another Amazon state, Pará, more than a thousand miles northeast. But thousands of grizzled veterans still spent four or five months a year on the Madeira's banks, hoping to make a strike before the government opened the lands around the mining sites to waves of new pioneers.

I never actually saw the Madeira, or the Mamoré River, which joined it about the midway point on my 228-mile bus trip. The rivers and the old Madeira-Mamoré Railway were completely obscured by the thick Amazon jungles. There had been a brief squall the night before, and the route turned muddy, sometimes slowing us down to a mule's pace. The only vehicles passing our bus were occasional trucks hauling refrigerated containers of Bolivian beef for the Rondônia settlers. Finally, twelve hours after the departure from Pôrto Velho, we pulled into the small river port of Guajará Mirim, the old terminal of the Madeira-Mamoré Railway.

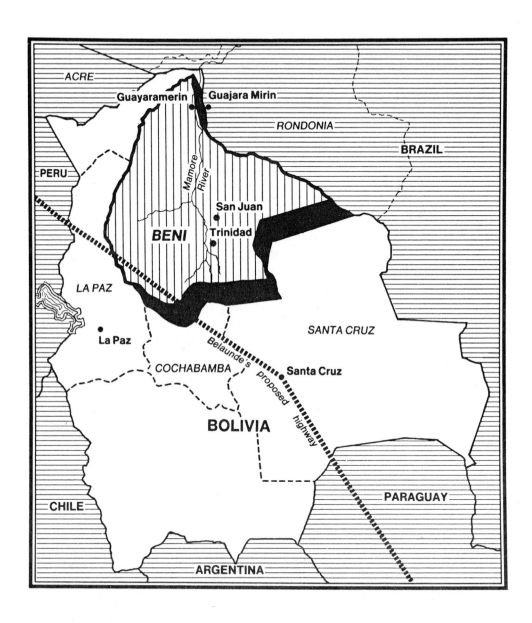

Across the Mamoré River was the Bolivian port of Guayara-merín. I intended to board a boat there and head another three hundred miles south into the heart of the Beni, Bolivia's northern province and the source of the meat cargoes that had lumbered past my bus.

The topographic map I retrieved from my duffel bag indicated that the terrain would shift soon after crossing the Bolivian border. The Amazon rain forests enveloping all of Rondônia spill across the Mamoré River into Bolivia and cover the northern quarter of the Beni. But the rest of the Bolivian province is a huge, flat, African-like savanna of natural pasturelands, dotted with only isolated patches of jungle where the ground swells into knolls.

Savanna exists along much of the periphery of the Amazon basin. In their entirety, the South American savanna lands are immense, about six hundred thousand square miles, an expanse greater than the area of Alaska. The Beni alone is large enough to accommodate all of England and Scotland. But the savannas are underpopulated, infrequently visited and rarely studied—marginal lands in every sense.

The Beni is a terrain of transition between the steamy Brazilian Amazon rain forest to the north and the cold, windswept Bolivian Andes and plateaus to the south. Almost by definition, it is unstable, with extremes of jungle wetness and baked prairie heat. The soils are somewhat more fertile than most Amazon lands, but also much less porous. During the wet season from December to early June, there are about seventy inches of rainfall in the Beni, just half the annual precipitation usually recorded in Amazonia. But the loamy clay earth of the savanna fails to absorb the torrential downpours and heavy overflow of the many rivers, and two thirds of the province becomes a vast, churning lake. Only the clumps of rain forest on higher, spongier ground resist the spectacular floods. Cattle, deer, rodents, jaguars and birds flee the rising waters to these scattered, drier havens.

In the dry season, the climate shifts dramatically. Temperatures, which hover in the seventies during the rainy months, soar above one hundred degrees. A relentless, fiery sun scorches the prairie, cracking the thin topsoil and bleaching the grass to a parched yellow.

If Belaúnde's transcontinental road is ever built, it is supposed to meander across the Beni. So, after a long detour through the Brazilian frontier, I was slowly returning to the trajectory of Belaúnde's imaginary highway through the continent's interior.

The shift from Brazilian jungle to Bolivian savanna marked a buffer between two completely different types of frontier experience. In Rondônia, the Brazilian government has spearheaded the opening of new lands by its extensive road-building programs, and the settlement of that territory has been dominated by peasants and small homesteaders. In the Bolivian savanna, the frontier is the domain of large cattle barons, and its development has unfolded with virtually no state assistance, barely without the awareness of the government. But no matter how dissimilar, the two frontiers are linked commercially because the arrival of so many Brazilian pioneers into Rondônia has created a profitable market for the Bolivian cattle ranchers in the Beni.

Guajará Mirim, where my bus journey south through Rondônia had ended, and Guayaramerín, on Bolivian territory a short ferry ride across the Mamoré River, were the staging bases for these large meat shipments. The two small ports are equally decrepit, with discolored wood and mud-brick shacks set on dirt alleys branching out from unpaved main streets and a butcher-shop smell wafting permanently in the air. The towns exist only because they are the last navigable points on the Madeira-Mamoré waterway before it breaks into rapids and cataracts on its northward course to Pôrto Velho. I decided to board a ferry and spend the night on the Bolivian side because I would have to look for a boat there to take me along the Mamoré southward deep into the Beni.

The Bolivian customs-immigration officer in Guayaramerín, a rotund, moon-faced man with dark glasses and black teeth, had apparently never seen an American passport. He turned it around from every angle until I pointed out the numbers etched across the top of the passport.

"Do you work for the American government?" he asked.

"No. I'm a tourist."

"American tourists never come to Guayaramerín," he said. "Why didn't you take a plane to La Paz?"

"I'm in no hurry to get there."

He was not in any rush either. He set aside my passport and ordered one of his aides to search my knapsack and duffel bag. The decayed, whitewashed, mud-and-wattle building used by the customs officers was an old turn-of-the-century rubber warehouse. Bolivian officials, clad in drab-olive fatigues, walked between bags and crates of Brazilian merchandise—machines and tools, all sorts of household equipment, canned goods—and scribbled notes on their clipboards. Outside the warehouse, by the docks, barges loaded down with refrigerated meat containers were being cursorily inspected by other Bolivian guards.

Judging from the amount of money passing between civilians and customs officials—with no accompanying documents—I gathered that virtually all the transactions were contraband or bribes. In my own small way, I made a contribution by agreeing to slip my immigration officer the Brazilian currency equivalent of five dollars to have my passport stamped and returned to me. His surliness evaporated and he cheerfully offered to buy any of my foreign currency. But a Bolivian cattle herder standing behind me whispered that there were better rates to be had once I got past customs.

Outside the warehouse, the ranch hand introduced himself as Guillermo Calderón. He was a tautly muscled, middle-aged man with a swagger and a warm smile that crinkled his eyes. He worked in the Beni as a foreman for a rancher, who had bought a dozen prize humpbacked zebu bulls with sharp, curving horns in Brazil for crossbreeding with his own livestock. Guillermo was accompanying the animals back to the ranch near Trinidad, the capital of the Beni, three hundred miles to the south. He strongly advised me to take a small taxi-plane to Trinidad. But when I told him I had planned all along to make the trip by river, he suggested that I ride the same boat he was taking the next morning.

The boat, about sixty feet long, was a two-tiered wooden barge powered by an ancient, smoky diesel engine. The livestock were kept on the open-air bottom section, practically at water level. The three-man crew and six passengers stayed on the bridge, a covered top section within sight and smell of the animals. There were no bunks, only hammocks. What I like most about a hammock is that it places the body in a position perfectly congenial for reading. But I never could fall asleep hanging in the air, stomach upward, with my back bent into a crescent. So I spread my sleeping bag on the hardwood deck.

Guillermo had two younger ranch hands with him. The two other passengers were an older couple who were protecting four large burlap sacks of contraband goods from Brazil. They were bronze-skinned small merchants of the Beni, who kept to themselves, whispering in a choppy Spanish. The barge pilot, unshaven with heavy-lidded eyes, remained morosely behind the wheel. He thumbed through a huge stack of comic books, and only occasionally looked up at the river to correct his course when the boat drifted too close to shore. One of the crew, wearing a tattered straw hat, hunched over the bow, sometimes dropping a line to measure the depth of the river. The other crew member was the cook, who spent most of his time playing a medieval Spanish card game with Guillermo and his ranch hands.

The crew and other passengers ate a watery beef stew and a mash of overripe bananas, corn, rice and peppers that looked so unappetizing that I initially mistook it for livestock fodder. The captain, completely perplexed by my steadfast refusal to join in the meal, kept repeating to me, "But it's free—comes with the passage." Fortunately, I had purchased several pounds of canned beef hash and tuna, a large bunch of finger-length bananas and a dozen bottles of mineral water in Guayaramerín. We bought fresh fruit, dried fish and turtle eggs at several riverside villages during the trip. Following Guillermo's example, I peeled off the top half of the leathery brown eggshell, squeezed gently so as not to dribble the white and popped the raw yolk into my mouth. It was grainy, with a faintly nutty taste.

The cruise was uncomfortable almost from the moment we left port. We were downwind from the tightly packed animals, and their deck was never cleaned out. The tropical sun seemed not so much to shine as to strike, and its rays exploded on the light brown waters with blinding effect.

The Mamoré, which averages about two miles in width, runs north for more than six hundred miles from its source in the Andean highlands of central Bolivia to its confluence with the Madeira in Brazil. For 120 miles south from Guayaramerín, the Mamoré traces the borderline between Brazil and Bolivia. It took our boat two days and nights to cover this distance. The Mamoré is then joined by a large tributary, the Guaporé, which continues to mark the Brazilian-Bolivian border for another three hundred miles southeast. But we kept to our southerly course along the Mamoré as it veered from the border and deeper into the Beni.

After the first day, I pretty much exhausted the conversational possibilities with my fellow passengers and the crew. The Bolivian merchant couple seemed to distrust everybody. The captain had been reduced to catatonic stupor by his comic books. Guillermo began to get on my nerves by insisting that I paint the United States in unblemished, glowing terms, and was obviously skeptical at my suggestions that most of my compatriots were not millionaires and that not many American women were buxom blondes. I suppose I annoyed him as much by repeatedly probing him about the excitement of ranching in the Beni, a life-style which he said he would unhesitantly trade for a one-way ticket to Miami. Occasionally, I joined in the card games, and then I would drift off to a corner to read my dwindling reserve of books.

When the boredom became unbearable, I would pull out a small pair of binoculars and focus on the abundant birdlife. Green-and-yellow macaws swooped low over the thickly jungled banks. Blue kingfishers made arrowy descents into the water and emerged with small fish grasped crosswise in their beaks. Flocks of storks sailed overhead, their long necks extended on a downward angle. Egrets clung to the trees like huge white blossoms.

I spotted a few large caimans—South American alligators—basking on sandbars at the river's edge near the rusting hulks of steam-powered paddleboats from another era. The waters were too murky to see fish, but sometimes, small pink dolphins bounded in and out of our wake.

Like dozens of other species whose normal habitat is the Atlantic Ocean, dolphins swam up the Amazon River millennia ago, somehow adapted to the fresh water and made their way into dozens of Amazon tributaries. On other trips, I had seen sea cows or manatees and even a few sharks along the larger rivers of Amazonia.

Perhaps because of its almost human intelligence and seemingly sly smile, the dolphin is the object of sexual superstitions throughout the Amazon. In parts of the Brazilian and Peruvian jungle, there are recurring legends of dolphins that transform themselves at night into hypnotically handsome men who seduce and then abandon young unmarried women. They may help account for some unexplained pregnancies. The scrapings of dried dolphin eyes are prized as an aphrodisiac.

The river traffic was light. There were canvas-covered passenger boats, barges heaped high with gravel, a few medium-sized cabin cruisers probably ferrying contraband, and the fishermen's dugout canoes, called *peke-peke* for the puttering sound of their long-shafted propellers.

Every afternoon, as the flaming sunset ebbed slowly away, the tedium returned, and so did the mosquitoes. They were inescapable, especially the tiny, whining pium flies, which had an uncanny knack for finding holes in the mosquito nets and left small, madly itchy blood blisters wherever they bit.

Although we were nearing the beginning of the dry season, torrential rains lashed our barge several nights. The roof of the bridge sprouted a dozen leaks and forced me to climb into the dreaded hammocks for a few sleepless hours. We had no lights, and parts of the river were too cluttered with driftwood to risk traveling in the dark. So at dusk, we tied up near one of the tiny villages at the river's edge, let the cattle graze and water along the banks overnight and, after herding the livestock back up a plank into the boat, set out again at dawn.

Most of the villages were clusters of thatched-roof houses set on tall stilts. But they looked like barges because the river had swelled and flooded during the rainy season, raising the water level to the very top of the stilts. As our boat approached, the inhabitants would paddle out in canoes, hawking food and wild animal skins—mostly jaguars and caimans.

Finally, after what seemed like six interminably long days and nights, we disembarked at a small port called La Loma, just north of Trinidad. Guillermo's cattle looked sickly, and he was worried that the yellowish-red dirt road to his ranch was impassable because of the recent rains. But the truck drivers who were waiting for him at La Loma said the sun dried out the road by midmorning. So we set out in a Chevy pickup and a larger Ford truck for the livestock on a thirty-mile drive eastward to the ranch.

The lushly wooded banks of the Mamoré had blocked the savanna from view during most of the river journey. And now that we were on the road—a relatively straight causeway elevated several feet above the flooded plains—the gigantic dimensions of the Beni came as a shock. The grass, in sharp, thick blades ranging from waist-level to a man's height, unfurled like a yellow-green sea. The rains had turned huge stretches of the prairie into deep, dark puddles, some as large as lakes. The cattle—stout, humpbacked zebus and thinner, longer-horned local breeds—waded in small groups through the swampy, inundated pasturelands or were driven in herds of up to two hundred animals by ranch hands on horseback along the dirt causeway. We passed some sluggish, creaking oxcarts, and a few motorcycles churning up the reddish earth along the road.

"In two months' time, in the middle of the dry season," said Guillermo, "you wouldn't recognize this landscape. We set the plains on fire. Hundreds of fires to clear away the old, yellow grass. The smoke is everywhere, and some days you can't see a thing. The smoke rises so high that planes have to fly on radar because the pilots can't see the horizon or the ground. Then the rains come and the new grass grows, green and thick for the cattle. Just a day or two after the first rains, the land turns green again. It always grows back. That's the way it has always been in the Beni—water and fire, water and fire."

The Beni is dotted with tens of thousands of artificial mounds and elevated fields that from the air look like discolored, rectangular patches. They were built by aboriginal Indian tribes in the centuries before the arrival of the first Spanish conquistadores around 1600. Their purpose evidently was to achieve water control for settlements and agriculture. By raising one- or two-acre plots of land a few feet above the plains, the Indians were able to guard their crops from all but the worst floods of the rainy season. Ditches were dug across these fields and mounds to further drain them of water. Many of the elevated dirt causeways that still provide the Beni with its only roads can be traced back to these pre-conquest tribes.

An American anthropologist and geographer, William M. Denevan, who is one of the few scholars to have researched and surveyed the remnants of aboriginal civilization in the largest part of the Beni's savanna, called the Mojos, speculates that as many as five hundred thousand Indians may have inhabited these plains before their discovery by Spanish explorers. If the estimate is correct, the Beni once had twice its current population.

"Evidence has been presented," wrote Denevan, "that in the Mojos savannas in the sixteenth century there were several hundred thousand Indians and large villages with palisades, moats, plazas, and streets; and there still can be seen at least 1,000 miles of causeway, several hundred thousand linear drained fields, and also numerous canals, large mounds, and small mound fields.... In a savanna environment with seemingly little opportunity for grassland cultivation because of flooding, drought, and low fertility, pre-Spanish people achieved a productivity and population density that have not been equaled since."

Despite their acumen for large-scale water-control works, these tribes produced no architecture comparable to the Inca temples and fortresses. Their pottery was more primitive than ceramics found in

Peru, Colombia and Mexico. By the time the Spaniards arrived in the Beni, the Indians were in organizational decline, divided among scores of tribes often hostile to each other.

Between 1580 and 1617, bands of conquistadores thrust into the province in their feverish search for El Dorado. They came to the Beni from their outposts in Santa Cruz, Bolivia, and Asunción, Paraguay, in the southeast and from Peru in the west, where the fabulous treasures of the Incas had only aroused their greed for even greater riches.

The conquistadores set their compass by rumors and myths passed on to them by tribes captured along their route. Often, the Indians were so terrorized that they lied about faraway treasures just to rid themselves of the Spaniards. Sometimes, the Indians ingenuously repeated legends of civilizations that may once have existed but had died out long before the arrival of the conquistadores. Both these explanations seem to have played a role in the initial Spanish incursions into the Beni.

The El Dorado legend in the Mojos savanna of the Beni revolved around a mythical empire called the Great Paititi.

"The Paititi is an extremely rich kingdom," wrote Father José Guevara, an eighteenth-century Jesuit historian. "This kingdom is isolated in the middle of a great lagoon surrounded by mountains of untold riches. Its buildings are all of white stone, and it has avenues, plazas and temples. From the center of the lagoon, the palace of the emperor of Mojos rises, superior to all the other structures in size, beauty and wealth, its doors chained in gold."

Guevara's description of the terrain—so different from the flat Beni savanna—has led other historians to believe that the Indian legends might have been inspired by the Tiahuanaco ruins on the edge of Lake Titicaca, which is high in the Andean plateaus between Peru and Bolivia and surrounded by mountains. The Tiahuanaco structures belonged to a civilization that preceded the Incas and disappeared centuries before Francisco Pizarro set foot in Peru.

In any event, the conquistadores found not a trace of El Dorado in the Beni. Cursing the warlike tribes and the absence of treasure, they moved on, but dutifully reported back to the Spanish viceroys that the area seemed propitious for livestock. Fifty years later, in the second half of the seventeenth century, Jesuit priests introduced cattle into the province and enticed the Indians to agricultural missions.

It was about this time that missionairies began to play a key geopolitical role for the Spanish court throughout the New World. The myth of El Dorado had evaporated after almost a hundred years of costly, frustrated expeditions, and the conquistadores were withdrawn to the established cities, most of them near the coasts of South America. The administration of the empire was turned over to bureaucrats, lawyers and judges brought over from Spain. The missionaries were a cheap solution to safeguard the frontiers of the empire, particularly from the Portuguese explorers and adventurers in Brazil. Spanish Jesuits in Paraguay, Argentina, Bolivia and Peru built self-sufficient agricultural missions and commanded large numbers of Indian troops who proved to be a powerfully dissuasive force against Portuguese marauders.

The Spanish conquistadores and missionaries introduced into the Beni the same European diseases that had decimated natives elsewhere in the New World. Denevan estimates that fully ninety percent of the tribal population of the savanna was wiped out by common influenza, small pox and other illnesses, so that by 1737, there were no more than fifty thousand Indians in the Beni.

But other scholars tend to laud the Jesuits for their efforts to protect the Indians from slavery imposed by Spanish and Portuguese settlers elsewhere on the continent. The missionary settlements of the Beni existed in relatively prosperous isolation for one hundred years until the Jesuits were expelled from Latin America in the latter half of the eighteenth century by jealous rivals who had the ear of the Spanish and Portuguese monarchs.

Drawing on missionary accounts of that era, modern-day Bolivian historian Gabriel René-Moreno has described the Jesuit settlements of the Beni as a lost utopia, the apogee of civilization in this part of the world. He wrote:

> No one was lazy here. [The Indians] worked communally under the tutelage of the priests, without individual holdings, without knowing about the use of money or the give and take of business. They received everything from the hands of the priests, from their clothing and food for their families to blessing and religious instruction, from the teaching of crafts and the example of work to temporal punishment and the examples of Heaven and Hell. They wove, tanned leather, carved wood, melted and forged metal, boiled sugar cane, sewed, spun, made shoes, played instruments, sang, cultivated and worked the cacao, and herded the three species of cattle. They produced everything they needed for this rudimentarily civilized life.

When the Spanish monarch's troops, two hundred soldiers at most, came for the Jesuits and confiscated their holdings, neither the twenty-three missionaries nor their twenty thousand Indian wards put up any resistance. Bereft of their Jesuit protectors, many of the Indians scattered in panic back to the virgin savanna and rain forests. The missions' cattle dispersed and multiplied into huge wild herds like Texas longhorns.

The Beni lapsed into the kind of lengthy oblivion that has often afflicted other frontier lands on the continent. Viewed from the perspective of South Americans, the frontier history of the United States has always had a marvelously linear quality about it. The progression was steadily westward until the Pacific Ocean was reached. Once a territory was conquered, the land was settled by ranchers and homesteaders. Trains and stagecoach lines brought it into the orbit of the established East. Government and private investment then ensured its economic and demographic growth. By and large, the winning of the West was a constant process of consolidation.

In South America, by contrast, since the arrival of the conquistadores, there has long been an unstable, predatory approach to the wilderness. When the early Spanish and Portuguese adventurers failed to find their El Dorado in the hinterlands, they retreated. In later centuries, when coveted mineral deposits and natural resources were exhausted or lost their markets, the frontier areas withered and were deserted. Often, towns and adjoining farms remained isolated, surrounded by wilderness in every direction. This was to be the Beni's fate following the collapse of the missions.

In the decades after the Jesuits' departure, the potential richness of the Beni continued to be noted by the few travelers who had the time, patience and stamina to venture into this wilderness. One of the most eloquent and determined of these visitors was the young French naturalist Alcides D'Orbigny. He explored South America about the same time that his countryman Alexis de Tocqueville was spending nine months in the United States analyzing American democracy. D'Orbigny stayed seven years in the hinterlands of South America, from 1826 to 1833, and wrote an encyclopedic but lively four-volume account called *Voyage à l'Amérique Meridionale*. He never gained a fraction of De Tocqueville's fame because the backlands of South America paled in importance to the emerging power of the former English colonies.

But D'Orbigny was often as acute an observer of politics, social mores and character as De Tocqueville. And he far surpassed his better-known compatriot in his knowledge of geography and nature. In the Beni, which he visited for several months in 1832, D'Orbigny described the remnants of the Jesuit communities, the listlessness of their former Indian trustees, the total isolation of the province and its wondrously large herds of wild cattle. Not given to flights of hyperbole, he nevertheless denounced the treatment of the Indians by the missionaries who replaced the Jesuits as the worst example of "slavery and despotism I have ever seen under a free government.... They are supposed to be employed for the good of the State, but in fact they are exploited by their administrators and priests, who do not give them a moment of rest."

D'Orbigny was awed by the extremes of dryness and inundation in the province, and he shivered through a fearful bout of malaria. But he remained convinced that "in this century when there are no insuperable obstacles to men of science and industry" the Beni had the natural resources and extensive river network to prosper. "It could even transform itself into the center of commercial operations on a vast scale that would take advantage of the inherent riches, now unutilized, in the core of this American continent."

D'Orbigny's predictions proved accurate fifty years later during the rubber boom that swept through the Beni and the Amazon. That boom produced a remarkable empire builder, Nicolás Suárez, a rubber baron who dominated the Beni as thoroughly as the seventeenth- and eighteenth-century Jesuits.

He was born in Santa Cruz, the capital of eastern Bolivia, but grew up in Trinidad, the Beni's capital, where his father was a modest rancher. As an adolescent, Nicolás Suárez became a trader in quinine bark—an antidote for malaria attacks—and explored the farthest reaches of Bolivia's northern rivers and jungles. With his thorough knowledge of the region's geography, Suárez was well equipped to take advantage of the burgeoning world market for rubber that began in the 1870's. He quickly gained control of the key waterfalls on the Beni River that fed into the Amazon River system flowing out to the Atlantic Ocean and the markets of Europe and America. Suárez created a crude but effective system of portages to carry rubber around the Beni River's cataracts and rapids and deliver it to Amazon boats.

He sent his brothers to London to establish an extensive network of buyers and creditors. By 1890, the Suárez family owned sixteen million acres of rubber forests—almost equal in area to all of Ireland—in the Amazon jungles that formed the northern periphery of the Beni's savanna. In the Beni itself, Nicolás built a string of communities and ranches to provide logistical support for his vast jungle operations. At his peak, he accounted for more than half of Bolivia's rubber exports.

Like many South American frontier giants, he turned his back on the capital and its social circles. He bragged that he had visited La Paz only once in his life. And his contempt for the central government was unbounded after it ceded Bolivia's rich northern rubber forests in Acre—including extensive Suárez properties—to Brazil in 1903, despite the fact that Suárez and his Indian army had successfully held off the Brazilians for months.

The rubber boom collapsed in northern Bolivia as it did throughout South America in the second decade of this century when cheaper Asian rubber cornered the world market. The Beni slipped again into deep economic lethargy and isolation. But Suárez himself remained a very rich man. He built a huge mansion in the northernmost Bolivian jungles, planted an orchard and bulldozed a dozen miles of roads to drive his imported American limousines for pleasure. He continued to vacation abroad, taking his own yacht down the Madeira to the Amazon River, and then boarding a steamer in Manaus bound for Europe. When his wife died, he erected a monument of Italian marble over the Beni River and buried her there. He himself lived until 1940 to the ripe old age of eighty-eight.

Although the life of rubber workers in northern Bolivia was certainly brutal, Suárez was largely unscathed by accusations of wholesale atrocities that gained worldwide notoriety for some of his counterparts in Peru and Brazil. In La Paz and elsewhere in Bolivia, he is a forgotten figure. But in the Beni, he is still remembered as the "Rockefeller of the Rubber Trade." His company name—Casa Suárez or Hermanos Suárez—appears in faded letters on old warehouses throughout the province. His yellowing photographs, showing a short, bullish man with an unsmiling visage, hang in some municipal offices and in the ranch houses of a few of his descendants who stayed on in the Beni.

The Jesuit missionaries brought the Beni its first period of economic vigor following the Spanish Conquest. Rubber and Nicolás Suárez stoked another boom. I was now arriving in 1982 in the midst of the Beni's third great economic surge—in cattle and drug smuggling—both of them enterprises that were historically linked to the two previous eras.

It was the Jesuits who were responsible for the Beni's cattle fortunes. The small herds, which they brought over from eastern Bolivia three hundred years ago in punishing journeys through hot plains and tropical highlands, had multiplied prodigiously and now stood at 2.5 million animals, about ten times the size of the province's human population.

Nicolás Suárez's responsibility for the Beni's current boom was more indirect. His grandnephew, Roberto Suárez, had recently emerged as the kingpin of Bolivia's cocaine trade. By reviving some of the business and organizational methods of his ancestor, Roberto Suárez had become even more wealthy and powerful and notorious than old Nicolás in his heyday.

I had not yet heard of Roberto Suárez or the Beni's reputation for cocaine as I drove across the province's pasturelands with Guillermo and the Brazilian bulls we had accompanied along the Mamoré River. To me, the Beni was only synonymous with cattle.

Guillermo had told me that his boss owned several cattle operations throughout the province and might not be on hand to welcome us at his ranch. The owner, in fact, was not at home when our trucks rumbled onto the property. It was about eight thousand acres, small by Beni standards. Judging from the ranch's primitive, worn-out appearance, Guillermo's boss seemed to be an indifferent cattleman. Most of the livestock were mangy descendants of the wild herds that had roamed the savanna since missionary times. I saw no evidence of fences along the property, and the animals—bulls, cows, steers and calves—mingled freely and grazed anywhere they pleased, even on the grass-patched airplane runway. The ranch house was a rambling turn-of-the-century building badly in need of a new coat of whitewash. Its decaying wood porch listed to one side.

It was late in the afternoon, and I decided that since the owner was not around to invite me to stay, I would hitch a truck ride into Trinidad and spend the night at a hotel there. I thanked Guillermo for his help and company during the river trip.

The sun was setting in a fierce red ball over Trinidad when the truck driver dropped me in front of a small single-story hotel. I was far more tired than hungry, so I lay down as soon as I checked into my room. It was the first real bed I had seen in a week, and I slept until dawn.

The rooms of the hotel all faced an inner courtyard, where I ate breakfast amid the potted flowers and hummingbirds that glittered red and gold through a blur of wings. There were no other guests. The two waiters seemed astonished that I finished a plate piled high with toast and ordered two more along with another jar of marmalade and a whole pot of coffee.

I had the names of two people to contact in the Beni. They were Guillermo Tineo, a rancher and politician who apparently was well versed in the history of the province, and Carlos Schenstrom, a young rancher who had inherited one of the largest properties in the Beni. They had been recommended to me by mutual friends in La Paz, the Bolivian capital, when I was last there some months before.

It was too early to call upon anybody, so I decided to explore the town before the midmorning ninety-degree heat set in. Trinidad was the most substantial community I had visited since Pôrto Velho in Brazil, and a good deal more charming. About thirty-five thousand people live there, one out of every eight of the province's inhabitants. The town, located 270 miles northeast of La Paz, is built around a large tree-lined plaza dominated by a cavernous cathedral with twin, white Neo-Gothic towers. The streets are paved with yellowish-red bricks. Most of the vehicles are Japanese motorcycles, many of them hiring out as taxis.

The sidewalks are two feet above the streets because of heavy inundations during the rainy season. Most of the buildings are only one story, but have very high ceilings with slow overhead fans that keep the rooms relatively cool. The buildings' façades are monochromed pastels—purple, blue, green, turquoise, yellow—and their roofs are topped with red-brick tiles. The roofs jut out over the sidewalks and are held up by evenly spaced wood columns, making it possible to walk around the town protected from sun and rain. Like my hotel, many of the buildings have lushly vegetated, airy inner courtyards.

In short, Trinidad is a classic Spanish colonial town, unspoiled by department stores or high rises. Horseback riders and oxcarts still meander through the streets. The merchandise in the shops is dominated by basic frontier goods: farm machinery parts, diesel generators, tools, sacks of rice, flour and beans, rough flannel pants and blue jeans.

In physique and personality, the Benianos can hardly be more different than the natives of La Paz and the Andean highlands. The Indians of the Bolivian capital are squat, with deep brown, almost purple complexions and an unsmiling gaze that signals their aloof-

ness to the wealthy, powerful, light-skinned minority descended from the Spanish colonists. In Trinidad the inhabitants are mostly lithe and bronzed, garrulous and prone to easy laughter. Young women lean out of their ground-floor windows to flirt with boyfriends and stare with whimsical smiles at passersby. Any inquiry I made provoked a cascade of curious questions, invitations to coffee or offers to guide me around town.

There are relatively few cars on the broad streets, yet they honk loudly as they approach every corner. From the shops, radios play deafening Brazilian sambas interrupted by personal messages: "Pedro, tell Mom I found a job and will be sending money soon" or "Jorge, please come to Trinidad, a friend has arrived from San Javier."

About nine A.M., I walked into Guillermo Tineo's storefront office, the local cattleman's association. Tineo was drinking coffee and reading a two-day-old La Paz newspaper. He was short, about fifty years old, with a craggy face partially hidden by dark aviator glasses. His wavy hair was slicked back with brilliantine. A loose, white shirt fell over his soiled khaki pants covering a soft, ample belly.

Tineo traces his roots in the province through four generations, all of them cattle ranchers. He had been a senator in La Paz during one of those intermittent periods of constitutional government prior to the last three military coups. And he launched into a brief but detailed history of the Beni, as if he were delivering a speech on the senate floor. Almost all his information, though, checks out in history books I perused later.

Trinidad was founded in 1687 as one of the earliest Jesuit settlements in the province by Father Cipriano Barace, a revered missionary who was later martyred by a tribe of Indians he was attempting to convert. There are no buildings in Trinidad that can be traced to the missionary era. The impressive cathedral was built at the beginning of this century on the spot where the original Jesuit church burned down.

In one essential respect, according to Tineo, little has changed since the Jesuit era. There are still no roads from Trinidad to La Paz or the outside world, except for a dirt trail that winds 320 miles east to Santa Cruz and is washed out for most of the rainy season. The rivers connecting the province to the rest of the country are still navigable only at flood tide between December and June.

"When I was a boy, we used to hunt down the cattle like buffalo and send only the hides by boat southward along the river to Cochabamba and other towns," said Tineo. "The carcasses would just rot in the savanna because there weren't enough people to eat the meat."

About 1970, Tineo and a group of younger ranchers came up with the novel idea of buying old cargo planes, many of them vintage World War II models, to break the Beni's commercial isolation. The cattle are slaughtered and loaded on these rickety planes that lumber off dirt runways built on hundreds of ranches. Without pressurized cabins for high-altitude flights, the ancient aircraft wheeze through the Andean mountain passes to La Paz and the tin-mining communities beyond. The airstrips of the Beni are littered with wreckages of planes that were too heavily burdened for takeoff, or not agile enough to avoid skidding off muddy runways.

But the province has become the main source of meat for Bolivia, and has established an important market in Rondônia. The Beni has suddenly and unexpectedly entered its greatest period of prosperity since the rubber days. Like Rondônia, the province has dramatically reversed the history of technology. Airplanes preceded motor vehicles as the main source of transportation. And, undoubtedly, roads for trucks and cars will be built long before a railway connects the Beni to the outside world. Here, as in Brazil, is an inversion of the history of transportation on the North American frontier.

The possibility of finally getting the meat to market has sparked a real interest among the Beni ranchers to improve their livestock. Humpbacked zebu cattle, like the ones I accompanied along the Mamoré River, are being massively imported from Brazil and crossbred with the native criollo stock. The new breed, called a mestizo, produces more meat than the wild criollo and takes less time to fatten for slaughter. It also adapts well to the Beni. During the dry season, the mestizo can walk long distances looking for water while withstanding the intense heat. Tineo himself has imported more than five hundred zebu cattle, and half of his seven thousand animals are now mestizos.

Tineo displays the typical frontiersman's scorn for government. "Everything you see here is the result of local, private efforts," he said. "The government didn't give us a peso for the airplanes or the imported cattle. As a former senator, I can tell you that for years they have promised us a highway to La Paz, and those projects are still gathering dust in the government archives. There is not one kilometer of asphalted road in the whole of the Beni. If we had to depend on the government, this province would look exactly as it did two hundred years ago when the Jesuits were expelled. In La Paz, everybody's mind is set on the tin mines. They can't conceive of this country's agricultural wealth."

It was Tineo who first told me about the old rubber baron Nicolás Suárez and his more unsavory grandnephew, Roberto Suárez.

"Nicolás was the greatest figure the Beni ever produced, a man who changed the course of his country's history," said Tineo. "Roberto Suárez is an entirely different matter. He pretends to be a cattle rancher, but his real business is narcotics, cocaine. I have nothing more to say about him. You can find out from others, almost anybody here can tell you something about him. But I don't think it is such a good idea to take a close interest in him."

Tineo was far more upbeat on the subject of Carlos Schenstrom, the prosperous young rancher whose name had been given to me in La Paz. He urged me to visit the Schenstrom ranch and arranged by radio to have Carlos pick me up.

Tineo and I had lunch at a nearby restaurant. It was, of course, beef, served slice after slice until I had to beg the waiter to relent. Between us, we finished off ten bottles of beer. And I staggered back to my hotel for a siesta.

I was awakened by a telephone call from Tineo confirming that Schenstrom would fly in to meet me at the Trinidad airport the following afternoon. I had not forgotten about Roberto Suárez, but I decided to pick up his trail after visiting the Schenstrom ranch.

13

The airport, on the outskirts of Trinidad, was more than anything a huge depot for meat. Workers were carrying big slabs of beef from a crude, refrigerated warehouse to a cargo plane twenty yards away. The hundred-degree afternoon heat melted the thin layer of frost on the meat, and blood drenched the laborers' rough cotton shirts. A cloud of red dust swirled up as the propellers roared and the aircraft hurtled down the runway heading southwest to the tin mines high in the Andes.

The skies became overcast and it had started to rain by the time Schenstrom arrived an hour later in his small, twin-engine Cessna. He was only thirty-three years old, but had already spent twelve years ranching in the Beni. He was relatively short, barrel-chested; his head cocked slightly upward, and he had a booming laugh and voice that seemed to well up from his diaphragm. I took a liking to him immediately.

The family name came from Carlos's Swedish grandfather, but Carlos had been drawn into the frontier by his father's adventurous impulses. After World War II, the father began purchasing huge tracts of land in the Beni for as little as a quarter an acre. His friends thought that even at such piddling prices the older Schenstrom was tarnishing his reputation as a shrewd businessman. How in the world, they wondered, could he gamble that someday a way would be found to get his beef to market?

The father eventually amassed more than two hundred fifty thousand acres of savanna—almost four hundred square miles—and gathered a herd of twenty thousand lean, tough criollo cattle. He called his ranch San Juan, and gave it as an emblem the rhea, a four-foot-tall South American ostrich that abounds in the frontier plains. But he never lived to see San Juan operating as an efficient, profitable enterprise.

As a child, Carlos often accompanied his parents to the Beni. He loved the savanna and was determined to work the ranch, so he studied agronomy at the university in La Paz. When he married shortly after graduation, he moved up to San Juan with his wife.

Carlos did not want to linger at the Trinidad airport because heavier rains were soon expected, so we lifted off into rumbling black skies. A steady drizzle blurred the plane's windshield. The Beni had seemed swampy when I drove along its savanna by truck two days before. But from the air, the full impact of the wet season was truly jarring. I stared down incredulously at the rainwater lakes that immersed the province in all directions, sometimes merging into an enormous red-and-black sea. Ranch houses and old mission villages stood out like islands on the dots of higher ground. I could see cattle dog-paddling through the dark waters next to the bloated carcasses of drowned steers. All but a few of the elevated dirt causeways were submerged. Canoes and motorboats navigated the flooded plains where Jeeps and oxcarts normally tread during the dry season.

After only ten minutes, we were already flying over the huge Schenstrom estate, about forty miles north of Trinidad. Some of the land was underwater, but it looked more orderly than any of the ranches we had passed. Wire fences crisscrossed the property, dissecting the grazing areas into neatly geometric shapes.

"None of the fences were up when I first took over the ranch," said Carlos. "My idea was to graze the animals as efficiently as possible, and to separate them according to age so they could be more easily selected for slaughter. We figure that we need about four hectares [10 acres] per animal. So the herds are very spread out, and it means a lot of time spent rounding them up. Imagine trying to handle, say, just a thousand head of cattle spread over four thousand hectares [10,000 acres], and doing it all on horseback because there aren't enough roads for Jeeps. Then there is the problem of the rainy season. For six months a year, half my land is underwater. We have to guess what fields will be dry enough for grazing, and fence them off."

A few minutes later, Carlos banked the plane sharply and swooped down for a landing. We circled over silos and hangars, past the mud-brick homes of the ranch hands and the red-tiled roof of the large Schenstrom house. A small cluster of cattle, which had been huddling peaceably on a patch of higher dry ground, stampeded helter-skelter into puddles as the plane buzzed them during its final descent. Carlos set down the craft on his bumpy, dirt runway, and we clambered into a pickup truck and headed over to his ranch house. A brick road led up to the prosperous new two-story mansion into which Carlos had moved a few years before with his wife, Irene, and a growing brood that now included two daughters and a son.

Irene is a stunning, tall, dark-haired beauty with high cheekbones. She was obviously delighted that a guest, a foreigner yet, had unexpectedly arrived. As soon as I introduced myself and was handed a cold glass of beer, she started plying me with questions about the United States, Europe and Latin America, about politics, big cities, farms, anything and everything. She said their primary source of outside news was the shortwave radio, mainly the BBC Spanish-language broadcasts. Newspapers rarely arrived, and then only with a delay of several days to a week. "Mostly, they carry news from La Paz that we have already heard from radio conversations with our family and friends back in the capital," she said.

The adjustment to living in this distant frontier must have been difficult for a thoroughly urbanized, upper-class young woman like Irene. Most of the larger ranchers left their properties in charge of managers and maintained households in La Paz and Santa Cruz because their wives could not stand the isolation and their children lacked proper schools in the Beni. The distance between ranches, and the dearth of roads, also reduced social life to a minimum. But she betrayed no regrets.

Educational facilities were woeful in the Beni, particularly outside Trinidad. There was a schoolhouse at San Juan, near an old mission chapel and within easy walking distance of the two-room mud-and-wattle homes where the families of the eighty ranch hands lived. The Schenstroms helped subsidize the teachers. But they had brought over a Chilean woman as a private tutor for their own children to prepare them for secondary school and eventually university in La Paz.

The Beni, particularly after the rainy season, was wracked with malaria and yellow fever. Some years before, a deadly hemorrhagic fever had ravaged the population. In such emergencies, doctors had to be flown to the ranch, and once when the Schenstroms' oldest daughter fell ill, Irene decided to fly with her all the way to La Paz.

Irene had supervised the construction of the six-bedroom ranch house. Though massive, the building was well exposed to light to take advantage of the long hours of sun during the dry season. And its high ceilings ventilated the house so well that air conditioning and fans were not needed even in the hottest weather. Wood beams and luxurious plants gave it a properly rustic ambiance. The floors, laid in tile imported from Brazil, were easy to wipe clean of the inevitable mud tracked by work boots. A swimming pool in the backyard adjoined a large gymnasium equipped with an indoor squash court, a Nautilus exercise room and a Jacuzzi.

Construction of the mansion had been a tedious, slow process because materials had to be brought in from other parts of Bolivia and Brazil, and there were few skilled laborers in the Beni. Irene's cousin was the architect, but he could not absent himself too long or frequently from his practice in La Paz.

We were joined by Teddy Avila, who for thirty-five years had been manager of the San Juan ranch and was now easing into retirement. Tall, thin, extremely fair-skinned, with blue-gray eyes and salt-and-pepper hair, Teddy has about him the air of an English country gentleman. He has a dry wit, a mellifluous almost purring voice and a ready stock of anecdotes delivered between puffs on a long cigarette holder. Whenever Carlos's memory faltered, Teddy was ready to fill the gaps about the history of the province and the ranch, the special characteristics of different cattle breeds, the exact dates of cattle importations.

"There were hardly any vehicles in the whole province back then," said Teddy, recalling the beginnings of San Juan in the late 1940's when Carlos's father initially purchased the lands. "We did everything on horseback or on foot. We first set out to explore the properties because we didn't even know what paths and streams crossed the lands, or how much pasture they contained. Then slowly, we bought cattle from local ranches, and we herded the livestock on horseback, sometimes a hundred kilometers [sixty miles] back to the ranch. Later, we built the roads, even the big one that leads to the Mamoré River and the boats."

Carlos had practically doubled the herds he inherited from his father, and now had more than thirty-five thousand animals. He was among the first ranchers to take advantage of cargo planes to get his meat to market, and sat on the board of directors of the largest airfreight company in the Beni.

About six thousand head of cattle are slaughtered at San Juan every year. Most of the twenty-four hundred tons of meat are sold to the tin mines in the Bolivian Andes. But a rising proportion is being exported to the Brazilian Amazon frontier.

Carlos is also one of the Beni's biggest importers of Brazilian humpbacked zebu cattle. While the old-timers shook their heads in amazement, he made six major importations of zebu to crossbreed with his criollo herd. Although the criollo has a good flavor, it takes five years to fatten for slaughter and produces less meat than the zebu. The crossbreeding resulted in a hardy strain that was bigger and ready for market within three years.

But importing the Brazilian stock called for a journey that almost paralleled the ordeal undertaken by the Jesuit missionaries when they introduced cattle into the Beni from southeastern Bolivia three centuries before. Carlos bought his prize zebu bulls and cows from a rancher in the Brazilian Atlantic coastal state of Paraná. In that first importation, about two hundred animals were loaded onto fifteen trucks in Paraná and driven westward more than eighteen hundred miles through the Brazilian scrub forests and Amazon territories—a two-week trek.

"Not once did we allow the cattle off the trucks in all that time," said Carlos. "We rarely stopped even at night because we had two drivers for each truck. The cattle were watered and fed on the backs of the trucks. The idea was to keep the vehicles moving twenty-four hours a day so the cattle could arrive as soon as possible. The road was often hideous, like a swamp when it rained, or else like a dust storm. We lost cattle all along the route. But the worst part occurred toward the end, when we reached the Brazilian-Bolivian border. We let the cattle get out of the trucks and graze along the river before they were put on boats for the final stretch to San Juan. Many of them died from eating poisonous weeds. They just dropped like flies. We lost sixty animals there. It was heartbreaking."

Schenstrom once tried another route. He put his Brazilian cattle on a train from Paraná to Santa Cruz, the eastern Bolivian city. But there were no facilities at Santa Cruz to handle livestock. When the train arrived there and the wagon doors were opened, the three hundred head of cattle stampeded out of the central station and into the steets. A few of them were never found again. From there the cattle were loaded onto trucks and driven along the asphalted highway westward to Cochabamba, then by dirt road north to Puerto Villar-

roel, and finally by barge farther northward along the Mamoré River to San Juan. The trip took almost as long as the other way, and thirty to forty cattle were lost.

Most of the Schenstrom cattle have been crossbred into mestizos. But the quality of the livestock alone does not ensure the prosperity of San Juan.

The rising cost of fuel has sharply cut into the profits of air-freighting operations in the Beni. Building on this shaky flying wedge, Schenstrom and other ranchers have more recently increased their share of the meat market by modernizing their transportation facilities with refrigerated containers. During the rainy season, the containers are hauled onto river barges. In the dry months, they are hitched to trucks that make a tortuous five-day journey southeast to Santa Cruz along the 320-mile jagged, pocked dirt road. From Santa Cruz, the trucks double back westward along the asphalted highway to La Paz. When the road out of the Beni is too rutted and the rivers too low for barges, the ranchers undertake an old-fashioned, cowboy-led cattle drive to Santa Cruz.

"Someday a highway will be built to La Paz, and maybe another paved one to Santa Cruz, and on to Argentina and Brazil," said Carlos, unconsciously echoing Belaúnde's dream of a transcontinental road network that would link the inner frontier lands of South America. "Then the Beni will be another Texas. That day has to come. We could double, triple, quadruple our herds if we could only reach the markets by road all year around. This place doesn't need much investment. The cattle are all here, and they'll never be able to eat their way through all this grassland."

Besides the transportation dilemma, cattle raising in the Beni faces other serious problems. The price of meat is set once or twice a year by the government, sometimes at levels below production costs. This year, Carlos explained, the livestock industry was in real crisis. The rains had caused the worst inundations in three decades, drowning huge numbers of cattle and making it even more difficult to deliver meat to the distant markets. Inflation was galloping and the Bolivian peso had sunk by one half against the dollar in less than a month. But the government was holding fast to its price controls, and beef was now selling for an incredible twenty cents a pound—surely the lowest price in the world.

"The sad truth is that there is no stimulus for a rancher to improve the quality of the meat he produces," said Carlos. "A filet mignon from a tender calf sells for the same price as a tough steak from a ten-year-old cow."

Adding to the ranchers' problems is the fact that Bolivian politics are extremely unstable. By mid-1982, there had been 190 coups in the country's 157 years as an independent state. The turnover has been even more rapid in recent years, and each new president brings in a new economic team with new policies. As a result, Carlos, who keeps an office in La Paz, must visit the capital often to meet with agrarian and bank officials and figure out how best to adapt to new measures and credit lines.

He is constantly trying to devise ways of making inflation work in his favor. That means making investments in his ranch with government loans pegged at interest rates well below inflation. He has tapped cheap government credits to help finance the purchase of refrigerated containers to move his meat by boat and trucks. And he has recently diversified into corn and rice because he feels prices and storage facilities for these products are better than those for meat.

Night had fallen over San Juan by the time Carlos finished explaining to me the rudiments of cattle ranching in the Beni. He suggested that we continue the conversation the following morning, when he would guide me around his vast estate.

The next day, I woke up before six A.M. A half hour later, after a steak-and-egg breakfast, Carlos gave out the day's instructions to the ranch hands assembled on the front porch. He invited me to join him in a pickup truck.

Gray-feathered rheas strutted in large packs along the red dirt roads. They broke into frantic dashes as our vehicle approached, finally skipping off the road into the fields as we overtook them. The ranch hands never hunted the rheas, although they occasionally feasted on their large eggs, cooked in huge omelettes with onions and peppers.

We passed the squat, whitewashed homes of the few ranch hands who lived away from the main compound. In their yards, blankets of sun-dried beef, called *charqui,* hung on scaffoldings set high enough to discourage dogs but within easy reach of thousands of flies. Because there is no refrigeration, *charqui* is the staple of the ranch hands, who eat it fried or in a stew. To vary their diet, the workers hunt duck, deer and wild pig, or fish in the waters of the nearby Mamoré River and its side streams.

Corrals had been placed strategically around the large ranch near each of the grazing fields. Carlos recalled that in his father's time, it took up to a week to gather three thousand head of cattle for branding, castration and vaccination. But thanks to the wire fencing that concentrated the herds, the same tasks could be accomplished in a day or two.

Most of the corrals had their own crude slaughterhouses, open-sided structures with high wood roofs. I was not particularly anxious to witness the butchering. But a foreman explained to me that a steer was yanked above the ground by a pulley, its throat was slit and, after bleeding to death, it was hacked and sawed into large portions. Ranch hands lined up to receive gratis the heads of the slaughtered animals stuffed with intestines and other offals which were not marketed. The rest of the carcasses were placed in containers and hoisted on trucks and boats, or else loaded on cargo planes at Schenstrom's airfield. The aircraft brought in canned foods, flour, household goods, clothing, medicines and farm equipment and parts. But almost all essential foods, including rice, manioc, fruits and vegetables were grown at the ranch.

"Every two weeks or so, I try to complete a full round of the ranch, by pickup truck, horseback and plane," said Carlos. "But it's impossible to keep a tight schedule, because there are always specific problems that come up day to day. Fences that have to be repaired. Fields that have to be burned. Animals that get sick. Workers who have personal problems that have to be discussed. Then, I'll often have to fly to La Paz or Santa Cruz to talk with bankers and government officials and clients."

We drove over to the ranch's machinery depot at the far end of the airfield. There were a dozen huge plows and seeders and six tractors in the metal-roofed shed. The machinery was spotless, well-greased, with hardly any scratches. One of the tractors was almost fifty years old, but in perfect working condition.

"All the equipment and parts were originally brought over from the United States," said Carlos. "We don't have time to wait for new parts to arrive. Mostly, we make our own. So the workers in this depot must be real artisans besides being good mechanics."

Behind the machinery depot, next to the dirt runway, lay the skeleton of a wrecked DC-6, a four-engine meat cargo plane that had crashed eight years before while landing in a storm. The aircraft had been thoroughly cannibalized by the Schenstrom mechanics, who melted and reforged its propellers, pistons, valves, pumps and metal siding into replacement parts for farm machinery. "That plane has proved to be a real gold mine," said Carlos. "It has probably paid for itself ten times over."

Schenstrom had recently begun a large rice plantation at the ranch. Next to the machine depot, he had built a rice-husking plant and nearby a silo for grain. He had heard of a way to bake bricks by mixing the rice husks with the red savanna earth, and he was trying to figure out the most economical method of building a kiln. "We could save a lot of time and money if we could make our own bricks here," he said. "We might even be able to sell the surplus to other ranchers."

There seemed to be no waste in the ranch. Just as in the surrounding savanna and rain forest, everything here was being recycled.

The rice fields had become Schenstrom's main preoccupation. They were the first large-scale commercial attempt to grow the grain in the Beni. And Carlos was eager to show them off.

On the way, he explained how he had gone about the rice cultivation. The planting was done in only three harried days in December to give the seeds just enough time to sprout roots that would hold them in place during the torrential rains. Tractors ploughed up the fields sixteen hours a day, followed by mechanized seeders and then small planes swooping low with fertilizers. The first time, an American variety of rice was planted. But it quickly developed a fungal disease and was abandoned for a more resistant Colombian strain. Sometimes, the heavy rains came too quickly, washing away the seeds and forcing Schenstrom and his workers to repeat the laborious three-day planting effort. And once, a flock of wild black-and-white ducks, so dense that it looked like a dark cloud on the horizon, had ravaged almost an entire fledgling rice crop.

This was Schenstrom's third rice crop, and easily the most successful. The fields were a far deeper green than the surrounding savanna and extended for four miles and were two miles wide. They were bounded by wire fences to keep cattle away. But a dozen rheas were able to wade through the waist-high rice stalks until a pack of dogs sent them scurrying into the nearby rain forest.

Throughout our drive, I was impressed by the variety and quantity of birds. I had often traveled through the tropics and was almost always disappointed by the difficulty in spotting wildlife. But the heavy inundations of the rainy season in the Beni had concentrated the fauna on the islands of higher, dry ground where they sought

refuge. As we bounced along the dirt roads, I was stunned by the numbers of gray ostriches, blue-and-red macaws, yellow-breasted woodpeckers, heavy-beaked toucans, snow-white storks, egrets and herons, black-faced ibis with sickle-shaped beaks and dozens of other species I could not even begin to identify.

Schenstrom's chief foreman, Guido Montalbán, pointed out a large flock of wild ducks perched in a clump of trees a couple of hundred yards away. He scurried after them with an ancient .22 caliber rifle. We heard the weak pop of the gun and then saw Guido running back smiling, with a duck clutched in his left hand. The duck was large and black, with white patches on its wings and a red, warty face like a turkey.

When we returned to the ranch house late in the afternoon, Carlos suggested I might want to go fishing before dinner. He often went himself, he said, but he was a bit tired that day and asked Guido to accompany me instead.

It was pitch-black when we set out on the fishing trip shortly after eight P.M. Riding in the pickup truck along a narrow road that was slippery from earlier rains were four of us: Guido; myself; Juan Kuljis, a chunky, ebullient, young rancher of Yugoslav descent who managed a large Schenstrom corn farm in Santa Cruz; and Delfín, a stubby, taciturn ranch hand with a mustache that partially concealed his harelip.

We had to slow down several times to avoid running over herds of capybara, the largest of rodents. Surely one of evolution's most comical creations, the capybara has a dark brown, pig-shaped body with the head of an earless rabbit, and huge buck teeth that beamed back at our headlights in an imbecilic grin. Capybaras roam in packs of up to twenty, and did not panic when we approached. At the last possible moment, when our truck was virtually upon them, they shuffled unhurriedly to the edge of a roadside stream and plopped into the water, letting their nostrils surface between the thick reeds. Capybara meat is so foul tasting, and their hides so tough to cure, that it is little wonder the animals show no fear of humans.

The drive lasted almost an hour before we pulled up beside what seemed to be a straight water canal or stream. Guido said it was actually a road that had been inundated by the heavy rains. He preferred fishing here because it was easier to navigate along its straight course at night, and most of it was shallow enough to spot fish lurking at the bottom.

The four of us clambered into a long dugout canoe. Delfín took the stern, Juan and I rowed in the middle and Guido stood at the bow, poised with an air-powered harpoon gun and a blinding spotlight wired to a car battery. Tall, dark-complexioned and sinewy, Guido had stamina and balance that belied his middle age. His spotlight attracted hordes of mosquitoes that looked like minnows darting about an illuminated fishbowl. The dark silence was punctured by the loud croaking of frogs, the chirping of crickets and the splash of a lost calf scampering out of our wake.

At times, the water was so shallow that we had to jump out and push the canoe along. All of us except for Juan, who with fraternity-house humor pretended to be the coxswain and loudly cheered our efforts. Other times, when we neared the Mamoré River, swollen by the rains, our waterway was so deep that the trees to our sides were flooded to their branches. It was difficult to believe we were paddling along what was a dirt road in the dry season.

Guido's spotlight reflected a pair of eyes burning like red coals. They belonged to an eight-foot-long alligator that slithered into the water a few feet ahead of us. We saw a dim light in the far distance. Guido whispered that it was a boat of *lagarteros*—alligator hunters—and cursed them softly. It is illegal to hunt alligators, which have been declared an endangered species. But their skins still bring high prices. The *lagarteros* look for the red eyes of their prey and maneuver their canoes until they are almost on top of the beast, holding it mesmerized with their strong spotlights. Then with a .44 caliber revolver they blast it between the eyes.

Almost an hour had gone by when Guido motioned for us not to move. The boat glided silently, and Guido, as still as a statue, fired the harpoon. He had speared a large stingray. The fish writhed and flapped its sides wildly as Guido pulled it to the surface. Out of the water, it made a desperate sucking sound, almost like a muffled shriek, from the large fleshy mouth on its underside. Its barbed tail slashed about menacingly until Guido, with a deft swing of his machete, chopped it off.

Flat and almost round, the fish was about two feet in diameter, gray with red spots. In the Beni, the stingray is feared more than any other fish, including the piranha. It buries itself in the bottom of shallow streams and rivers and stings unsuspecting waders who accidentally step on its back. Though not fatal, its poisonous, lacerating tail can inflict horrible pain for several days. But the stingray is also prized—because of its liver, from which an oil is extracted. The local inhabitants swear by it as a remedy for any respiratory illness, from common colds to bronchitis and pneumonia.

Guido quickly sliced open the stingray's soft underbelly and ripped out its pink liver, as large as a human liver. He placed it at the bottom of the canoe and then heaved the mutilated fish overboard. It flapped weakly in the water. Then, suddenly, black shadows converged, and the water churned to a red foam as piranhas ripped the fish to shreds. In fewer than thirty seconds, there was nothing left of it.

We continued our course, paddling down the flooded road. Occasionally, Guido would signal us to stop. He would aim and fire his harpoon, never missing. The canoe filled with large catfish, called *surubí*, each between a foot and two feet long. They thrashed hopelessly against the barbed spear, until Guido reeled them alongside and battered them over the head with a wooden club, taking care not to be stung by their long, white, brittle whiskers or razor-sharp fins.

With enough fish to last us a week, we decided to head back. We stuck mainly to the inundated road, but occasionally explored a side stream. Sometimes we scraped against bushes, and tiny red ants clung to our clothes and stung us mercilessly. A few more alligators impassively stared at us with their bright red, unblinking eyes.

Suddenly, Guido stiffened, and I could sense his excitement. The spear gun fired, and in an instant, a giant catfish, bigger than any I had ever seen, struggled furiously, leaping out of the water and pulling the canoe on a crazy zigzag course. The fish jerked so violently that Guido dropped the spotlight and held on to the harpoon's cord with both hands. I quickly retrieved the light before it fizzled out. Guido screamed at us to hammer the huge *surubí* with the wooden club. I struck it twice to no effect. Then the fish plunged beneath the boat, heaving it to one side and capsizing us.

Our entire catch dropped overboard. Delfín managed to stay on his feet, but Juan and I landed on the muddy bottom on our haunches. The water was no more than three feet deep, but I was in a panic thinking about the black, unseen piranhas and stingrays. After another minute of struggle, Guido finally subdued the *surubí* and killed it with several machete chops to the head. Juan, Delfín and I turned the canoe upright again, retrieved our gear and most of the catch and clambered aboard.

We burst out laughing over our tumble. Juan's pointy Texas

leather boots, his pride and joy, were hopelessly waterlogged. But our giggling stopped as we got a close look at the fierce catfish. It was almost four feet long, and when weighed later, it proved to be almost sixty pounds.

As we paddled back to our pickup truck, Guido slit open the huge fish and cleaned out its entrails. I remarked that we had been lucky there were no piranhas around. "No, no, they were there," asserted Guido. "They were just frightened by the confusion." Then, to prove his point, he tossed the bloody fish guts overboard, and the waters swirled again as the piranhas devoured the bait.

We arrived back at our starting point and quickly jumped out of the canoe and into the pickup truck. I had become more conscious of the discomfort from the mosquitoes. My hands were swollen from their bites, and I was furiously scratching my back where the little red ants had moved just out of reach. Guido, Juan and I rode up front, while Delfín, a skilled hunter, remained in the back, armed with an old shotgun and spotlight.

Delfín ignored the packs of capybara along the road. But after a few miles, he banged his hand above our truck cabin, signaling us to stop. The rifle exploded, and Delfín grunted that he had wounded a deer. He bounded after it across a small stream and into the bush as Guido aimed the spotlight. After a few minutes of following a trail of blood, Delfín found the deer and dragged it back to our vehicle.

I pitied the poor animal. It was small by North American standards, no larger than a fawn, with tiny antlers like bumps on its head. The shotgun pellets had hit it under the shoulder, but it was still alive. I had a large knife in my hand, and Delfín told me to finish the deer off. But I couldn't, and turned the blade over to him. With a quick, brutal stroke, he ripped open the throat, practically decapitating the animal. The deer gasped desperately and its entire body convulsed. Blood gurgled up from the huge wound, and the animal finally collapsed in a heap.

I was a bit depressed and silent during the rest of the drive. Guido, perhaps trying to cheer me up, remarked it would have been far worse for the deer if it had scampered away wounded and slowly bled to death. The fish and deer, he said, would be a welcome change from the steady diet of dried beef. But I knew I would never be a hunter.

It was close to midnight when we arrived back at the Schenstrom ranch house. We had kept everyone waiting late for dinner, but they seemed delighted to hear about our escapades, and roared with laughter as Juan detailed the capsizing of the canoe. The meal began with catfish, marinated in a spicy sauce with onions and corn on the cob. We then had huge slabs of beef, with rice and salad, all washed down with Chilean wine.

Over coffee and cognac in the living room, we talked about piranhas. Teddy Avila remarked that despite their ferocious reputation he had never actually seen piranhas kill a human being.

"Oh, I've seen plently of people who were bitten, sometimes badly," he said. "But they always got out of the water in time, or managed to scare away the fish. I remember once years ago, a German moviemaker showed up around here to do a film on the piranhas. He wanted to record the scene of a steer being eaten alive by the fish as it crossed a stream. So we went to the slaughterhouse for the head of a steer. Then I climbed out on the branch of a tree overhanging the river and held the head by the horns in the water, and slowly pulled it up as the German was filming. I suppose that the people who saw the movie back in Germany were convinced that the piranhas had eaten away the rest of the steer."

The following day was dreary and wet. A hot north wind was blowing from the Amazon. The sky swelled yellow, gray and black until it burst over the ranch house in an explosion of thunder, lightning and water. Grape-sized drops splattered first in a slow staccato, and then like the steady flow from a giant, overturned cistern. The torrential, slanting downpour pummeled the thick savanna grass. The ponies in the Schenstrom's backyard bent their heads forward, like sailors leaning into a gale, and strained to reach the skimpy shelter of palm trees.

The Schenstroms had to postpone a flight back to La Paz to visit their two daughters, who were vacationing there. Carlos horsed around with his four-year-old son in the living room, flipping him in the air and catching him just above the floor. Under a large Viennese crystal chandelier, an old family heirloom, I lingered at the breakfast table listening to Juan Kuljis defend male supremacy and female servility on the frontier.

"Of course, a woman has a right to feel protected," he was saying, as Irene Schenstrom smiled sardonically. "But in the evening, when her husband comes home from a hard, long day of work, I really think that a wife should always be conscious of how important the right phrase, the smallest gentle gesture, is for her husband. The last thing he wants to hear is a complaint or a problem."

Chiding him, Irene muttered something to the effect that it sounded like a sure prescription for divorce.

"On the contrary," rebounded Juan. "That's why you see fewer divorces in the countryside than in the city. I feel sorry for all those divorced women in La Paz. If they had only realized that with a small effort every day to be more understanding to their husbands, they would still have them. Instead, they end up unwanted except as somebody's mistress. And they finish their lives alone in their old age."

Sensing the implacability of Juan's arguments, I tried to shift the conversation and asked Irene about her daughters. She said they were being taught by a private tutor, a Chilean woman who spent eight or nine months of the year at the ranch.

"The school near here would not be very good for them," she explained. "It isn't only the quality of the education. But also, frankly, the girls around here tend to think only about getting married from the age of fourteen on. I don't want that for my daughters. I want them to look around a bit, to get a sense of their worth before getting married and settling down."

I glanced at Juan, and thought I detected a dubious look that indicated he would go about his own daughters' upbringing differently.

The rain let up just enough for me to dash across the ranch's main compound for lunch with Fernando Muñoz, a bearish, red-faced man who would soon replace Teddy Avila when he retired as manager of the Schenstrom estate. Fernando was in his mid-thirties and had been a classmate of Carlos's in agronomy school. He and his wife, Ana, and their two children live in an old mud-brick house that the Schenstroms occupied before they moved into their mansion. Ana, a handsome, broad-shouldered woman with short, dark hair, was a native of the Beni, where her parents owned a ranch. She was breeding chickens in a coop behind the house, and had prepared one of them for lunch.

I remarked that she was probably fortunate to have been raised on a ranch, instead of moving from La Paz and having to adapt to country life.

"Actually, I grew up in Trinidad and visited my parents' ranch mostly on weekends," she said. "Trinidad may seem small. But it was a real city for me. At first, I found living on this ranch a bit hard to get used to, being away from friends and neighbors."

The pests and some of the more exotic wildlife around the ranch sometimes drove her to distraction. I could certainly empathize with her horror over tarantulas, which were mainly a red, furry variety here. Whenever she found one crawling around the house, she would place a bucket over it and wait for Fernando to appear on the scene for the kill. During the rainy season, her chicken coop was occasionally terrorized by anacondas, twenty-foot-long snakes that could snap up a hen and swallow it in a gulp.

But over the years, ranch life has become more comfortable. The diesel-powered generators have been expanded, and now provide electricity for all but a few hours a day. Fernando has an airplane for his own use, enabling Ana to visit her family and friends in Trinidad frequently. The videotape recorder had recently become available throughout the province, and Fernando has bought one. At night, he sets up a large screen in his living room and invites over ranch hands to view Spanish-dubbed John Wayne westerns.

Here again, like the introduction of air transportation before highways, was an example of the Beni skipping a stage in its technological evolution. No broadcasting stations could reach the province. But people who had never seen a television program in their lives were now watching video-cassettes, bootlegged in from the United States and Panama.

A similar technological breakthrough is occurring with small, portable, wireless telephones—mostly Sonys and Panasonics. There are painfully few telephone outlets installed in the Beni. But these hand-held, wireless phones, beaming in on a central switchboard a few hundred yards away, can reach the outside world. A rancher riding horseback can actually field and place calls to La Paz—and if he is patient enough, to Buenos Aires and Miami.

Fernando, who had taken a postgraduate degree in veterinary science at Texas A&M, was brimming with ideas about expanding cattle production at San Juan. He was overseeing the results of an experimental feed for calves. Normally, the cows in the Beni are fertile only once every two years because they are not receptive to impregnation while they are weaning their calves. Fernando and Carlos had concocted a liquid concentrate of soy and corn for two-month-old calves as a substitute for milk until they were able to graze on the natural pasturelands. The experiment was working: the cows were now being impregnated every year, and births had doubled.

But the slump in meat prices was frustrating Fernando. "As things now stand, we actually lose money on every kilo of meat we sell," he said. "It's irritating to see old-fashioned cattlemen doing nothing to improve their herds, investing little in production and yet being no worse off for it."

Fernando had agreed to manage the Schenstrom property until he saved enough money to take over and improve his father-in-law's ranch. But the inflation and devaluations had evidently cut deeply into his savings.

Remembering the boom-and-bust history of the Beni, I asked him if he thought the province could suffer a lengthy economic eclipse again. He shook his head vigorously.

"Some setbacks are possible," he said. "But look at this whole frontier zone. People are on the move. Brazil is expanding and is offering us markets. This country needs a strong agriculture. It can't afford to import food. And don't forget, growth in the Beni has happened without government money. You might say even in spite of government obstruction. As a rancher, I wouldn't consider living anyplace else."

The morning of the next day, the rains relented for a couple of hours, and I joined the hurried exodus to Trinidad. Carlos, Irene and their son were flying from there to La Paz, and bid me a warm good-bye. Juan Kuljis caught a plane to Santa Cruz. But I decided to linger in Trinidad to find out what I could about Roberto Suárez and the cocaine trade, which seemed to be as much a part of the Beni as cattle ranching.

Trinidad was in near panic over the almost unprecedented rainfall. The Mamoré—a gentle, almost sluggish river in the dry season—had burst its bed and splayed out over the flat terrain, enveloping large chunks of savanna. Radio bulletins detailed the inundations of nearby communities like fortresses falling before an advancing army. The waters had burst through the streets of Santa Ana and Santa Rosa to the north and west of the capital, and had reached the outskirts of Trinidad itself. The dirt roads stretching out from the city like the spokes of a wheel were built about six feet above the plains. This was high enough to cope with normal flood levels and also to create a primitive system of dikes. But the present downpours had been so severe that trenches were being cut across the roads in an effort to level out the waters around Trinidad. If that tactic failed, the center of the city would be flooded in a matter of days.

I joined in a saint's day procession that had the air of a pagan ritual to appease the gods of rain. It began at the cathedral after a mass by the bishop and wound its way, gathering thousands of the faithful, to the gates of a Catholic hospital. The wooden, eight-foot-tall saint, his outstretched arms draped with strings of biscuits, was hoisted above the crowd. Bare-chested *macheteros*—field hands wielding long, broad-bladed machetes—danced in a rocking, swaying motion in front of the effigy, which was followed by a horn-and-tuba military band playing a slow, lugubrious tune. At the end of the march, the faithful leaped up at the wooden saint to snatch at the rain-soaked biscuits. A thunderburst sent everyone scurrying back home, the musicians running with their shirts wrapped over their instruments.

Back at my hotel, I joined the owner for tea. His name was José Lorgio Sanbrano, and he had once been mayor of Trinidad. He was enormously overweight and preferred to hold court from his large leather easy chair off the hotel's inner patio. Swinging a flyswatter languidly in one hand, he needed only a fez on his head to render a credible impersonation of Sidney Greenstreet as the bazaar merchant in *Casablanca*. I told him I had spent a few days at the Schenstrom ranch and that I was greatly impressed by the operation.

"Schenstrom is a very special young man," said Lorgio. "If all the ranchers around here ran their properties the same way, the Beni would be the cattle center of South America. But unfortunately they don't, and the Beni is instead the narcotics center of this continent. Almost all the cocaine that leaves Bolivia passes through this province from those hundreds of little ranch airstrips. The police and military look the other way, to put it charitably. Every day I see bankers and businessmen flying into Trinidad from La Paz. They're not here to buy cattle or to take in the sights. They come here with suitcases full of pesos to exchange for dollars, cocadollars from the traffickers. They can buy dollars for ten percent less then they cost in La Paz because we have such a surplus of dollars here from the cocaine trade. Drugs and money exchange—those are the real industries of the Beni. The cattle are becoming purely decorative. There are twenty or thirty cocaine smugglers here who are richer than

Schenstrom or any legitimate rancher. And Roberto Suárez is the richest of them all. He could buy out a hundred Schenstroms."

Suárez rarely surfaced in public anymore. But a rancher staying at the hotel gave me the name of a cousin of Suárez's, and told me I was certain to find him at the Café Beni, a saloon off the central plaza frequented by the province's cattlemen.

There were several Jeeps parked outside the Café Beni and a few horses tied to wooden posts. Inside, there was a long bar against a wall with a mirror behind stacked liquor bottles. The ceiling was fifteen feet high with a long-bladed fan cutting slowly through the smoky air. Ranchers in Texas-style boots crowded around the dozen tables swapping horror stories about the weather. Many of them were absentee landlords who had flown in from La Paz and Santa Cruz to get a firsthand look at the damages the rains had wrought on their properties. A huge walrus of a man bellowed in anger at his losses between puffs on his long, thick cigar. Sitting next to him, a ferretlike rancher moaned that his new twin-engine plane had floated out of its hangar during the flooding and wrapped itself around a tree. One man held court at a center table, offering to rent out pontoons to ferry cattle and equipment.

I asked a hawk-nosed bartender if Suárez's cousin was there. He pointed him out at the table next to the open window. I introduced myself, and decided that the best way to broach the subject of his notorious relative was to ask first about Nicolás Suárez, the old rubber baron. He said that as a child he had visited Don Nicolás several times at his mansion near the Brazilian border and had played in his orchard. After a few rounds of cheap, harsh brandy, I asked about Roberto Suárez. He agreed to talk about him, but with evident reluctance.

He described Roberto Suárez as a tall, ruggedly handsome man about fifty years of age, with a full head of unruly black hair, who was once well liked throughout the Beni for his jovial and generous ways. But that was before his involvement in the cocaine trade became well known. Now, Suárez was a feared figure on the frontier. As his wealth and notoriety had increased, he had become a total recluse. The few former friends who occasionally caught a glimpse of him described him as thin, almost emaciated, moody, a heavy smoker of marihuana and cocaine base—the foul-smelling and highly addictive substance from which the cocaine itself is refined.

"I last saw him about a year ago," said the cousin. "He flew into my ranch unannounced and walked up to the house with two bodyguards—foreigners, speaking German, I think. I hardly recognized him he was so skinny. And he didn't make much sense. He said he felt badly that he owed me money for such a long time. And then he opened this big piece of luggage. It was filled with fifty- and hundred-dollar bills, and he said there was fifty thousand dollars altogether. I looked at him like he was crazy, and I said, 'Roberto, this has to be a mistake. I never lent you any money.' And it was the truth. He just looked at me kind of strangely, closed the luggage and walked back to the plane."

I left Suárez's cousin with the other ranchers in the Café Beni when it became obvious he wasn't going to offer me any more information. The rain had stopped, and I walked through the plaza to clear my head of smoke and alcohol. The small park was fragrant with jasmine and the smell of perfume from women strolling with their husbands and boyfriends.

When I returned to my hotel, I discovered two other Americans had checked in earlier in the day. I found them in the bar. They were agents of the United States Drug Enforcement Administration, and they also were interested in Roberto Suárez. One of them, Doug, was tall, beefy and prematurely white-haired for his forty-four years. Steve, the other agent, was a darker, mustachioed Mexican-American of medium height, maybe ten years younger. They were based in La Paz, attached to the American Embassy, but traveled throughout Bolivia monitoring the cocaine trade and gathering as much information as they could on the biggest drug traffickers. They made no effort to hide their identities, explaining that they wanted to encourage local people to seek them out. About their only concession to security were the guns that bulged in their leather handbags. Theirs was tedious labor, seeking out the few reliable and honest elements in the provincial police forces. They talked again and again with ranchers, lawyers, doctors, businessmen, trying to separate fact from hearsay in an attempt to update their assessments of cocaine production and smuggling.

"You'd be surprised how many people come forth voluntarily with information," said Doug. "There are girl friends who are pissed off at their dealer-boyfriends. Dealers who want to squeal on rivals. Straights who are honestly outraged over the cocaine business. We don't take any legal testimony. We're not here to make any arrests. We just want to make ourselves available, without pressure, to anybody who wants to talk."

What they wanted most of all was information on Roberto

Suárez. According to the DEA men, cocaine and Suárez ran together like a single strand through the Beni and the rest of Bolivia. In a few short years, he had achieved a meteoric rise to wealth and power by imposing his control over the cocaine trade that led from Bolivia, across the Brazilian Amazon to Colombia and eventually to the United States. The DEA had come close to trapping Suárez in a spectacular undercover operation two years before. And therein lay a tale that unraveled a lot of the mystery surrounding Bolivian cocaine and Roberto Suárez.

14

Statistically, Bolivia is among the most economically backward nations in South America. Coca—the raw material of cocaine—has long been part of this culture of poverty. For hundreds of years, perhaps for millennia, the Indians of Bolivia and Peru have harvested the leaves of the coca plant, whose natural habitat is the Andean slopes. Their descendants chew wads of the leaves daily to stifle hunger, overcome the drudgery of heavy work loads and, supposedly, stimulate sexual prowess. In their unprocessed form, the leaves bear little chemical resemblance to cocaine, and are perfectly legal to harvest and distribute in Bolivia. So ingrained is the practice that factory workers, miners and rural laborers often have specified monthly rations of coca leaves written into their employment contracts. Bolivians would no sooner accept a prohibition on coca than Americans would stomach a ban on coffee.

Throughout most of this century, portions of the coca harvest have been processed into cocaine and smuggled into the United States. The conversion involves pouring kerosene over the dried leaves, stomping on them overnight until they become pasty, then using sulphuric and hydrochloric acids to turn the paste into a light-brown, malodorous powder base, and finally, through a combination of ether and other chemicals, producing the snow-white cocaine hydrochloride crystals. Once in the United States, the powder is cut down with borax and other substances to a purity of only twelve percent or less before sale on the streets.

Until a decade ago, cocaine remained a low-priority target for American drug enforcement officials, whose main efforts were directed at disrupting street sales and intercepting shipments as they reached American shores. But by the late 1970's, cocaine's popularity had grown so explosively that consumption was being estimated at twenty to thirty tons a year, with a street value of $25 billion and more.

The lion's share of these profits is being reaped by Colombian drug traffickers. Thanks to their relatively sophisticated chemical industry, Colombians have enjoyed a much better reputation than the Bolivians for converting cocaine base into a finished, high-quality powder. Their proximity to the United States, and their smuggling expertise through their use of ships or clandestine flights, also have established the Colombians as the middlemen of the cocaine trade. Today, less than a quarter of Bolivian cocaine is exported in finished crystal form. Virtually all the rest is sent as paste or base to the Colombian laboratories.

But Bolivian drug dealers still manage to earn about a billion dollars a year, more than the entire value of the country's legal exports of mineral ores and natural gas. Cocaine has far surpassed the revenues of the great tin-mining era in the first half of this century. And before that, during the sixteenth and seventeenth centuries, only the legendary silver mountains of the Andes produced as much treasure in Bolivia.

Those mineral riches were confined to the mountainous western portion of the country, where the bulk of the population has always lived. The cocaine boom has brought the neglected northern and eastern regions of Bolivia into the political and economic mainstream. Like oil, minerals, cattle and agriculture, cocaine has become one of the great sources of wealth in the frontier lands of South America. In recent years, all of Bolivia's endemic disadvantages—its landlocked borders, inaccessible interior, wretched rural poverty, political instability, ingrained governmental corruption and long-standing tradition of contraband—have quickly emerged as pillars of strength for the cocaine industry.

The geography of cocaine in Bolivia extends along a roughly diagonal axis running from the Beni in the north, through the Chapare in the center-east and on to the province of Santa Cruz still farther east.

The Chapare, the long-ignored tropical highland between the Beni and Santa Cruz, has proved a natural greenhouse for new coca plantations. The leaves that grow there are too bitterly acid to chew, but produce a high-quality cocaine base. The shortage of roads in the Chapare poses no real economic hardship and ensures privacy. Brigades of machete-wielding peasants have cut hundreds of miles of footpaths. An even larger army of campesinos carries fifty-pound loads of coca leaves along these trails to clandestine laboratories. In fact, the only asphalted highway in the Chapare is used by coca growers mainly to dry their leaves in the sun before they are compressed into bundles for the pack carriers. On an average day during the harvest season, a four-mile stretch of the highway—roughly the distance along Broadway from the edge of Harlem down to Times Square—is blanketed on one side with dehydrating coca leaves, while traffic is diverted to a single lane.

Most of the clandestine cocaine laboratories are now installed north of the Chapare in the Beni, which is even more isolated and inaccessible in its furthest reaches. It was the cattle boom that led indirectly to the Beni's importance in the mushrooming cocaine trade. Many of the small, secluded airfields built to handle the transport of meat out of the savanna have become staging points for the sophisticated network that ferries processed and semi-processed cocaine through Bolivia, across Brazil, and into Colombia, and then to Florida.

The business-and-banking capital of this cocaine trade is Santa Cruz, the principal city of eastern Bolivia. It is the gathering place of Colombian and American buyers, and the garrison for the Army and Air Force contingents who offer cocaine smugglers protection and secure contraband routes.

Like virtually all the Bolivian cocaine barons, Roberto Suárez is a man of these frontier lands. From his family, descendants of Nicolás Suárez who controlled the country's rubber trade at the turn of the century, he inherited some modest cattle ranches in the Beni, the Chapare and Santa Cruz. An accomplished small-plane pilot, Suárez developed a profound feeling for the geography of the Bolivian interior, something which gave him a sizable advantage over his competitors in cocaine smuggling—much the same way that his granduncle, Nicolás, had used his knowledge of the Beni's rivers and rain forests to cash in on the rubber trade one hundred years before.

By the early 1970's, Roberto Suárez was flying contraband goods into the country from Brazil and Argentina. He also had begun selling small quantities of cocaine base abroad, usually no more than twenty or forty pounds per shipment. When the boom came after

1977, Suárez was far better positioned than most of the other small smugglers. He had contacts in customs, the police and the armed forces. Rather than simply expand his own production of cocaine, he hit upon the notion of acting as a middleman between the many small Bolivian smugglers and the few big Colombian buyers. The idea appealed to corrupt military and police officials because it made the cocaine trade more manageable. And it drew converts among the smaller traffickers because the arrangement relieved them of the expense of bribing the security forces and transporting the cocaine abroad.

By the beginning of the 1980's, Roberto Suárez had become the cocaine king of the world. He controlled fully half of the cocaine smuggled out of Bolivia—about twenty-five tons a year—and was conservatively grossing $400 million annually. He was more powerful than the Bolivian president or any Bolivian general. He was de facto chairman of the board of Bolivia's largest economic enterprise. Not even the proverbial tin mines of the Andes produce as much revenue or employ as many people as the cocaine industry. His payroll and associates included generals, colonels, majors, captains, customs officials, cabinet ministers, industrialists, businessmen and thousands of peasants. He had an army of bodyguards—mostly Argentine, Swiss, Austrian and German neo-fascists—recruited and trained by Klaus Barbie, a former Nazi SS colonel who found refuge in Bolivia more than thirty years ago. They were spread over a dozen different locations in northern and eastern Bolivia because Suárez, out of a caution bordering on paranoia, rarely spent more than two days in any one place.

For several years, the US Drug Enforcement Administration had been aware of Suárez's role in the expanding narcotics traffic. The DEA reasoned that the best way to ensnare Suárez was to play on his growing resentment of the Colombian middlemen. By skimming off the profits in the cocaine trade, the Colombians were on a collision course with Suárez and the other Bolivians. In late 1979 and early 1980, Suárez in fact had a series of fallouts with his Colombian buyers. After receiving a large shipment of particularly bad quality cocaine base from Suárez, the Colombians castrated one of his couriers as a warning. A few weeks later, five Colombian buyers were gunned down in Santa Cruz by Suárez hitmen.

Suárez started to complain about the untrustworthiness of the

Colombians and sought a direct access to the American market. Getting wind of Suárez's discontent, DEA agents in Bolivia spread rumors that there were American underworld figures willing to bypass the Colombians and deal personally with Bolivian traffickers.

In April 1980, the DEA succeeded in making contact with a lieutenant in the Suárez organization. Mike Levine, an agent working out of the American Embassy in Argentina, met with Marcelo Ibañez in a Buenos Aires bar. Ibañez, a former rancher from Santa Cruz and a close associate of Suárez, had been told by a go-between that Levine was a Florida-based Mafia figure with an extensive cocaine distribution network in the United States. Levine, who came to the DEA with a professional acting background, was a tall man in his early forties with dark Mediterranean looks and seemed to fit the role of an American racketeer.

Levine commiserated with Ibañez, acknowledging that the Colombians were a wild bunch, violent and prone to rip-offs. He claimed to have a large organization working the entire East Coast from Miami to New York. Levine assured Ibañez that key American customs officials were on his payroll, making it easy to bring drugs into the country. And he said he had a fully equipped laboratory, employing bona fide chemists, to process the cocaine base into pure crystalline form.

Ibañez responded enthusiastically. Suárez, he confided, had been dealing with half a dozen Colombian syndicates, and now he wanted to simplify his operations by finding two main buyers—one of them Colombian and the other an American. The Bolivian suggested that the Suárez organization sell Levine about a thousand kilos (twenty-two hundred pounds) of cocaine base a month.

This was a far larger amount than the DEA had ever thought of handling. A single monthly shipment would have surpassed the total seizures made in Miami during all of the previous year. More to the point, the agency would have been unable to come up with the $18 to $20 million necessary to show Suárez that it could purchase that much cocaine. Levine countered Ibañez with an offer initially to buy five hundred kilos of cocaine base. If that deal went through smoothly, he said, he was ready to absorb a thousand kilos a month. In the meantime, Levine invited Ibañez, Suárez and his son, Roberto, Jr., up to Miami to inspect his organization and his laboratory, even spend some time at his home, where they could meet his family and associates.

With little haggling, Levine agreed to pay $18,000 a kilo, or $9 million for the five hundred kilos (eleven hundred pounds). Once refined and then sold on the streets, the shipment would have brought more than $200 million in 1980 prices. Levine told Ibañez that he and Suárez would be shown the $9 million on their visit to Miami, well before the delivery of the drugs.

Ibañez returned to Bolivia to consult further with Suárez. Levine flew back to Miami to mull over the mind-boggling quantities of cocaine he was being offered, and to set the scam in motion. Until the Buenos Aires meeting, the DEA had been uncertain just how much cocaine base was being smuggled out of Bolivia. As late as 1977, the agency had been divided on whether Peru or Bolivia was the larger producer. It now became evident that the Bolivians had spurted ahead, and that Suárez was the single biggest cocaine merchant in the world.

After being briefed by Levine on his return to Florida, the DEA decided to finance one of its most expensive undercover operations. A three-bedroom house was rented during May 1980 in Fort Lauderdale, just across from the beach. It was stocked with Johnny Walker Red and Tanqueray gin, and wired with salsa music which Suárez supposedly enjoyed. Two Lincoln Continentals were leased. Women agents were brought over to Miami to act as maids and escorts for the Bolivians. A warehouse in Miami was outfitted with funnels and cookers as a cocaine laboratory, and an agent was recruited as its chief chemist. Finally, $9 million in one-hundred-dollar bills was borrowed from the Federal Reserve and deposited in six giant safe-deposit boxes at a Miami suburban bank to impress upon the Bolivians that the Levine organization was prepared to pay cash on delivery of the cocaine.

Mike Levine installed himself in the beach house, along with a young, attractive, Spanish-speaking agent from the DEA's San Francisco office who posed as his wife. Richie Fiano, a short, chunky, bearded agent in his early thirties, was designated as Levine's chauffeur and chief lieutenant in the Florida area. After a number of phone calls to Bolivia, it was agreed that Ibañez, Suárez and his son would arrive in Miami on May 15, 1980.

"Myself, Mike and a couple of other agents, we go out to Miami airport early that morning to pick up the Bolivians on the flight from Santa Cruz," Fiano, an Italian-American from the Bronx, recounted to me when I met him in Miami much later. "But the only guy who shows up is Ibañez. He gives us some reason or another why Suárez couldn't make it. So we say no big deal, and we drive Ibañez back to the house."

"Now, we thought we had rented a pretty impressive place," said Fiano. "Hell, we're paying twenty-five hundred dollars a month. It's a great neighborhood. The house is big, has its own swimming pool, and it's right across from the ocean. But Ibañez looks at the place like it's good enough for hired help. And he tells us that back in his ranch in Bolivia our swimming pool could pass for a small duck pond."

The DEA agents didn't quite know what to make of Ibañez. A couple of inches under six feet tall, thin, clean-cut with wavy dark hair, in his late thirties, he could have easily passed for a successful young businessman. His mood oscillated sharply between supreme self-confidence and deep anxiety. "We were planning on a party with the girls, maybe a quick trip to Vegas, even a couple of Broadway shows," said Fiano. "But Ibañez didn't want any of it. Wouldn't even touch a drop of booze. He just wanted to leave as soon as possible."

Ibañez spent most of the day closeted in the beach house on the phone with Suárez, who was in Santa Cruz. He emerged only to take a brief drive along the waterfront with Levine, Fiano and Pepe, a Spanish-speaking agent. He didn't even ask to see the $9 million or the cocaine laboratory. He turned down a suggestion that the Suárez gang deliver the cocaine base in the Brazilian Amazon or Colombia, and insisted that the pickup be made in Bolivia with a plane supplied by Levine. Some of the agents suspected that the Suárez people might be setting a trap of their own.

"I argued that Ibañez was leveling with us," said Fiano. "In fact, I thought he had bought the whole story hook, line and sinker. He was just nervous. I thought maybe he had a personal stake in seeing this thing through. He was the guy who had set the whole deal up for Suárez, and maybe he was thinking that if it went through he would move up in the organization. Anyway, he did seem nervous. He was getting along best with Pepe, maybe because Pepe's Spanish was so good. So that night Pepe took him to dinner, calmed him down and assured him there would be no problems."

After dinner, a final meeting took place in the beach house to sort out the details of the flight to Bolivia. Three pilots, military veterans working for the DEA, came to the house and talked to Ibañez about the route to Bolivia, the terrain and the length of the clandestine airstrip where the landing would be made. Ibañez placed a last phone call to Roberto Suárez to inform him of the type of aviation fuel the plane would need for its return trip to Florida, and to receive precise instructions. He was told by Suárez that a Bolivian pilot would meet the plane when it made an intermediary stop in the Brazilian Amazon city of Manaus, and guide the flight into the Bolivian hideout. Suárez agreed that his emissaries in Miami would collect the $9 million once the plane had taken off from Bolivia with five hundred kilos of cocaine base.

Early the next day, May 16, just twenty-four hours after his arrival, Ibañez drove with the DEA agents to a small airfield near Fort Lauderdale to begin the trip to South America. The plane was a forty-year-old, twin-prop Convair. Ibañez was startled by its poor quality, and commented to Fiano that it was the kind of aircraft used in Bolivia to transport meat. "We were worried that such a low-class plane might cause us some credibility problems, but it really was the only aircraft we could afford," recalled Fiano. "Ibañez said to us he couldn't understand how we were willing to risk $9 million dollars in cocaine with this piece of shit."

Carrying Ibañez, Fiano and the three pilots, the Convair took off from Florida, refueled in Puerto Rico and laid over in Barbados. Ibañez made several phone calls to Suárez, and then, without any real explanation, told the DEA agents that it would take several more days before the cocaine would be ready for a pickup in Bolivia. The next four days were spent sunbathing and deep-sea fishing in Barbados. Finally, on May 20, the Convair took off again and landed that afternoon in Manaus. At a downtown hotel, in a sweltering room so small that only one person could stand up at a time, the Convair's passengers were joined by Renato Roca Suárez, the thirty-year-old nephew of Roberto Suárez. He was an experienced pilot and brought along aerial maps of the landing zone in Bolivia.

The destination was to be an isolated ranch in the savanna of the Beni. Roca Suárez marked off an airstrip on the edge of a large lake, called Rogaguado, as the site of the rendezvous with the cocaine shipment. The dirt runway, however, was shorter than the minimum requirement of the Convair. One of the DEA pilots pointed out that while the strip might be long enough to land upon, it would be difficult for the plane, fully loaded and refueled, to take off again.

"We argued it back and forth," said Fiano. "But in the end we figured what the hell, we're this far along, and we gotta go for it."

The next morning, the Convair set out for Bolivia. The pilots filed a flight plan with the Bolivian Air Force control tower in Santa Cruz. Then, following Roca Suárez's instructions, they informed Santa Cruz that they were turning back to Brazil because of technical problems. But instead, they flew at low altitude toward the secluded ranch in northern Bolivia. Roca Suárez told Fiano that they could probably remain an hour on the ground before Santa Cruz wondered why they had lost radio contact and sent out search planes for them.

"As we're landing," recalled Fiano, "all these Bolivian Indians come scurrying out of their hootches, running toward us, and I'm thinking what's to stop them from holding us hostage and ordering Miami to release the nine million dollars. The whole scam is being done without the knowledge of the Bolivian government. Hell, the Bolivian Air Force would be out looking for us because we lied about our destination. So who are we going to complain to if we end up getting ripped off?"

Fiano relaxed a bit when he saw the Indians carting large gasoline drums to refuel the Convair. Within minutes, a small, single-engine plane circled above and then landed. Ibañez went over to talk to the pilot, who was Roberto Suárez, Jr., and brought him over to meet Fiano and the other agents. Short, thin, dark-complexioned and in his mid-twenties, the son of Roberto Suárez spoke a perfect Texas dialect, which he had learned as an agronomy student some years before at Texas A&M University.

Roberto, Jr., explained there would be a short delay, no more than an hour, before the shipment of cocaine base arrived. Meanwhile, the Indians would form a bucket brigade to refuel the Convair.

"At this point, we're not only worried that the Bolivian Air Force is going to catch up with us," said Fiano. "We're also concerned that this is just one big hummer. Now, over in Miami, you can go out and hum all day for a guy who says he'll bring you a kilo of coke and never does, and it's no big thing. But for this operation, we had spent like thousands and thousands on the plane, the beach house, the cars, the agents. It was going to be one big embarrassment if these guys didn't come through."

In less than an hour, another small plane landed. It was carrying dozens of black plastic garbage bags filled with cocaine base in light brown powder form. Ibañez explained that the delay was due to the relatively poor quality of the initial shipment. This load, he said, was 854 pounds—less than the promised 500 kilos—but the quality was supposed to be excellent.

Then, handing Fiano a kilo of pure white cocaine, Ibañez said, "I want you take this present from Suárez to Mike to show him that our word is good, that we're friends, and we're sorry for any problems along the way. We want this arrangement to work out."

Roberto, Jr., who had been monitoring the radio, reported that the Bolivian Air Force had sent out planes to search for the Convair, and that a takeoff would have to be made quickly.

"Now Ibañez says to me that he's going back to Santa Cruz, and to please, please, as soon as we were in the air to call Miami and have the money released," recalled Fiano. "He let us know that he was way out on a limb, that he just hoped everything would work out okay. He pleaded with us not to rip him off. I guess it was at that point that I was really relieved. I smiled and I told him he didn't have a thing to worry about."

"Our only problem was taking off," continued Fiano. "The hydraulic system for the front wheel was ruptured on the landing. With the eight hundred fifty-four pounds of cocaine base and the fuel tanks loaded, we were carrying a lot more weight. We started down the runway, hitting all those potholes, and we just missed the lake at the end of the strip. Too little wind under the wings and we would have nose-dived right into the water."

Back in Miami, Mike Levine had already met with another Suárez henchman, Alfredo Gutierrez, and had shown him the money in the bank safe-deposit boxes that would be turned over as soon as the Convair flew out of Bolivia. Gutierrez, a dark, stout, middle-aged man, was a former president of the Santa Cruz Chamber of Commerce and owner of a fleet of small airplanes in Bolivia. He was accompanied in Florida by Roberto Gasser, son of one of the wealthiest Santa Cruz industrialists.

After hearing from both Ibañez in Santa Cruz and Fiano enroute from Bolivia that the cocaine base was being flown back to Florida, Levine picked up Gutierrez and Gasser at their Miami hotel and drove them over to the bank. John Lawler, another DEA agent posing as a bank security guard, welcomed them. As Gutierrez went into the vault and placed the key in a safe-deposit box, Levine and Lawler drew their guns and arrested the two Bolivians.

A few days later, after stopping in Barbados for repairs, the Convair hobbled into Miami with its cache of drugs. Fiano and his colleagues had completed an odyssey of seventy-five hundred miles—the equivalent of a round trip between New York and Paris—in a forty-year-old aircraft designed for hauling passengers and goods only a quarter of that distance.

The US Drug Enforcement Administration had pulled off what was until then the greatest sting operation in narcotics history. It had been a classic stroke of undercover work. But the seizure of the cocaine proved far easier than the legal and diplomatic morass involved in bringing any Suárez associates to trial. And in the long run, the impact on the Bolivian cocaine traffic was negligible. In fact, the sting operation against Suárez inadvertently helped to spark a coup in Bolivia that brought to power military officials whose chief concern was to protect the cocaine empire of Suárez and other large traffickers against this kind of outside disruption.

The arrest of Gutierrez and Gasser in Miami had brought a flood of official protests from Bolivia. Cabinet ministers, generals and industrialists had sent letters and documentation to Washington attesting to the character and honesty of the two men. Roberto Gasser had long been suspected by the DEA of laundering drug money for Suárez and other cocaine traffickers. But his lawyers successfully argued that he had innocently accompanied Gutierrez to the bank thinking that Gutierrez was going to pay him back money he owed him. In court, Gasser stuck by his story, and he was released after all charges against him were dropped.

Gutierrez was indicted on charges of conspiring to smuggle and distribute cocaine in the United States. His bail was set at a million dollars. In July 1980, Gutierrez's son presented two cashier's checks totalling $1 million to the clerk of the court. His father walked out of detention and fled to Bolivia.

Meanwhile, back in Bolivia, just a few weeks after the DEA's undercover operation against Suárez, a small group of Santa Cruz industrialists had met at a social club in their city with General Luís García Meza, commander in chief of the Bolivian Army. The businessmen, led by Erwin Gasser, father of the detained Roberto, were there to convince the general to carry out a military coup against the tottering civilian government in La Paz. A suitcase containing more than a million dollars was passed across the table to García Meza, according to participants at the meeting. The money included contributions from Roberto Suárez and other traffickers who were concerned that the civilian government was about to clamp down on the cocaine trade because of a wave of adverse publicity and strong pressure from the American government.

A few days before, the cocaine mafia had turned over large payments to other ranking military officers, along with promises of much more money in the months ahead.

On July 17, 1980, General García Meza carried out one of the more brutal military coups in Bolivian history. Thousands of people were arrested, and numerous cases of torture and killings were reported. Although the ostensible motivation for the coup was the fear that a left-wing civilian government would take power, it quickly became apparent that the cocaine bonanza played an even more important role. Paramilitary groups swept through government buildings in La Paz, burning all records of drug cases. The military officers most suspected of having close links with the cocaine traffic were given key government positions.

General García Meza emerged as president. Army Colonel Luís Arce Gómez, a cousin and close associate of Roberto Suárez, was appointed minister of interior, controlling the police and other security forces. The colonel already had a big stake in cocaine traffic through his joint ownership of a fleet of airplanes in the Santa Cruz area. A private airplane owned by his partner, Army Colonel Norberto Salomón, made a forced landing in the Beni in February 1980, and more than fifteen hundred pounds of cocaine base were found on board. Colonel Salomón was cleared and reassigned as Army attaché in Bolivia's embassy in Venezuela.

The United States reacted to the García Meza coup by withholding recognition of his government. The American Embassy staff in La Paz was scaled down, and the ambassador was recalled. Almost all American economic aid to Bolivia was rescinded. Then, when the military regime's strong links with the cocaine trade became obvious, President Jimmy Carter cut off the American anti-drug program in Bolivia.

With the election of President Ronald Reagan, the Bolivian government made an attempt to restore ties with Washington by carrying out a cosmetic crackdown on the drug trade. In February 1981, García Meza forced Arce Gómez to resign as minister of interior. In the following weeks, dozens of small cocaine smugglers were arrested and numerous small drug shipments were seized.

But only a few days after his resignation from the cabinet, Arce

Gómez, who still continued in active military service, called a gathering of the largest cocaine traffickers in the country to explain the government's true intentions. The meeting took place in the Santa Cruz mansion of one of the biggest smugglers. Arce Gómez warned that for diplomatic reasons the government felt constrained to launch a highly publicized roundup of drug smugglers. At the colonel's suggestion, the major cocaine figures transferred most of their drug operations away from the more visible Santa Cruz region to more secluded zones in the Chapare and the Beni. And to ensure continued government protection, Arce Gómez announced that more payments would have to be made to García Meza and other officers. As a first contribution, he collected half a million dollars from his audience.

The farcical campaign to stamp out the cocaine trade ended a few months later, failing to convince Washington. Not even the lucrative profits from drug smuggling could make up for the deepening crisis in Bolivia's legal economy and the failure of the government to attract international credits because of its lamentable image abroad. So in September 1981, another military commander, General Celso Torrelio Villa, became president.

In an effort to repair relations with Washington, General Torrelio made at least one telling gesture. Late in 1981, Alfredo Gutierrez, who had skipped bail after getting caught in the DEA's undercover operation against the Suárez gang, was brought back to Miami under Bolivian police escort. A few weeks later, Marcelo Ibañez, who had negotiated most of the 854-pound cocaine deal with the DEA, was also flown up to Florida. Both were convicted and sentenced to prison terms. Then, in 1982, Suárez's son, Roberto, Jr., was arrested in Switzerland for entering that country with a false passport and was extradited to Miami to stand trial for cocaine smuggling.

Neither the DEA nor State Department officials believed that General Torrelio himself was involved in the cocaine trade. But he was far too weak to clamp down on the traffic. In July 1982, he was briefly replaced by General Guido Vildoso, who in turn was succeeded a few months later by Hernán Siles Zuazo, Bolivia's first democratically elected president in more than a decade.

Siles Zuazo reaped considerable goodwill abroad by extraditing Klaus Barbie, the notorious Nazi fugitive who had supplied Suárez with his army of bodyguards, to France in 1983. As head of the Gestapo in the German-occupied city of Lyons between 1942 and 1944, Barbie was accused of murdering hundreds of French Resistance members and deporting thousands of French Jews to death camps.

But despite these setbacks, Roberto Suárez has held his wealth, organization and power intact. The US State Department still has a standing demand for his extradition from Bolivia. DEA agents have repeatedly pinpointed his hideouts. But they are having a good deal more trouble finding a military or police commander who will dare arrest him.

oug and Steve, the two DEA agents I had befriended, left Trinidad for Santa Cruz and gave me the name of a hotel where they could be reached there. I followed them a few days later.

I was still journeying along the northwest-to-southeast course traced by Belaúnde's projected highway across the South American frontier lands and was determined to reach its end. In a straight line, roughly paralleling Belaúnde's imaginary road, Santa Cruz lies 250 miles southeast of Trinidad. My commercial jet flight took only half an hour. Below me, the flooded savanna of the Beni was quickly cut off by the jungle highlands of the Chapare. Then the city of Santa Cruz rose amid lush agricultural fields carved symmetrically out of subtropical plains and forests. As the aircraft circled for a landing, a rainbow glowed through the fading rain in front of the purple Andean foothills about thirty miles to the west.

When Belaúnde first proposed his transcontinental road more than two decades ago, Santa Cruz was still a wild frontier town, struggling to overcome its economic isolation and loosen the stranglehold that La Paz—the Bolivian capital 330 miles to the west—exercised over its political affairs. Santa Cruz was founded in 1561 by Spanish conquistadores seeking El Dorado, or at least a route from the Atlantic to the Inca lands in Peru. The province—bearing the same name as the city—was always recognized as a breadbasket. But with the construction of a railroad from the Pacific to the rich Andean mines of western Bolivia at the turn of this century, La Paz decided it was cheaper to import foodstuffs from abroad rather than transport them overland by mule trains from Santa Cruz. Even as Santa Cruz sank into depression, the government in La Paz pre-

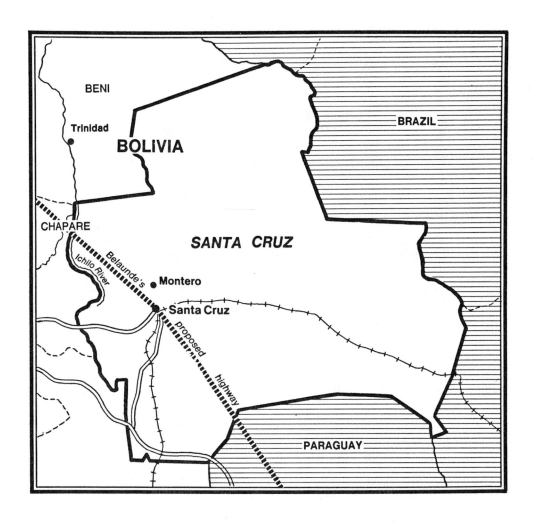

vented the building of road and rail links from eastern Bolivia to Brazil and Argentina out of fear that a secessionist movement might gather momentum in Santa Cruz. It was the discovery of sizable oil and gas reserves in the province during the 1950's that finally stimulated the construction of asphalted highways, railroads and pipelines connecting Santa Cruz to La Paz in the west, Argentina in the south and Brazil to the north and east. Since the 1960's, Santa Cruz has enjoyed a prosperity stoked by hydrocarbons and agriculture. The cocaine boom has multiplied the region's fortunes many times and has given further impetus to its growing dominance over the rest of the country.

The city has about three hundred thousand inhabitants, only a third the population of La Paz. But I now had the feeling that I was flying into the real vortex of power in Bolivia. Most of the recent military coups in the country have been hatched and financed in Santa Cruz. Politically ambitious officers seek to be garrisoned here. The more corrupt ones find the bribes from contraband easier and more lucrative than anywhere else. The roles of capital city and backward frontier have been reversed: Santa Cruz clearly overshadows La Paz, forging ahead with a buoyance and optimism that the old capital lacks.

Santa Cruz's new status underscores the different ways in which the frontier has been perceived in North and South America. Generations of North Americans have grown up with the firm conviction that the frontier, continually thrusting into new lands, was the most important element shaping their character and sense of nationalism. The experience of overcoming a virgin wilderness was what set them apart from the Old World.

In South America, the frontier has always been viewed far more ominously. The Spanish court, which ruled over most of the continent for three centuries, feared the growth of powerful settlements on the periphery of its New World empire. Even after independence from Spain in the nineteenth century, the South American governments inherited this same reflexive anxiety about the emergence of rival power centers in the frontier lands beyond the reach of the established capitals.

In his masterpiece, *Facundo*, the nineteenth-century Argentine statesman and writer Domingo Sarmiento articulated this anti-frontier ideology in South America. He warned his countrymen and the rest of the continent's inhabitants that their civilized capitals faced the permanent threat of barbarism from the frontier lands. In his own day, Sarmiento believed this danger was embodied by the Argentine dictator Juan Manuel Rosas, whose gaucho army from the pampa provinces took Buenos Aires by storm.

Buenos Aires, wrote Sarmiento, "is the only city in the vast Argentine territory which is in communication with European nations; she alone can avail herself of the advantages of foreign commerce; she alone has power and revenue. Vainly have the provinces asked to receive through her, civilization, industry, and European population; a senseless colonial policy made her deaf to these cries. But the provinces had their revenge when they sent to her in Rosas the climax of their own barbarism."

Substituting La Paz for Buenos Aires, Santa Cruz and the Beni for the Argentine pampa and Roberto Suárez for Rosas, one can construct a striking analogy between nineteenth-century Argentina and twentieth-century Bolivia. Perhaps Ché Guevara, the Argentine-Cuban revolutionary who grew up absorbing the myth of Rosas, had some of these parallels in mind when he set out to lead a guerrilla movement in eastern Bolivia. But Ché was not a *cruceño,* à native of Santa Cruz. Shortly before being captured and killed by the Bolivian Army not far from the city in 1967, he wrote despairingly in his diary that his exhortations for rebellion fell on deaf ears because the local peasants were "like stones."

It took a man of the backlands like Roberto Suárez, who could offer peasants, businessmen and soldiers the tangible, quick wealth of cocaine, to stir up Santa Cruz and its neighboring provinces. If Rosas were alive today, he would probably feel at home in eastern Bolivia as a drug racketeer with a private army. More than any other frontier region I visited, Santa Cruz—by weaving together a military-civilian cocaine alliance—seems to have borne out the long-standing South American nightmare of an uncontrollable, centrifugal force whirling out of the hinterlands.

Yet there is nothing sinister about the city's appearance or the personality of its inhabitants. Visiting Santa Cruz 150 years after the French naturalist D'Orbigny passed through, I would readily concur with his assessment that it was the most desirable of all Bolivian communities. He was seduced by the friendliness of the populace, the beauty and informality of the women, the fecundity of its fields. When he arrived bedraggled at the city's gates after a cold, foot-blistering descent from La Paz and a wet, fever-wracked trek

through the Beni and Chapare, he felt he had reached an oasis. And when he left Santa Cruz reluctantly to begin his journey back to France after a seven-year odyssey through the continent's hinterlands, he penned a warm homage to his favorite South American city:

> The more generous a place, the more difficult it is to abandon. Nowhere did I feel as much sadness in leaving as I felt parting from this hospitable city where I was received like a compatriot, as one of their own. Never will I forget Santa Cruz!

While I never journeyed there on foot, aching and hungry like D'Orbigny, I always had a feeling of ebullience arriving in Santa Cruz, and this time was no different. At the airport, there was the usual near pandemonium of whole families squealing, jumping, waving to welcome or send off friends and relatives. I squeezed through the crush in the lobby and sped away in a taxi. In the rain's wake, the plants and trees growing thickly along the route into Santa Cruz were washed and sheathed in moisture. The rich scents of dripping flowers and red mud mingled in the cool morning air.

Five years had passed since I last visited the city. Back then, before it had become a narcotics center, Santa Cruz was renowned for its rustic, Spanish colonial charm. Attracted by its warm climate, cheap land and low-cost farm labor, a few wealthy Americans living in Florida had purchased substantial ranches there as vacation spots. They could board Thursday- or Friday-night flights in Miami, arrive nonstop the next morning in Santa Cruz, spend the weekend ranching, fishing and hunting and be back in Florida on Monday morning after another direct overnight flight. But the narcotics trade has scared them away. Land is no longer cheap. It is difficult to find ranch hands because so many of them have been lured by higher salaries as pack carriers and processors in the cocaine trade. And the flight from Santa Cruz to Florida has become so notorious for drug smuggling that passengers risk being stripped down and detained for several hours by zealous customs agents at Miami's airport—an ignominious experience I once shared returning to the United States from a trip.

The cocaine boom has mightily transformed Santa Cruz. Its downtown district still has a nineteenth-century colonial style recalling Trinidad. Tall weeds sprout from the orange tile roofs of squat, one-story, white-stucco buildings that are old enough to have lodged D'Orbigny. But around the leafy plaza the hulking red-brick cathedral is now dwarfed by a few taller, modern buildings. The shops are stocked with the latest stereo and video equipment, most of it contraband financed by cocadollars. Santa Cruz probably now has more BMWs and Mercedes per capita than any other Latin American city. Some of the policemen patrol the streets in their own Datsun sports cars, marred only by sirens on their roofs. A black-and-gold Cadillac, with Miami limousine license plates still screwed to its trunk, blocks the entrance of a steak house. The owner, I was told later, had liked the car so much when he was chauffeured around Miami Beach that he bought it on the spot and had it smuggled into Santa Cruz without making an alteration.

The really jarring metamorphosis has taken place away from the city center. Along six concentric roads on the outskirts, the newly rich *cruceños* have given full vent to their fantasies. Mud roads have been paved and tropical woods mowed down to make room for sprawling, gaudy mansions, vaguely mimicking Palm Beach and Beverly Hills architecture. Here is a California ranch house with so many split levels that no two windows are on the same plane. There is a Georgian-style plantation house, white neoclassical columns vaulting twenty feet high from its front porch and black-faced plaster jockeys bidding a permanent welcome to guests from the lawn. One of the wealthier cocaine smugglers has built a Versailles-style palace, so huge that his neighbors have dubbed it "the little Holiday Inn" to distinguish it from the only slightly bigger American chain hotel nearby.

Affluence has brought a new sense of self-importance to the community. Santa Cruz, with its unlikely mixture of Indians, Spaniards, Germans, Italians, Mennonites and Japanese, has always chided the La Paz upper class for its aristocratic pretensions. Yet in recent years, wealthy *cruceños* have vied to erect statues of obscure ancestors. The metal and concrete effigies, placed strategically at traffic rotundas, bear plates explaining the alleged historical roles of these forgotten personalities.

The most visible of these statues is a large, heroic representation of Ñuflo de Chavez, the sixteenth-century Spanish explorer who founded Santa Cruz. In the late 1970's, a famous Spanish sculptor was commissioned to design the statue, but when his drawings arrived, there was a widespread sense of outrage in Santa Cruz. Ñuflo looked positively haggard, almost like a beggar, with a walking stick in one hand and a tattered roll—presumably the document authorizing him to found the city—clutched in his other hand. The artist had wanted to convey the full hardship of Ñuflo's journey from Paraguay through hundreds of miles of baking scrub forest at the head of a small band of adventurers.

The city fathers were aghast, yet too timid to reject the design outright. Instead, they prevailed on the most eminent local historian to pen a flowery letter to the Spanish sculptor explaining that popular sentiment was running strongly against his conception. Modifications were eventually made, and Ñuflo now stands with a proud, conquering gaze, a sword in his hand instead of the cane, and a flowing cape covering the wrinkled knapsack the artist had orginally designed on his back.

No matter how inflated their sense of pride, the *cruceños* at least have the good grace not to conceal the illegitimate source of their wealth. Many, perhaps most, of the businessmen and farmers I met during earlier visits to Santa Cruz have become involved either straightforwardly or indirectly with drug smuggling. A travel agent who was selling three-day round-trip tickets to Bogotá and Miami and Amsterdam remarked that "trips like those, you know the clients aren't going for vacation." A banker recounted how he had repeatedly extended large loans to a cotton farmer who reputedly used the money to finance a laboratory to process coca leaves into cocaine base. In three years, the farmer had not had one cotton harvest, but he had repaid all his loans on schedule, maintaining his excellent credit rating. A doctor at a rural clinic said that his patients, most of them peasants who had always been penniless, were paying for his services on the spot with thick wads of crisp dollars—they had not even bothered to change them into pesos.

Cocaine was not a taboo subject for the newspapers. Colonel Arce Gómez, the former minister of interior whose involvement in the cocaine dealings of his cousin, Roberto Suárez, was notorious, made a public statement calling for the execution of known drug traffickers. The following day, a columnist tweaked him by printing an item to the effect that his martyrdom was expected soon.

Widen Razuk, a former prefect of Santa Cruz, was so strongly rumored to be using his fleet of small airplanes for drug smuggling that he felt compelled to speak out. So he wrote the United States Immigration Office in Miami asking if he was wanted in the United States for cocaine trafficking. An immigration official wrote back stating that no charges were pending against him, so Razuk twice took out ads in the local newspapers, reproducing the letter as proof of his innocence.

I walked around the central plaza of Santa Cruz, past a milling group of money changers carrying briefcases stuffed with dollars and pesos, and small, light folding tables. Their meandering path on the edge of the plaza, usually on the corner farthest away from the cathedral, is known as "little Wall Street." It is here, amid the rapid opening and folding of the little portable tables, that the small change of the cocaine trade is laundered and circulated—the larger currency being invested in real estate or placed in American and Swiss banks. Politely declining their business offers, I threaded my way through the money changers and walked over to the Café La Pascana, in the shade of the cathedral. I was supposed to rendezvous there with Jaime, a banker I had met twice before in the 1970's.

It was the afternoon of an ordinary weekday, yet scores of men and women wandered about the café's terrace, apparently having nothing better to do than flaunt their jewelry, cars and clothes. Jaime provided a running commentary about their recently acquired fortunes and how they were being spent. I expressed amazement that even some of the leading industrialists, people with honorable reputations, had become involved with cocaine.

"It would never occur to many of these guys that they are doing anything so reprehensible," Jaime explained. "In the course of normal, legitimate business, they had to pay off the police and the Army and customs and other government officials. Anytime they brought in a car or television set or refrigerators, they would have to pay bribes. Once they have done that year after year, they figure what's wrong with paying off the same people to move cocaine. The stuff isn't a social problem in Bolivia. It's too expensive to sell here. It's an American problem. If Americans are stupid enough to pay all that money to sniff cocaine, well, if we don't sell it to them, someone else will. That's the way most people here justify it."

But by mid-1982, at the time of my visit, a backlash against the cocaine trade was mounting, even in Santa Cruz. The economic crisis in Bolivia was reaching tidal-wave proportions. Inflation was soaring, and the peso was falling daily against the dollar. The prices of legal exports like tin, oil, gas and agricultural products were in the doldrums. With a foreign debt of almost $4 billion, the government banks had no dollars left to finance imports or extend other loans. Hundreds of bankruptcies were sweeping industries and farming. The chamber of agriculture took out ads in a Santa Cruz newspaper complaining that coca had become the only profitable crop in the country and had created a rural labor shortage by offering workers much higher salaries than legitimate farming. A group of two hundred enraged mothers stormed the Central Bank branch in Santa Cruz and held the employees hostage for several hours until the government promised to give them dollars to send to their children, university students who were stranded abroad.

Only a relatively small proportion of the estimated $1 billion a year in cocaine revenues was now being repatriated to Bolivia. Cocaine smugglers had just about satiated their appetites for real estate, ranches, cars and luxury goods. There were no other investments they wanted to make in Bolivia. The bulk of their profits were stashed abroad, in Miami and Zurich banks. About the only financial game that interested them in Bolivia was the money market. Desperate businessmen were willing to pay higher and higher prices for cocadollars, which were being doled out in dribs and drabs.

I drove through a posh suburban neighborhood, past palms and eucalyptus and orange trees in full blossom, to one of the larger mansions, the headquarters of the Comité Pro-Santa Cruz. The Comité was the biggest booster organization for the city and the province. It claimed a diverse and powerful membership of business, agriculture, labor and professional groups, and advocated something approaching total separatism from La Paz. On the second-floor balcony of the house fluttered a green-and-white flag with a gold crown atop a red cross, the emblem of an independent Santa Cruz.

I had been invited to visit by Luís Dario Vázquez, the secretary-general of the Comité, to discuss Santa Cruz's development and its thorny involvement with cocaine. Vázquez is a short, thin man with white hair, piercing blue eyes and an enviable suntan. His contempt for La Paz and fervor for Santa Cruz know no bounds. In support of his arguments, he mustered economics, politics, history, even race.

"You have to go back to ethnic differences to begin to understand why La Paz and Santa Cruz have developed so differently," he said. "It is no secret that here we had the best Indians in Bolivia—the Chiriguanos and Guaranís—hardworking, headstrong people, like the white *cruceños*. Our first governor was the Duke of Osuna, a real duke, not an adventurer. And then we had such a long tradition of semiautonomy because we were physically isolated from the rest of the country for so long. We had to survive by our wits. We had to become virtually self-sufficient. La Paz began to take an interest in us only after oil and gas were discovered here in the 1950's. Well, I say that's about four hundred years too late. The people in La Paz claim that because we are richer than the rest of the country we should share our wealth. But when the tin mines were booming, only La Paz developed. We were ignored. That's understandable because charity begins at home; only a saint would do the opposite. Now, it's our turn to behave the same way. We are no longer a wild frontier. We have all the characteristics and qualities of a real nation, and someday we may have to stand alone. There are a lot of people here who believe as I do that the rest of the country is deadweight. And like any ship that wants to remain afloat, we should try to throw the deadweight overboard."

I remarked that it seemed somewhat unjust that so much of Santa Cruz's current wealth was based on cocaine, and that La Paz appeared to be reaping all of the consequences and few of the benefits of the drug trade.

"In the beginning, all of us thought the cocaine trade wasn't such a terrible thing," conceded Vázquez. "A lot of the profits were being reinvested here. There were dollars to spare. They became an important source of capital. But in the end, the cocaine people corrupted everything. They have a stranglehold over us."

Vázquez suggested that I speak to Erwin Gasser, one of the earliest and most powerful local industrialists who had also helped fund General García Meza's July 1980 coup. Vázquez even offered to make the appointment, as I had hoped he would.

Gasser was born of German parents in Santa Cruz in 1916. He was an old muleteer, driving his pack animals loaded with dry goods back and forth between Santa Cruz, Cochabamba and La Paz during the 1930's and 1940's, before the advent of highways and railroads. With two brothers, he bought a large rural property in 1940, not far to the north of Santa Cruz. It became the cornerstone of his fortune, producing more sugar and alcohol than any other plantation and refinery in the country. He had a nefarious reputation as a civilian power broker for ambitious military officers. But he preferred to think of himself as a civic spirit, the man who helped create

the cooperatives that brought electricity, telephones and savings-and-loan associations to Santa Cruz. He was paunchy, balding, slightly stooped and wheezed after every puff from his mentholated cigarettes. Unlike other wealthy businessmen, he declined to move his offices into one of the modern high rises or the outlying mansions. So we chatted in the one-story Spanish colonial building he had been using for thirty years, in the heart of the city, along a narrow, cobblestoned street behind the cathedral.

His son's arrest in Miami, he said, had been a terrible mistake. Yes, he and his son knew Roberto Suárez, but only casually and had no dealings with him. Cocaine was bringing only trouble to Santa Cruz. He also was finding it difficult to recruit farm labor because of the far more competitive wages offered to peasants by coca growers and smugglers. Apparently, the drug trade had made it difficult even for honest businessmen to contract the services of colonels and generals.

"The military governments have been a total disappointment," said Gasser. "They keep changing cabinet ministers so quickly that by the time we can educate them about the country's economic problems, they are thrown out of office. And, of course, there is the corruption problem. What makes it different from other countries is that these guys steal more money than the government has."

I returned to my hotel late in the afternoon. The sun dropped in the salmon sky, but it was still warm enough for a swim. Lounging around the pool, I found Doug and Steve, the two DEA agents. They had spent the last few days making "reconnaissance" forays into the province—fifteen miles north to Montero, called the "white city" because of its many cocaine laboratories, and to the streams and jungles farther west, where peasants trekked with their coca-leaf packs toward other clandestine narcotics factories.

The DEA men were awaiting the arrival of a small entourage of diplomats from the US Embassy in La Paz, who were traveling to Santa Cruz to press Washington's campaign against the cocaine trade.

I gathered that a fairly clear split had developed within the American government on how best to bring the narcotics traffic from Bolivia under control. Officials in the State Department tended to argue that no quick, dramatic breakthroughs were possible. Instead, honest elements in the Bolivian government had to be encouraged through the extension of economic aid and diplomatic support; peasants had to be offered electricity, roads and markets for legitimate crops that could replace their profitable coca harvests; only then could law enforcement be most effective against the cocaine smugglers. The DEA, while agreeing with this overall assessment, maintained that enforcement was still the key and insisted that it was handicapped by a shortage of personnel and money in its pursuit of men like Suárez.

Summarizing the State Department arguments, one of the diplomats visiting Santa Cruz, a man with long experience in narcotics, described the cocaine problem.

"This country has always been potentially wealthy," he said. "First, in silver, then rubber, then tin and now cocaine. But it always remained dirt poor because everybody exported everything and never reinvested enough here to create a prosperous economy. When one looks at drugs, it's undeniable that the cocadollars that were repatriated at first had a salutory effect. In economists' terms, they had a multiplier effect: creating jobs, new businesses, financial liquidity. And not only in La Paz or in Santa Cruz, but in the interior, in places where nobody had ever seen any wealth. But I also believe that one can now demonstrate that the negative economic effects outweigh any benefits. Just look at the country's image abroad—never good, it's now worse than ever. It is almost impossible for it to obtain foreign credits.

"The damage that cocaine has caused to this country in terms of further corruption of government, the police and the military may almost be irreparable. The hierarchy of the officer corps has been destroyed. There are colonels who are more powerful than generals, and captains who are more powerful than colonels because rank doesn't count unless you have drug connections. Even if you had a dozen honest generals and colonels who came together in an attempt to crush the drug trade, they could not command the loyalty of many of the officers under them. And even if the military got its act together and tried to sweep through the Chapare coca fields, they would face a full-scale peasant insurrection. Those campesinos are making real money for the first time in their lives. So what we are facing is a nation that doesn't have state power as we understand it. A nation with no political consensus or clear sense of identity. And you can't cut a deal with a government if no one is really in charge.

"So what to do? Slowly, you have to develop a crop substitution program in the Chapare, particularly the Chapare because it doesn't have a long tradition of coca growing. When you add up the installation of electricity, the road building, credit facilities for new crops, that's going to be a minimum of fifteen to twenty million dollars a year. Then you find the elements and tendencies in and out of government that work in our direction. And also, of course, you beef up law enforcement. You know we spend a billion dollars a year in the United States coping with narcotics—five hundred million dollars in treatment programs and five hundred million dollars in enforcement. And we spend only five percent of this abroad. Yet we know that we get a hundred percent more bang for the buck the closer we spend it to the source of the problem."

Doug, the DEA agent, had no qualms with the diplomat's assessment. He had few illusions that any progress was being made by the DEA in suppressing Bolivian narcotics traffic. Yet, he was clearly obsessed by the notion of bringing Roberto Suárez to heel. Over a mountainous plate of deep-roasted wild duck in a restaurant on the outskirts of Santa Cruz, he spoke with a mixture of awe and contempt about the cocaine king.

"Roberto Suárez is probably the best-known person in Bolivia," said Doug. "Ask any kid on the street, and he can tell you who he is. His name is more recognizable in Santa Cruz than the president's. We're not going to pull another scam on him. We tried that once, and it didn't work. He's too smart to fall for that kind of thing again. But there are so many pressures on this guy that he must be going nuts. Look at the way he's constantly moving about. Never spends more than a couple of days anywhere. He has to be pretty paranoid by now. Think of all those people he has to pay off, all those accounts he has to juggle, all those little and big things that could go wrong and explode in his face. Who's to say that someday enough military officials aren't going to figure that he is a real liability for any government that wants to reestablish this country's image abroad? Who's to say that maybe somewhere in his organization there isn't an ambitious lieutenant who thinks he can do a better job than Suárez? I'm not saying anything like this is happening now. We know that the coca harvest this year will set an all-time record, and that Roberto Suárez is richer and more powerful than he has ever been. But maybe he figures now is the time to cut the best possible deal with us. He won't get off scot-free. But he won't end up with a bullet in his head somewhere in the boonies either."

I had decided to leave Bolivia the following Monday. But with the weekend at hand, I accepted an invitation from Jaime, my banker friend, to visit his family's ranch along the banks of the Ichilo River, about ninety miles northwest of Santa Cruz. From the ranch, we would motorboat on the river. Besides fishing, Jaime wanted to give me a glimpse of the cocaine trade at its grassroots level.

The Ichilo flows north into the Mamoré River, and roughly divides the rolling plains of Santa Cruz from the tropical highlands of the Chapare. Its tan waters, lighter than the Mamoré, teem with succulent catfish and *tambaquí,* a fierce fighter with a taste that resembles trout. But in recent years the river and its banks had become the lairs and corridors of the *cocaleros*—the coca-leaf runners and processors—who had scared away most of the sport fishermen and duck hunters. Jaime said that his family, like many other nearby farmers and ranchers, wanted nothing to do with the drug trade, but they had been forced to permit the *cocaleros* free passage through their lands in return for a measure of tranquility.

It was still dark when we walked a mile from the ranch house to the motorboat. Anselmo, a wrinkled, gap-toothed Indian foreman with a milky cataract in one eye, led the way to the river. Roosters began to crow, and a batrachian chorus of metallic croaking erupted on the water's edge. I could barely make out the silhouettes of the cattle, but I could hear them cropping, pulling away mouthfuls of grass and chomping loudly.

Tugging powerfully at the cord wound around the engine, Anselmo started up the boat with a roar. Slanting rays descended through rents in the broken eastern sky as we headed north at dawn.

Hoping to shake off my drowsiness, I sat up and let the wind whip briskly past my face. The din of the outboard motor shattered the early-morning stillness. A skein of ducks, black with white-tipped wings, raced overhead, quacking loudly in alarm. On the shore, a willow tree, laden with egrets like a crowded dormitory, disintegrated into a flapping of white wings. A panicked heron arched over to the other bank and landed on a sandbar in a clumsy, falling-apart stance, one long leg shakily touching the ground before the other. Smaller blackbirds dived, skittered and twisted in a wild acrobatic display. As we rounded a sharp bend in the river, a brown hawk burst out suddenly low over the trees and in a flash climbed high above us as it passed the boat.

A pungent, acrid smell began to drift about us. Anselmo, with his

one good eye, was the first to signal the source, wisps of smoke rising at several points along both banks of the river a few hundred yards ahead. He slowed the boat, and Jaime said that we were coming to the cocaine-base factories. Here, the coca leaves, having been mixed with kerosene and stomped on through the night, were being processed in huge vats of sulphuric acid. As we drew nearer, the jungle air had the smell of an industrial suburb.

Five ragged figures in greasy blue jeans appeared on the river's shore, grim-faced men with machetes or guns tucked in their belts. Jaime raised his fishing pole as if to explain our purpose. Recognizing him as a local family member, the men relaxed their vigil and waved. Without cutting the motor, Jaime shouted a good-morning and asked whether the fish were biting farther downstream. A short, wiry man with knotted forearms, who appeared to be the leader, shrugged and waved again—more a gesture of warning away than friendliness. All smiles now, we shouted good-bye and moved on as slowly as we could without giving the impression that we wanted to spy on the numerous shacks housing the cocaine laboratories along the banks.

Small vans puttered along unmarked dirt roads. Through cleared patches in the woods, we could glimpse peasants silently trudging toward the small factories. They wore tattered sneakers or rubber-soled sandals and carried their *tambos*—fifty-pound packs of compressed coca leaves—flat against their backs, with harnesslike straps about their heads. Some were women, and a few were adolescents. Unable to move their heads under the strain of their *tambos,* they followed our boat's slow passage out of the corners of their eyes. There were scores of them. They seemed a guerrilla army, recreating what I imagined the Ho Chi Minh trails must have looked like during the Vietnam war. I remembered the American diplomat's warning that any sudden attempt to crush the cocaine trade militarily could set off a full-scale peasant uprising, and seeing the vastness of this illicit enterprise I had no doubts he was right. Here were people who had never before ventured far from their plots on the Andean slopes, now marching hundreds of miles away from their homes, weary and bent by their burdens, but earning several times what they could expect from fieldwork. I also recalled that the American diplomat had mentioned $15 to $20 million as the minimum annual cost of US government aid to wean away these peasants from the cocaine trade. It now sounded like too optimistically low a figure to me. What legal crop could ever command the steadily higher profits of cocaine as long as demand for the drug remained so high in the United States? The DEA's cloak-and-dagger approach seemed even less promising. How silly, I thought, to believe that capturing Roberto Suárez or a dozen other major smugglers would dismantle this enormous industry. As I saw all the factories and the runners, Suárez dwindled in my estimation. He possessed no irretrievable secrets. If he ceased to exist, these frontier lands would reinvent him.

As we turned back to Jaime's ranch under the glare of the mid-morning sun, I chuckled perversely at the thought that if all these cocaine trails, running from the edge of the Beni southeastward to Santa Cruz, were ever paved, they would account for a good chunk of Belaúnde's proposed transcontinental highway through the Bolivian frontier.

16

From Santa Cruz in Bolivia to the Paraguayan capital of Asunción, Belaúnde's imaginary highway runs its most desolate stretch 670 miles southeast through the sparsely populated Chaco wastelands.

After the Amazon rain forests of Peru and Brazil, after the savanna and tropical plains of northern and eastern Bolivia, I yearned for a familiar, temperate landscape. But I knew I would not find it in the Chaco.

From the four-mile altitude of my commercial jet, the Chaco was an immense prairie of silver-and-rust grass dappled with darker green patches and ugly, small rivulets splayed out like brown varicose veins. It blankets 115,000 square miles—an expanse bigger than Arizona—joining together Bolivia, Paraguay and Argentina.

I had seen the Chaco years before at ground level. The terrain is a bewildering mosaic of sandy deserts and clay-based shrub forests, tropical jungles and impassable swamps. Sometimes all these elements blend incongruously like vast, unkempt botanical gardens. Tall palms spread their feather-duster fronds above redwoods so hard they are called *quebrachos,* or axe-breakers, and other stocky trees whose bulging trunks and staggering silhouettes have earned them the sobriquet "drunken sticks." Below the thickly knit branches of this forest grows an even more unexpected profusion of thornbushes and cacti with sharp spikes protecting crowns of white-and-pink flowers. The landscape harbors an equally contradictory menagerie of jungle and desert wildlife: monkeys and jaguars, armadillos and peccaries, rattlesnakes and aquatic anacondas.

A superficial glance at the meteorological chart might lead an observer to mistake the Chaco for a temperate zone. Its annual precipitation of forty inches is comparable to parts of the American Midwest. But here the rain falls in heavy cloudbursts, mostly from December to March, diminishing its agricultural benefits. Between these torrential downpours, a blistering sun sends temperatures soaring above a hundred degrees, and the leaves of the Chaco's undergrowth wither from the heat while the roots and stems drown in the waterlogged clay soil. During the long, dry season from April through November, a gray dust covers the parched prairies, and the tall grass of the marshlands collapses into yellow straw clumps. The palm fronds of the Chaco forests wilt and only the cacti at their base seem alive, curling their long arms around the tree trunks in a thorny embrace.

For the sixteenth-century Spanish conquistadores, the Chaco was a green hell that had to be endured in the search for El Dorado. They did not linger here. Between their base camp in Asunción and their newer colony to the northwest in Santa Cruz—the distance separating Washington from Chicago—they founded no settlements. Even the Jesuits who followed them were unable to tame this wild land, and confined their missions to the Chaco's periphery in Paraguay, Bolivia and Argentina, where the wooly terrain tapered into more tractable and fertile plains.

The Chaco dozed in its heat-haze, forgotten and almost ignored, until the twentieth century. The wider swathes of prairie could support only the hardiest cattle, whose meat was too tough to be eaten except in leathery, sun-dried strands or overcooked stews. The *quebracho* trees, with their axe-breaking trunks, were the land's only exploitable natural resource. Their wood was so hard it could be used instead of asphalt to pave provincial roads and village streets. The *quebracho*'s bark also produced a tannin extract to cure leather hides.

Then, in the 1930's, these barren wilds became the unlikely battleground of South America's bloodiest conflict in this century. Oil was discovered on the southwestern margins of the Chaco in Bolivia. Rumors swept La Paz and Asunción that enormous petroleum pools lay beneath the Chaco's repulsive terrain.

In June 1932, after months of mounting tensions, two small Paraguayan and Bolivian Army garrisons facing each other across a salty lagoon on their disputed borderlands traded fire, and the three-year Chaco war was on. The Bolivian forces were led by an eccentric former German officer, General Hans von Kundt, who resurrected his World War I tactics of frontal assaults against enemy trenches. The

Bolivians at first gained the upper hand and marched deep into the Paraguayan Chaco. But their tanks soon bogged down in the marshes. Their communications and supply lines became overextended, and Paraguayan counterattacks annihilated whole columns of Bolivian troops. Then the Paraguayans strayed too far into the Bolivian Chaco, straining their own supply lines and suffering terrible losses.

The conflict began to resemble the bloody stalemate of trench warfare in Europe two decades before. Along with the Japanese invasion of Manchuria, the Chaco conflict was front-page news around the world as the first major tests of the efficacy of the League of Nations, which had ingenuously banned the use of war to settle disagreements between nations. The League convoked emergency sessions in Geneva. It issued outraged statements noting that Bolivia and Paraguay had violated the world organization's covenant on the illegality of military force. But the League's calls for an immediate end to hostilities and direct peace negotiations to fix new boundaries in the Chaco were ignored by both the Bolivians and Paraguayans.

One of the great journalists, Peter Kihss, a former colleague of mine who recently retired from *The New York Times,* is probably the only American correspondent from the Chaco war still alive today. He covered the conflict mostly from the Paraguayan side and was kind enough to dig up some of the old dispatches that he filed in 1933–34.

Because of heat, exhaustion, thirst and disease, Kihss estimated, as many as one out of every ten Paraguayan soldiers died before even reaching the front. The casualties were far greater once they entered the battle zone.

"The Paraguayan water supply was brought, a glass per soldier per day, from distances twenty-four hours of traveling away," wrote Kihss. "And it was not brought when weather conditions were bad, as they frequently were, or when Bolivian airplanes pierced the forest veil with bullets. . . . In such country, wounds or exhaustion meant death. World War [I] correspondents used to estimate the wounded by multiplying the number of dead by four. In the Chaco, a man wounded was a man for whom death's rattle was preciously close. It took so long to get wounded men back to first aid that their bodies were covered with white grubs before suffering could be alleviated. Then surgeons made swift incisions, spread ether and waited until the worms drew away before they could even begin to see the wounds drilled by bullets. Nurses in Asunción hospitals reported that most of their care was not for wounded men but rather for men drained by the campaign. There were men there who resembled rag bags emptied of their contents."

Always, recalled Kihss, there were the snipers from the trees, the silent commandos wielding machetes against the stragglers who lost their way in the Chaco forest, and the deadly ruses of the enemy.

> There was a Bolivian machine gunner who, when the armies lay in trenches only thirty yards apart, yet invisible for the screen of forest, suddenly shouted: "Quick, a mechanic! This damn gun is out of order!"
>
> Gleeful Paraguayan eavesdroppers rose from their trenches and rushed the site. The grinning trickster mowed them down with a perfectly working gun.

When the war finally ended in 1935, the Paraguayans could claim victory in terms of territorial gains. The peace treaty ceded most of the Chaco to their country. But measured in terms of booty, it was a worthless triumph. No oil was ever found in the disputed wastelands. Almost a hundred thousand soldiers died, probably ensuring that more people lie buried beneath the Chaco than will ever live peacefully on its surface.

For all its horrors, the Chaco war was only the latest in a series of frontier conflicts that scourged Paraguayans over the centuries. Since Spanish colonial times, their country has had the misfortune of being a buffer state separating larger neighbors. And as a result, Paraguay's frontier lands have often been contested by Brazil, Argentina and Bolivia.

Throughout most of the colonial era, the task of holding the wilderness frontiers fell upon the Jesuits, whose prosperous, populous Indian missions dominated the Paraguayan landscape and staved off the *bandeirantes* of Portuguese Brazil. Following independence in the nineteenth century, a trio of Paraguayan dictators sought to insularize the country against the expansionist pretensions of Brazil and Argentina. That unsuccessful effort culminated in a war that almost wiped Paraguay and its inhabitants off the face of the map.

It began in 1864, when the Paraguayan ruler, Francisco Solano López, fearful that the Brazilians were about to invade his country, declared war on them. Brazil forged an alliance with Argentina and Uruguay. and troops from all three nations plunged into Paraguay, massacring almost any inhabitants they came across. In 1870, Brazilian soldiers caught up with Solano López in the tiny village of Cerro Cora, in eastern Paraguay. Fatally wounded during the battle, Solano López was reported to have cried out, "The nation dies with me!" And he was very nearly right. Only 221,000 Paraguayans emerged alive in 1870 from a prewar population of 525,000. And only about 28,000 men survived, most of them too young or too old to have been conscripted into military service. A fourth of the country was annexed by Brazil and Argentina.

In light of the Jesuit-*bandeirante* conflicts, the 1864–70 holocaust and the brutal Chaco war, it is little wonder that Paraguayans have long associated their frontier lands with national catastrophe. Until a decade ago, the vast majority of the three million inhabitants in this landlocked, California-size nation huddled in the central zone—in Asunción on the Paraguay River and in the rich farmlands spreading in a small half circle east, north and south of the capital.

Then, in the early 1970's, the Paraguayan frontier lands began to yield an unexpected treasure. On the Paraná River separating eastern Paraguay from Brazil, the two countries decided to build the world's largest hydroelectric project, the Itaipú Dam.

By the end of the 1980's, when Itaipú is operating at full capacity, it will generate the equivalent of five hundred thousand barrels of oil a day. This is six times the energy pouring forth from Egypt's renowned Aswan Dam, or as much electricity as all of New York State, including New York City, consumes. At current prices, Itaipú's output would save well over $5 billion a year in petroleum purchases for Brazil, a country that imports almost ninety percent of its oil as it staggers under a foreign debt of more than $90 billion. Paraguay has agreed to sell its half of Itaipú's power to the Brazilians. So the dam could convert that poverty-stricken smaller country into a hydroelectric equivalent of an oil emirate.

Itaipú's potential riches far surpass Bolivia's cattle and cocaine bonanza, the agricultural windfall of Brazil's western Amazon settlements and the petroleum finds in the Peruvian jungles. The giant dam has made Paraguay the greatest beneficiary of South America's recent thrust into its inner wilderness. No other country on the continent has been transformed as rapidly by newfound wealth on its frontiers.

Thus, as I flew southeastward from Bolivia's Santa Cruz province into Paraguay, following Belaúnde's imaginary highway to its termi-

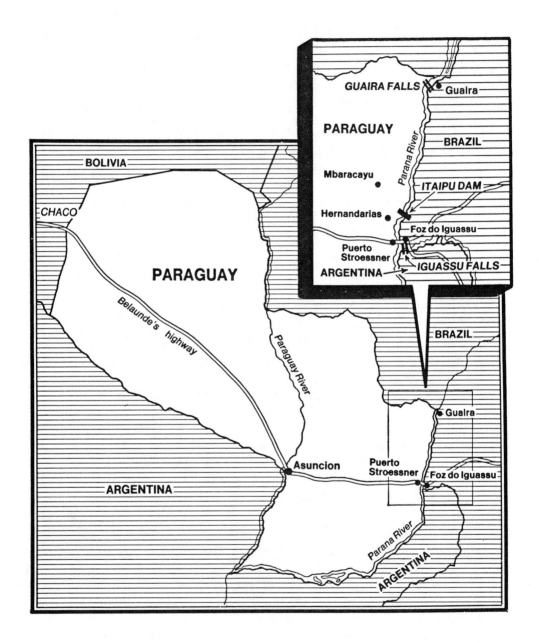

nal point at Itaipú, I was approaching the pot of gold at the end of the South American frontier rainbow. I decided to break this final segment of my continental odyssey by stopping first in Asunción before proceeding to the dam at the eastern end of Paraguay, 190 miles away from the capital. My plane skimmed low over the Chaco as it ended its ninety-minute flight. The sluggish Paraguay River, glinting silver and blue, flowed from north to south, sometimes splitting into coves and channels, then pulling together in great molten bends. To the west of the river lay the green-and-bronze mottled wastelands of the Chaco. On the river's eastern banks, around Asunción, the terrain changed into rich red earth and lush green farmland.

I arrived in the Paraguayan capital in 1982, after an absence of six years, during which the economic ripples of Itaipú had been washing over the city with the force of monsoon waves. The old airport, no larger than a freight terminal, had been replaced by a huge structure shaped like a glass-and-concrete crab. Only the bigger-than-life portraits of the dour, medal-bedecked Paraguayan strongman Alfredo Stroessner hanging in the marble lobby were familiar.

The rutted road into Asunción had been smoothed and broadened. Decrepit shacks had given way to ample country homes, nightclubs and barbecue restaurants. Inside the capital, along Mariscal López Avenue, there were mansions with garden sculptures and cool, deep verandas. The downtown streets were bustling with Mercedes-Benz taxis that had replaced rusty postwar Fords and Chevrolets. The stores were stocked with the latest Asian electronic goods and European fashions. A Kentucky Fried Chicken restaurant and other American-style fast-food outlets were doing brisk business. Dozens of large multistoried buildings now soared above my hotel, the Guaraní, the only high rise in the city a bare seven years before.

From the vantage point of my hotel room on the twelfth floor, I could see that the construction boom had not yet effaced Asunción's colonial charm. Amid the newer office towers, there were still many tufts of green foliage and older, smaller buildings with red-tiled roofs and whitewashed stucco walls that shimmered in the afternoon sun. The city slanted gently down toward the squat, gray legislative and presidential palaces, the old cathedral and then the broad, curving Paraguay River.

On the radio, I listened absentmindedly to the nasal chirping sound of a news bulletin in Guaraní, the Indian language spoken by most Paraguayans when conversing among themselves. *Stroessner* was the only word I could make out. When I flipped the dial to a Spanish-language broadcast, the announcer was enumerating the good deeds accomplished by the Excelentísimo Presidente Stroessner that week: the inauguration of a school, a shopping center, a gas station. No project was too small to dispense with his presence and guiding hand.

President Stroessner, a hero in the Chaco war and now a balding, stocky septuagenarian with heavy jowls, is Latin America's longest reigning dictator. Most Paraguayans were not even born when he came to power in 1954. A million of them fled the country, partly because of political repression and mostly because of economic misery, under Stroessner's rule. Until the early 1970's, the nation's most profitable business was contraband. Grains, narcotics, tobacco, liquor, automobiles, household goods and luxury items are still abundantly smuggled in and out of the country by gangs under the control of Stroessner's family, his military cronies and the chieftains of his Colorado party. The contraband is so prolific that international organizations and financial institutions often complain that it is impossible to get a true picture of Paraguay's balance of trade. Some years ago, a thoroughly bewildered official of the United Nations' Food and Agriculture Organization wondered out loud how Paraguay, without any known wheat farms of its own, was reporting exports of the grain. The mystery was solved when it was later discovered that sizable quantities of wheat were being smuggled into the country from neighboring Argentina and then sold abroad.

The once legion number of political prisoners in Paraguay has dwindled over the years, as both the regime and its critics have accepted the hopelessness of opposition. But the secret police—known as *pyragües,* or "people with hairy feet"—still creep around silently, detaining and torturing alleged Communists, overly vocal critics, dissident peasants and laborers and, occasionally, hippies and homosexuals.

"The price of peace" has been the slogan used by Stroessner's defenders to justify every government transgression, large and small. School textbooks recall the dark ages of military and civil strife that preceded Stroessner's iron rule. Radio and television commentators offer paeans to the president's brilliance in keeping the country isolated from the social and political upheavals that have rumbled through South America over the last three decades. Though considerably less shackled than they used to be, the newspapers still avoid direct criticism of Stroessner and his closest collaborators. Even the hardest hitting exposés of corruption and brutality fall back on the well-tested formula: "If Stroessner only knew what his underlings have been perpetrating . . . "

The Itaipú project has given Stroessner a golden opportunity to rewrite his heavily blemished historical legacy. Like any other undertaking by the regime, the giant dam is steeped in controversy. There are no parallels in South America, nor perhaps anywhere else in the world, for a binational effort of such magnitude as Itaipú. But in spite of the official rhetoric from both the Brazilian and Paraguayan governments about equal partnership, the fact remains that the planning and construction of Itaipú, and the distribution of its profits, have been thoroughly dominated by Brazil.

Itaipú was conceived by the Brazilians at a time when Richard Nixon was proclaiming "Project Independence." Its construction got underway just as Jimmy Carter was calling for a "moral equivalent of war." These American promises to deal with the world energy crisis now have a hollow, ingenuous ring. But Brazil, with far less fanfare and far more single-mindedness, has been carrying out a monumental drive to substantially lessen its dependence on costly petroleum imports.

Itaipú is the linchpin of this effort. Brazil has raised the entire financing for the project, estimated at $17 billion. It has assembled and trained an army of tens of thousands of engineers and workers, with a logistical support and organizational structure that would have satisfied two division commanders. Brazilian diplomacy, combining forcefulness, subtlety and at times deviousness, has extracted the most favorable conditions from Paraguay and kept another suspicious neighbor, Argentina, at bay.

Brazilian planning has taken into consideration even the remote possibility that a Paraguayan government might someday emerge seeking to alter or abrogate the terms of the Itaipú accord. Today, such an eventuality sounds as farfetched as the idea of the United States giving up sovereignty over the Panama Canal must have seemed a half century ago. But Brazil is taking no chances. As a future bargaining chip for any contingency, several hundred thousand Brazilian settlers have spilled across the Paraná River boundary and now constitute a heavy majority of the population in eastern Paraguayan farmlands around Itaipú.

Asunción lies almost two hundred miles west of Itaipú. And here, in the capital, the myth of Paraguayan control over the giant dam and the eastern frontier lands is intact. Itaipú is officially extolled as the inspired creation of President Stroessner, just like those schools, shopping malls and gas stations he inaugurates every week.

The day after I arrived in Asunción, I was joined in the hotel bar by a diplomat I had known years before in Argentina. He had been following the progress of Itaipú and its impact on the Paraguayan economy. The statistics of prosperity he reeled off gave me some notion of the radical transformations that had taken place since my last visit to the country.

Once among the poorest South American nations, Paraguay now boasted the fastest growing per capita annual income on the continent—from $260 in 1970 to $1,400 a decade later. Unemployment was minimal. Although inflation was galloping, wages were rising even faster. Across the country, land prices had soared by five hundred percent in six years, and by ten thousand percent in parts of Asunción, making thousands of property owners wealthy overnight.

"Itaipú is better than an Arab oil field," said the diplomat. "It has created an enormous construction boom, and there's nothing quite like a construction boom to produce a trickle-down effect in a developing country. Some people have gotten very much richer than others. But just about everybody has benefited one way or another. Not even a thoroughly corrupt, inegalitarian system like this one could prevent wealth from seeping down. Now, what happens after this spending orgy is over I don't know. I don't see any money going to build up new industries or any other sort of productive investments. Like everybody else, I've got to wonder just what is going to happen in eastern Paraguay with all those Brazilian settlers. That part of the country already thinks of itself as more Brazilian than Paraguayan."

A few days later, I had lunch with a Brazilian who had spent several years in Paraguay as a top-ranking engineer for the Itaipú project. We were supposed to confine our conversation to the technical aspects of the dam, but again and again, he drifted toward the subject of graft with an almost perverse fascination.

"I try to lead a very quiet social life, just hanging around with my wife and kids," he said. "I avoid as many parties as possible because the word gets around that I do something important at Itaipú and then I get approached for favors. A major asked me if I couldn't have some of Itaipú's laundry sent to his sister for cleaning since she lives nearby. A colonel says he'll give me a commission if I let him sell bananas from his plantation to the labor force at the dam. I have to laugh because it would take a whole factory, a major business to meet our needs. But everyone still wants their piece of the action. I have been in some heavy corruption countries, places like Haiti and Bolivia. But this is the big leagues. Here, you think that buying off the president will solve problems. But you have just gotten started. You have to bribe everybody and everything that moves. A man making a good salary will feel terrible if he is not paid off. I guess it is this incredible mentality of corruption that explains what has been happening in the eastern part of the country. It is the generals and the Ministry of Interior and even the agrarian reform agency who have sold all that land to Brazilians. They don't even wait for the Brazilians to come looking for land. They go after them all the way to São Paulo. Itaipú may turn out to be our Panama Canal. But we're going to be a lot smarter than the Americans. We're going to out-populate the Paraguayans around Itaipú the way the Americans never did in Panama."

At considerable risk, a few Paraguayan voices have been raised over this state of affairs. The loudest has come from Domingo Laíno. He is an economist and leader of the Paraguayan political opposition in the legislature, which is thoroughly controlled by Stroessner's Colorado party. Laíno has written two books—mostly collections of his legislative speeches—about Itaipú and the over-whelming Brazilian presence in eastern Paraguay. They were printed abroad, and were not available in Asunción's bookstores. By the decayed condition of his home, I gathered Laíno was not being sustained by royalties from his writings. In fact, he seemed to be one of the few Paraguayans whose personal fortune had declined in the boom times of Itaipú.

His rambling colonial-style house was surrounded by a large garden that was more weeds than lawn, its trees unpruned and planted haphazardly. The paint was peeling off the high ceiling in the living room. On the cracked walls hung family portraits of men with muttonchop whiskers and women in dresses bulging over crinoline underskirts. Small, cheap, plaster busts of Pope John XXIII and John F. Kennedy sat on a mantle near the fireplace. The few pieces of furniture were wooden and uncomfortable, with cushions flattened from overuse. From a back room, the laughter of a child and the footfalls of her mother echoed through the near emptiness of the old mansion.

Laíno was young, not quite forty years old. He was good-humored, heavy-set, with unruly brown hair and a scruffy beard. He wore stained khaki pants and scuffed shoes without socks. Before pouring me a whiskey, he held a glass up to the bare light bulb hanging from the ceiling to check whether it was cracked or dirty. "The kitchen is too far back," he said sheepishly.

We had met years before during one of the political campaigns that had predictably reelected Stroessner by a landslide margin. Laíno had no Marxist antecedents. He enjoyed good relations with the American Embassy, though things had been better when President Carter was in office pressing his human-rights crusade. Nowadays Stroessner felt secure enough to avoid the diplomatic embarrassment of jailing Laíno. Instead he preferred to mete out little humiliations.

There was the business of the phone, for instance. Despite a record expansion of the country's communications network in recent years, Laíno's application for a telephone had gotten nowhere. The waiting list was very long, he was told, even for a legislative leader like himself. By depriving Laíno of a phone, the police saved themselves the annoyance of bugging his calls. This also forced any of Laíno's friends and sympathizers to abandon discretion and openly visit him under the watchful gaze of Stroessner's agents.

Then there was the problem of the fence. Laíno had tired of the plainclothesmen with walkie-talkies staring from across the street. So he put up sheets of corrugated metal around his garden. Within a day, they had been ripped away. He planted a hedge on the garden's perimeter, and it too was soon uprooted.

"The police chief told me that maybe I was planning to hide terrorists in the garden," said Laíno. "I heard later that Stroessner himself had taken an interest in the fence. His limousine passes in front of my house every day, and he said what is Laíno up to, and why was I not kept under unobstructed surveillance."

An old school chum of Laíno's dropped by to discuss a passport problem. Twenty years ago, he had participated in a student demonstration at his university during which the rector's house was stoned. He had been arrested and released a few weeks later. When he applied for a passport, it was denied him, but he left the country anyway and had been living abroad using a stateless person's document issued by the United Nations. He had returned to visit his aging parents, and had reapplied for a Paraguayan passport. He was turned down again.

"A clerk at the Ministry of Interior told me that a computer check uncovered the fact that I had participated in a violent demonstration," Laíno's friend explained. "What a memory this regime has! I told the guy that the charges against me had been dropped decades ago. He said I was probably right, but that they hadn't gotten around to updating their computer and the waiting list was very long."

Laíno could do little more than commiserate. "Maybe you should apply for my telephone and I should apply for your passport," he said with a shrug. The conversation turned to politics, and after a while the friend emptied his glass and left.

Laíno then plunged into his favorite topic, Itaipú, dredging up its earliest history. The diplomatic maneuvering around Itaipú began to unfold in 1964, long before the world heard of OPEC or the energy crisis. What was then a new Brazilian military government started to consider ways of further harnessing the power of the Paraná River to service the growing industries of southern Brazil.

Running for twenty-eight hundred miles—more than the distance separating Seattle from Miami—the Paraná is longer than any other South American river except the Amazon. It is the seventh longest river in the world. Born in Brazil, the Paraná descends southward, curls around eastern and southern Paraguay, winds through northern Argentina and delivers its muddy waters to the broad Río de la Plata, which flows past the Argentine capital of Buenos Aires into the Atlantic Ocean.

The Brazilians had already constructed numerous hydroelectric projects along their portion of the Paraná River. They would have preferred to build another huge dam entirely within their country. But their engineers determined that the Paraná's greatest potential power lay between the giant waterfalls of Guaira and Iguassú, precisely the stretch of the river shared by Brazil and Paraguay. The problem was that Stroessner had long claimed both sides of the Guaira Falls for his own country.

The territorial dispute came to a head in May 1964, when Brazilian troops occupied the falls and unceremoniously barred the Paraguayan deputy foreign minister from visiting the area.

"The Brazilian message was clear," said Laíno. "The Paraná's hydroelectric potential would be developed by Brazil with or without Paraguay's participation."

Stroessner, always a pragmatist, signed an agreement in June 1966 with the Brazilian government, stating that the energy resources of the Paraná River around the Guaira Falls would be shared equally between both countries. A series of studies in the following years considered fifty possible sites for dams, but finally settled on the option of one giant project located just north of the Paraná River island of Itaipú—a Guaraní word that means "singing rock."

The Treaty of Itaipú was signed between Brazil and Paraguay in 1973. This was followed a year later by the statutes creating an entity called Itaipú Binational, staffed with officials from both countries, which was made responsible for overseeing the construction and operation of the dam.

The decision to build Itaipú raised hackles in Argentina. Paraguay had long sought to balance its relations between its two giant neighbors, and the Argentines correctly foresaw that the mammoth dam would firmly place the Paraguayans in the Brazilian economic and political orbit. The Argentines, who have plans for their own joint hydroelectric projects with the Paraguayans farther downstream on the Paraná, also feared that the size of Itaipú might reduce their share of the river's energy potential. But years of acrimonious negotiations between Buenos Aires and Brasília have only led to an uneasy compromise which has permitted the Brazilians to move full steam ahead.

It is in Paraguay, however, that the Itaipú accord has been most controversial. Under the terms of the agreement between Brazil and Paraguay, each country has the right to half of the power generated by the dam. But since Paraguay's economy and industrial structure are so small, it is doubtful that the country could use even a fraction of Itaipú's electricity in the foreseeable future. And the treaty obliges Paraguay to sell all the unused portion of its fifty percent share of the dam's power to Brazil.

Brazilian negotiators further extracted from Paraguay an agreement that the electricity exported to Brazil would be paid at the extremely low rate set in 1973, before energy prices began to soar around the world. If no adjustments are made, Paraguay will collect only $41 million a year from 1988 on, after its share of construction costs have been subtracted. This is a paltry sum for exporting to

Brazil the energy equivalent of 250,000 barrels of oil a day. Elsewhere in the world, agreements to export hydroelectricity tend to run seven or eight times above the purchase price that the Brazilians secured at Itaipú. Nobody expects the original Itaipú price accords to last, and, in fact, negotiations are underway to increase the revenues Paraguay will receive from the project.

"But let's be realistic," said Laíno. "Paraguay has very little leverage at this late date. It has no alternative than to accept what Brazil will be willing to pay. We are in this predicament because of a combination of Brazilian negotiating savvy and Paraguayan ineptitude."

After leaving Laíno, I met again with my diplomat friend. He agreed with Laíno's version of events surrounding Itaipú, and added a few observations of his own.

The Brazilians, whose resources enabled them to control the planning and to tap the financing for the project, deliberately underestimated the dam's cost in order to dampen Paraguayan expectations of profit. In 1973, when the Itaipú treaty was signed, Brazilian officials were asserting that only $2 billion would have to be spent on the project. But year after year, the cost has escalated, and the latest estimates placed it at about $17 billion. Part of this huge leap can be attributed to inflation and the skyrocketing interest rates on loans. "But probably just as important," said the diplomat, "has been Brazil's determination to build the dam as quickly as possible, no matter what the cost. The Brazilians' reasoning is quite simple. The sooner Itaipú starts operating, the less money they will be spending on oil imports. They probably could have cut the costs of Itaipú substantially by slowing down the project a few years. But they would have ended up losing a great deal of money on petroleum purchases.

"I would say that Paraguay's interest would have been to keep the cost of the project much lower even if it took more time to build. Instead, the Paraguayans are going to have to pay half of the $17 billion cost of Itaipú by exporting their share of electricity to Brazil at cheap prices. It's going to be many years before they finish paying off that huge debt and start making any money."

The next day I boarded a commercial jet for the thirty-minute flight east toward Itaipú to visit the dam in its final stages of construction. As the plane approached the Paraná River, the contrast between the Brazilian and Paraguayan sides of the border was as startling as a map on which both countries were clearly labeled. The

Brazilian landscape was all rich red soil and lush green fields, a terrain clearly shaped by human hands. The Paraguayan territory was far less homogeneous, a checkered pattern of dense forest and farm clearings, a wilderness that was still under assault.

From the air, Itaipú looked like a whitish-gray mountain straddling the Paraná River. It dwarfed the majestic Iguassú Falls just twelve miles downstream, near the corner where the borders of Paraguay, Brazil and Argentina join together. The plane landed in the Brazilian city of Foz do Iguaçú, almost midway between Itaipú and the waterfalls, and I spent the night in a hotel there.

It was only the following morning when I visited Itaipú's construction site that I had a true sense of the dimensions of the project. The mighty Paraná had been diverted slightly off its course through a canal on the Brazilian side so that the main dam could be erected on the dry riverbed. From this foundation, the dam soared an astonishing 735 feet high, more than half as tall as New York's World Trade Towers. Cranes hoisting six cubic yards of concrete mix in their huge buckets rose above the height of St. Peter's Basilica. The seventy-five-ton trucks lumbering into the work site had wheels that dwarfed a six-foot man. Laborers clinging to the scaffolding on the upper reaches of the dam looked like ants.

Accompanied by Aluisio Mauro Rezende, one of the chief Brazilian engineers, I walked through the bowels of Itaipú along a straight half-mile-long tunnel passage between Brazil and Paraguay above the riverbed. Looking down into the holds where the turbines would be placed, I got a severe case of vertigo. And then, under the roar of power drills and the shower of sparks from blowtorches, I could feel a sense of claustrophobia enveloping me.

"We have poured more than twelve million cubic meters of concrete into this project!" shouted Rezende, a pear-shaped little man in his fifties, trying to make himself heard above the din. "With the same amount of concrete, we could have built two hundred of the largest soccer stadiums in the world, or a city for four million people!"

The actual construction work on Itaipú began in late 1975. A million tons of earth and stone were removed every month as laborers gouged the canal to divert the Paraná off its course and make way for construction of the main dam on the dry riverbed. For miles around, the ground shook every day, and a cloying smell of explosives lingered in the air. Finally, toward the end of 1978, a deafening blast more powerful than all the others shattered the last wall of stone and knocked the Paraná River off its natural path and into the canal.

"It took more than a year for the riverbed to dry out enough to allow us to begin work on the main dam," said Rezende. "We used this time to start building flood barriers on both banks of the river."

When the laborers and engineers started to construct the main dam, they discovered that the riverbed was not as solid as they had expected. So they excavated more earth, drilled more than five miles of tunnels under the dam's foundation and filled them with several million tons of concrete.

For all its size, Itaipú is a model of simplicity. Its main dam will house eighteen to twenty turbines connected to an equal number of generators. The river's water, backed up behind Itaipú in a huge, 564-square-mile, fern-shaped reservoir, will be directed through immense funnels near the top of the dam and will crash down on the turbines, generating enough power to supply one third of Brazil's electricity needs by the end of this decade.

On the Paraguayan side of the river, the main dam connects to a giant spillway which receives excess water from the reservoir behind Itaipú. The spillway is capable of discharging enough water back into the river as it emerges through the dam to prevent any flooding. Then, as an added precaution, along the Brazilian side the main dam is linked to a three-mile-long barrier of earth and rock fill to ensure the countryside against an inundation of even biblical proportions. In all, Itaipú's structures run a length of almost five miles.

When I visited Itaipú, the reservoir did not yet exist, and the Paraná was still flowing through its diversion canal, while building of the dam neared completion on the dry riverbed.

Itaipú employed thirty-seven thousand Brazilian and Paraguayan workers. Though the Paraguayans accounted for half of the labor force, they tended to occupy the most unskilled jobs and were responsible for pouring only a tenth of the concrete. To accommodate this huge population, along with dependents, a virtual city was built from scratch, including homes, churches, movie theaters, sports facilities, clinics and hospitals and shopping centers. Itaipú was a year-round, twenty-four-hour-a-day project. There were two work shifts, each eleven hours long. The intervals between the shifts were used for dynamiting.

Again and again, Itaipú officials resorted to military images to explain the scope and organization of the project. Rubens Vianna, a tall, gaunt Brazilian engineer who oversaw construction of the dam, likened the workers to foot soldiers, called his foremen "my sergeants" and considered the engineers as officers.

"Of course, it is not nearly as rigid as the military," said Vianna, fifty-seven years old. "We have more camaraderie between engineers and workers. But in the end, the organizational pyramid is much the same as in the armed forces."

Vianna, who had spent thirty-two years working on dams, qualified as a field marshal. He started in 1950 as a young engineer at Brazil's first large dam, a project erected in the northeastern part of the country.

"We had so little experience back then," he recalled. "We imported all our equipment and hired a lot of European and American technicians and engineers. I have some foremen who first worked with me back then as carpenters and skilled laborers. They were the first *barrageiros.*"

The term comes from *barragem,* the Portuguese word for dam. *Barrageiros* connote a nomadic army of laborers who spend their active lives wandering from one giant project to the next. They are as much a part of the Brazilian frontier as the pioneer farmers of Rondônia. Along their odysseys, they have developed their peculiar rootless life-style and even an extensive dialect of their own.

I had no trouble deciphering the logic of slang like "running the gauntlet" (leaving one job in search of the next), or "the white-shoed man" (a doctor), or "cowboy" (a foreman who rides roughshod over his crew). But what to make of a phrase like "shouting a dog to death" (to be heavily in debt)? The expression that most intrigued me was "radio peon." It referred to the whole grapevine system through which workers learn about new dams and job openings. Once a *barrageiro* finds employment at a new project, he sends out letters to his friends about available jobs, the quality of the employers and foremen, the food, safety conditions, and, of course, the pay. With construction in its final stages, radio peon was operating full blast at Itaipú. If I asked an employee what he would be doing next year, he would sometimes say he was "keeping his ear to the radio." Others answered with a shrug or sullen silence.

"There is a devastating psychological impact as projects near their completion," said Andre Luiz de Souza, the chief of personnel for the Brazilian employees and himself uncertain about where he would be working next. "We see more illnesses and a recurrence of old ailments among the workers. Our clinic and hospital attendance goes way up. There is a rise in criminal delinquency. When we are about to make a sizable cut in our labor force, we let the local police know a month ahead of time so they can prepare themselves for the bar brawls and petty robberies that are bound to follow. As strange as it sounds, this becomes a very depressing environment just as the project reaches its climax."

The anxieties extend to the engineers as well. Vianna, the dean of Brazilian dam engineers, spoke with some distaste about hanging around Itaipú until the first turbine started churning. "It will be a bittersweet victory," he said. "I know I'm going to feel a momentary triumphant surge. But then, the letdown will hit me. I would never want to stay on as an operating engineer at a dam. It would be such boring, monotonous work watching those turbines turn and turn and turn."

For all the uncertainty and arduous work of the *barrageiro*'s life, there are some very definite attractions. Salaries tend to be twice as high as normal city construction jobs, and even higher when the overtime hours are added on. Civil engineers, who often measure their experience in terms of tons of poured concrete, find the opportunities for career advancement more frequent on the frontier than in urban settings. For a minority of the workers, there is also a chance to get ahead.

According to De Souza, the personnel chief, only about a third of the workers have lifelong careers as *barrageiros*. They move up slowly, as unskilled workers, then truck drivers and finally as foremen and heavy-equipment operators earning two or three times the two-hundred-dollar monthly salaries that are usual for beginning laborers. Besides income, the *barrageiros* benefit from free housing and medical service, at least two free meals a day and subsidized food for their families, and schools that tend to be several notches above what their children could expect in urban slums.

"But the disadvantages are many," said De Souza. "This is really backbreaking work. A laborer is under constant control and pressure. He usually feels like a cog, anonymous, without individuality. Often he is unrecognized unless he screws up, and then he's out of here before he knows what happened to him. This is the sort of project where we try to isolate workers from civilian life. We try to seal them off from political and social currents. The usual worker comes here as a farm laborer, illiterate or maybe with a couple of years of elementary schooling at most. He is probably very family or clan oriented, and used to keeping his own hours. A project like this comes as a huge shock to him. The hours are precise and the work is repetitive. He may be seeing real money for the first time, and he spends it all because he knows no better. When this nightmare ends—and that's what it is for most of them—he escapes back to farm work and a lower standard of living."

Except for a few secretaries and clerks, there were no women working in Itaipú, nor at any other construction project I visited throughout the Brazilian frontier.

"It's discrimination pure and simple," said De Souza. "A woman professional, like an engineer, won't even come looking for employment because she knows she won't find it. Among a hundred fifty engineers here at the headquarters building, there was only one woman, and she didn't stay long. I could say something simple like the frontier is no place for a woman engineer. But the real explanation is plain, old-fashioned machismo. We're a lot more reactionary than people in São Paulo or Rio. There is no tradition of women professionals on the frontier, and we're under no pressure to change."

I spoke to the wife of an engineer about her peripatetic existence. She and her three children had followed her husband through three dam projects over the last fifteen years. Itaipú would be the last frontier zone they would live in because their oldest daughter was ready for university, and they wanted to move to a city where she could be at home with them while attending classes.

"If I were starting out today, I would never agree to live in places like this," said the woman, in her mid-forties. "My husband's salary may be better than he could get in São Paulo. But today, if I were a recent university graduate, I could also get a good job, and between us we would be making more money than his salary here. But back when I started, we didn't have that option. You lose out on many things living in a place like this. Itaipú is better than other dams because at least there is a decent-sized city nearby. Still, I have no local friends, only the wives of other engineers. And this is a very rigid society, like the military or the diplomatic community. The wives measure their social position by their husbands' ranks. The wife of a junior engineer doesn't tend to be very close to the wife of a more senior engineer. Then you get caught up in all the other stupid status games. Take the homes, for example. There are four or five different types of prefabricated homes here. Each type is supposed to be exactly the same dimensions, with exactly the same size garden. But my neighbor's house was just a little better than ours. The living room was a little bigger, the porch had a better floor, there were a couple of trees in her garden and none in mine. And her husband was exactly at my husband's professional level. So I felt slighted, and I started to complain. But then I realized it was all so idiotic. I was just letting myself take this too seriously.

"The happiest women here are the mothers of very young children who want to spend all their time with their kids. The rest of us are just trying to fill our days. The administration here encourages all kinds of social clubs and sports activities. Pretty soon you start trying to get interested in as many things as you can handle, because otherwise boredom sets in. Some of the wives of the older engineers have moved back to the cities with their children. Their husbands are senior enough so that they can commute back and forth over the weekends. But that's no kind of solution."

At the end of the road, after twenty or thirty years at dam sites around the Brazilian interior, the veterans of this construction army seem to think about returning to their roots. João Antonio Pereira, a forty-two-year-old bulldozer operator from the northeastern state of Minas Gerais who had spent more than seventeen years as a *barrageiro,* pictured himself owning a small grocery store back in his hometown. "In the evenings, I'll be sitting on the porch talking to the old friends who stayed behind," he said. "My wife will be in the kitchen, and the kids watching television."

The yearning to return home seemed just as prevalent among the engineers, most of whom also came from provincial towns rather than big cities. The zaniest retirement scheme I heard about was from Arnaldo Pasquarelli, a portly, redheaded young maintenance engineer, who was planning eventually to move back to his small community in São Paulo state and buy a hundred-acre farm. Chatting in his office near the dam site, he showed me the only two nontechnical books on his shelves. The titles were *The Well-Bred Frog* and *Raising Rabbits for Fun and Profit.*

"This could be a really good retirement business," he asserted. "I mean, how many times do you go to a good restaurant and ask for frogs' legs or rabbit listed on the menu, and the waiter says, 'Sorry, we're out.' I think there's a real market out there."

Unlike the pioneers of Rondônia or the Beni, not a single person at Itaipú seemed attracted enough by the frontier to stay on. They would concede that Foz do Iguaçú, the nearby Brazilian city, was now a comfortable, modern place, with more amenities than many of their hometowns. But the homeward pull was so great that none would consider settling there even if jobs were available.

Under the impact of Itaipú, the population of Foz do Iguaçú had quadrupled to almost a hundred fifty thousand people. It was no longer just a sleepy frontier community catering to tourists visiting the famous waterfalls of Iguassú on their way to Rio or Buenos Aires. Construction industries had sprouted, and the road improvements that the dam had wrought also fostered an agricultural boom. Just across the Paraná River, in Paraguay, Puerto Presidente Stroessner had been transformed from a small, mud-clogged ramshackle town into a modern, bustling city with dozens of high-rise buildings.

But the most spectacular change in Itaipú's wake had taken place in the eastern provinces of Paraguay along the frontier with Brazil. I had first traveled through the zone in the early 1970's, and I remembered it as a sparsely inhabited, almost impenetrable forest. Now, large swathes of the woods have been mowed down and replaced by endless acres of soy, rice, corn, mint and bean fields. The overwhelming majority of the population is Brazilian. As many as three hundred thousand of them have moved into eastern Paraguay over the last decade, drawn by cheap land, easy credits and low taxes. They are mostly people of modest to middle income. Few of them would claim to be there for political reasons.

But if years from now Itaipú becomes a troublesome issue between the two countries, these Brazilian settlers, living in a tight arc on the Paraguayan side of the dam, will become a formidable force of dissuasion at the disposal of the Brazilian government. Already eastern Paraguay has far stronger economic ties to Brazil than to Asunción. Portuguese, rather than Spanish or Guaraní, is the most prevalent language in this zone. Brazilian money is the common currency. Virtually all the local harvest is transported to Brazil, which also provides almost all of eastern Paraguay's imports.

Brazilians now account for about a tenth of Paraguay's population, and two thirds of the inhabitants in the eastern provinces. Nowhere else in the western hemisphere has a country been settled in so short a time by such a large proportion of foreign migrants. Not even the large flow of Mexicans into the United States comes close to the sudden, overwhelming impact of these Brazilians in Paraguay.

It is the kind of Brazilian influx that the rulers of Paraguay had sought to prevent for almost four hundred years. Back in the early seventeenth century, eastern Paraguay was the cutting edge of the frontier between the Spanish stronghold in Asunción and the Portuguese empire in Brazil. As a barrier against the Portuguese, the Spaniards encouraged the Jesuits to establish their greatest missions in the New World along the Paraná River, southward into Argentina and eastward into Uruguay. For 150 years, the Jesuits ruled over their Indians, gathered in disciplined, self-sufficient agricultural communities. Besides providing a steady tax flow of crops and cattle for the Spanish communities around Asunción and in Argentina, the Jesuit missions recruited a powerful Indian army to hold back Portuguese-Brazilian incursions into the Spanish empire. The wealth and autonomy of these missions eventually inspired the envy of the Spanish court, and led to the expulsion of the Jesuits from Paraguay and the rest of Latin America in the second half of the eighteenth century. But by then, the borders between Portuguese Brazil and Spanish Paraguay were more firmly set.

In the two hundred years that followed the departure of the Jesuits, eastern Paraguay never regained its economic vitality. Most of its population was annihilated during the horrendous war of 1864–70. Well into this century, the area was divided up into huge, feudal agricultural estates, some of them several million acres large, which used a harsh peonage system similar to serfdom to extract timber and maté, an herb tea popular in Argentina and southern Brazil.

Small numbers of Brazilian settlers drifted into eastern Paraguay in the early 1960's. But the really heavy migration began after 1966, when Stroessner caved in to Brazilian pressure and signed the treaty to develop the hydroelectric resources of the Paraná River. In a move that attracted little notice at the time, Stroessner also agreed to lift restrictions on the sale to foreigners of land near the country's frontiers. Such restrictions are common throughout South America because of the long history of frontier disputes between countries, and still exist on the Brazilian side of the border.

Brazil then built a bridge over the Paraná River and helped finance the asphalting of the Paraguayan highway from Asunción east to the Brazilian border. This provided a direct link from eastern Paraguay to Brazil's Atlantic ports, where Paraguayan goods were granted customs privileges and export-tax exemptions.

The conditions were now established for a massive movement of Brazilian settlers across the border. Beginning in the early 1970's, they came in truck caravans, at times rivaling the numbers of pioneers making the much longer trek westward to the Brazilian Amazon lands of Rondônia. Like the Rondônian settlers, these migrants were forced to search for cheap, virgin land because of rising farm prices and the growing mechanization of agriculture in southern Brazil. The Brazilian government welcomed the exodus both as a safety valve for rural discontent and as a way to buttress Brazil's security around the crucial Itaipú project.

Supporters of Stroessner claim that he viewed the Brazilian influx as the quickest way to develop the backward eastern provinces of Paraguay. The Brazilians, with their higher technical prowess, were supposed to teach modern agricultural methods to Paraguayan peasants and maybe eventually become Paraguayans themselves. But with Brazil so close by, it is doubtful that the migrants will loosen their strong cultural and economic ties to their homeland. And if South American history is any guide, the smaller, less efficient farming practiced by the Paraguayans is not likely to survive in the shadow of the mechanized agriculture of the Brazilians.

Stroessner appears to have had more short-sighted political reasons for accepting the huge wave of Brazilian settlers. It was a way to reward his followers in the military and in the upper ranks of his political movement. The government's agrarian reform agency, which was supposed to distribute eastern lands to peasants, instead sold large expanses at cheap prices to military officers and Colorado party leaders. They in turn sought partnerships with Brazilian real-estate companies and split the large profits from land sales to Brazilian pioneers.

In a rented Volkswagen, I crossed the concrete bridge over the Paraná River from Brazil into the traffic-clogged main avenue of Puerto Presidente Stroessner on the Paraguayan side. Hugging the river, I headed north past another large town, Hernandarias. And from there, using a crude map provided by the Paraguayan agrarian reform agency, I drove northwest along a wide dirt road to Mbaracayú, the largest Brazilian settlement in Paraguay.

For two hours, I traveled through gently rolling hills and broad valleys. This was a healthier, less forbidding, more temperate region than Rondônia and the western Amazon. In winter, the thermometer can occasionally drop to near the freezing point at night. But on this fall morning, the air was pleasantly warm. Pine trees grew alongside cedars and palms where the forest cover had not yet been stripped away. Threshers harvested what remained of the soy and corn crops. Other fields were brilliant with the gold of sunflowers, rising high above a man's height until their plate-size blossoms drooped heavily sideways.

About twenty thousand Brazilians, mainly of German and Polish extraction, lived in Mbaracayú, clustered around a dozen villages. I drove into the largest of these communities, past bright pastel wooden houses with neat hedges and white picket fences. The town square was planted with soy instead of trees and grass. From this focal point, rutted dirt streets radiated out like crooked wheel spokes. I stopped at a two-story clapboard building, the Munich Hotel and Restaurant, judging by the Jeeps and horses gathered outside that it had a sizable clientele.

Standing at the bar were five Paraguayan gauchos wearing loose pantaloons and boots that sagged like accordions. A Lufthansa poster displayed a bird's-eye view of Mad Ludwig's castle in faded technicolor. A red-cheeked waitress, in a fluffy Alpine dress, held six steins of beer in her hands. When I sat down at a long table, she offered me a choice of two four-course lunches, with either chicken or veal as the main dish.

"The schnitzel is better," volunteered a man wolfing down his meal at the end of my table.

Jorge Schmid was his name. He was tall, muscular, blond, blue-eyed and sunburned, in his mid-forties. He was almost handsome except for a small, weak chin and a mouthful of jagged shark's teeth. A third-generation German-Brazilian, he had moved to Mbaracayú six years before from his farm in Rio Grande do Sul, Brazil's southernmost state. He invited me to his home for coffee.

I followed his Jeep to his five-hundred acre property, where he cultivated mostly soybeans. His four-room house, with geraniums growing from window boxes and a heavy, slanting shingled roof, had a passably Bavarian style. Lace curtains hung from the windows, and airline posters from Germany and Brazil covered the living-room walls. On a battered, upright piano sat a large, white plaster bust of Stroessner. It had been bought from a local government official who strongly advised all Mbaracayú settlers that no house could be properly decorated without one.

Schmid introduced me to his wife and children, and embarrassed his eldest daughter, a plump teenager, by overpraising her looks and pastry. Her strudel was, in fact, very good. Over coffee, Schmid played "The Trout" on a battery-powered turntable and sang loudly to disguise the scratchy parts of the record.

"Ah, Germany, what a culture," he sighed, professing a deep nostalgia which I found particularly curious since he had never visited the land of his ancestors. "Someday I will go, but not while all those Socialists are in power," he promised.

He reeled off a long list of German statesmen, extolling Frederick the Great, Bismarck, the Kaiser. He stopped short of Adolf, and could think of no postwar politician worthy of mention.

"Bach, Beethoven, Brahms, Mozart—all Germans," he bragged. When I pointed out that Mozart was Austrian, he offered a compromise: "To me, Austria is German. I will admit others don't think so."

In Mbaracayú, Schmid had settled on land that was part of fifty thousand acres granted by the Paraguayan government to a Chaco war veteran, a Captain Fernández. In 1968, the aging captain took a Brazilian real-estate speculator, Luiz Lanius, as his partner, and they began to sell off plots to Brazilian settlers.

Schmid had had a hundred-acre farm in Brazil, but it was too small to compete with the increasingly mechanized, larger estates around him. He had sold it, and with half the profits he was able to buy five hundred acres in Paraguay. With part of the rest of his capital, he had purchased a tractor and hired bulldozers to clear his new property. The sales of timber alone, smuggled across the border to Brazilian sawmills, were enough to recover the amount he had paid for his land.

Schmid had considered joining the land rush to Rondônia. But eastern Paraguay seemed to have so many more advantages: it was a lot closer to Brazilian markets and ports; it was near a developed road network; there was easier access to machinery and replacement parts; profits from his soybean sales would be greater because his crop was produced in Paraguay and would not be subject to export taxes at Brazilian ports; and income taxes were far lower and easily avoidable in Paraguay.

On the negative side, Schmid was a foreigner living in a country where no one could count on the protection of law. In 1978, two years after Schmid arrived in Paraguay, Captain Fernández and Lanius, the two real-estate partners who had developed Mbaracayú, had a severe falling out. Lanius, the Brazilian, struck an alliance with another Paraguayan officer, a more influential man than Fernández. Soon, Lanius and his new partner began to try to gouge Schmid and the other Brazilian settlers for more money, claiming that the deeds sold to them by Fernández were not valid. Fernández told the settlers that if they sided with him they could stay—for a smaller additional sum than was being demanded by Lanius and his new partner.

The settlers held several meetings and decided to ignore all further requests for their money. But legal recognition for many of their titles was being mysteriously held up by government agencies. Schmid felt certain that President Stroessner, himself of German ancestry, would never allow his fellow Teutons to be chased out of the country. "The reason he let so many Brazilians settle here is that so many of us are of German stock," said Schmid. "We have brought progress to this wilderness."

He was uncertain about what would happen after Stroessner died. He himself had no intention of applying for Paraguayan citizenship or cutting his ties to Brazil. Except for a few local peons in his employ, he had no contacts with Paraguayans, and a very low estimation of their farming capabilities.

"You look around and you won't find a single decent farm in eastern Paraguay owned by a Paraguayan," said Schmid. "There has to be a reason. They were offered the same opportunities as we were to buy and develop this land. But they don't have the stomach for hard work. They never save. Put a bit of money in their pockets, and they spend it on drink."

Late that Saturday afternoon, I began the journey back to the border. All human activity had ceased. The threshers and tractors lay abandoned in the fields. Freshly plowed furrows of red earth alternated with long rectangles of unharvested corn, their leaves flowing like banners in the breeze. Fluffs of cumulus piled up in the sky, and cloud shadows raced my car up and down the hilly road. A couple of hundred yards ahead, a man traced a stiff arc with his right arm, thumb stuck out in an exaggerated hitchhiking gesture.

He was a small Paraguayan gaucho with large syrupy eyes and a thin, silky mustache. He thanked me for stopping, and said he would be getting off at Santa Fé, another largely Brazilian settlement a few miles down the road. His name was Augusto Cañete, and he worked for a Brazilian-German farmer at Mbaracayú, but lived on a twenty-acre farm of his own in Santa Fé. That morning, his horse had gone lame and he had decided to leave it with his employers over the weekend. He was in a hurry to reach Santa Fé because horse races were being held there that afternoon.

"Good riders, the best," he promised.

Following his directions, I turned off the main road onto a bumpy lane. By the thick cloud of dust ahead of us, I could see that the races had already begun. Cañete was right: these were skillful riders. Between the races, they vaulted from side to side of their galloping horses, holding on precariously to the horns of their saddles. Some of them rode backward, yelping in mock panic, or leaned low from their saddles to deftly snatch colored handkerchiefs on the ground as their stallions accelerated to full speed. At times, a horse seemed riderless as it galloped with a gaucho completely hidden on one side of the saddle.

The Brazilians stood in clusters at the edge of the field, cheering on the riders but aloof to the larger crowd of Paraguayan spectators. Heavy grills were laid over burning embers, and a gaucho, wielding long metal tongs, took charge of cooking strips of beef, heart, kidneys, intestines, even udders and testicles. The pit was so large, hot and smoky that he danced around the edges holding a handkerchief to his eyes and nose.

I was still full from the meal at the Munich and the generous helpings of strudel at Schmid's house. But I accepted a maté from Cañete. He stuffed a wad of the green herb in a silver-inlaid gourd and poured boiling water into it. I drank from a metal straw. The maté had a pleasantly bitter taste, and I soon broke into a refreshing sweat.

A woman's scream pierced the air, and a commotion erupted near the throng of Brazilians. A young Paraguayan ranch hand, apparently drunk, had placed an arm around the waist of a Brazilian girl. Her father punched the man, who fell to the ground and got up groggily with a knife in his hand. Before things could grow uglier, an older woman, the mother of the ranch hand, pinched him firmly by the ear and dragged him cowering away. The races resumed, but among the Brazilians, at least, the festive mood vanished, and some of them began to drift away.

I asked Cañete about friction with the Brazilians. "That idiot was drunk," he said. "But the Brazilians are tight-asses. They really don't want to have anything to do with us."

Cañete was originally a peasant from Caaguazú, a farming region to the west, halfway between the Paraná River and Asunción. A decade before, in his mid-twenties, he had moved to the edge of Mbaracayú, where the government land reform agency had alloted him a fifty-acre block of virgin forest. He managed to clear only a few acres, and soon hired out as a farmhand for a Brazilian family who bought a three-hundred-acre property next to his. He rented his land to the Brazilians and then sold it to them. With the money, he purchased a smaller, cleared plot of land from his father-in-law in nearby Santa Fé.

"Everybody says the Brazilians are such hard workers, and it's true," said Cañete. "But they have what it takes to work. They come here with money and tractors and bulldozers and power saws. We Paraguayans only have a machete and ax. We plant manioc just trying to eat, while the Brazilians harvest soy and corn and mint to sell. It takes us ten times the effort to accomplish what they do with their machinery and capital."

Other Paraguayans—their eyes hidden under their flat, broad-brimmed gaucho hats—joined the conversation. They sat on their haunches and cupped their hands around their maté gourds and complained about land problems. They had been promised farms and credits by the agrarian reform agency which encouraged them to move there. Many of them never received plots. Others were never able to finish paying the government for their land and were refused titles. It was a vicious circle: without titles, they could not apply for bank credits to finance the planting and harvesting of crops; without a harvest to sell, they could not earn enough money to meet the mortgage payments for their land and receive the titles that they needed for bank credits. In the end, they all sold their properties to the Brazilian settlers and went to work for them.

"I don't know if someday we will wake up and find out we are all Brazilians," said Cañete. "But I do know that the Brazilians here will never become Paraguayans."

The sunset clouds glowed pink, and soon the field around us sank into a deep purple twilight. A breeze made the dying embers of the barbecue pits glitter like fireflies. Cañete and three of his friends squeezed into my car, and I dropped them off in Santa Fé. When I headed back to the Brazilian side of the frontier, the black sky was studded with bright stars to the far rim of the horizon.

A few days later, I flew from Foz do Iguaçú north a hundred miles to the Guaira Falls. Below the small, twin-propeller plane I had hired, the Paraná swelled to a four-mile-wide blue lake, then, splitting into eighteen falls, its waters cascaded 250 feet into a canyon only 300 feet wide and pulled together again as a boiling, white, raging river. The Guaira Falls are the largest in the world, at flood level more than eight times the volume of Niagara. I wanted to witness their awesome spectacle before they were obliterated. For in only a few months' time, these majestic curtains of water would be completely inundated by Itaipú's reservoir as it backed up behind the dam.

Public outcries against this cataclysmic event were few and ineffective, and virtually ended when a bridge spanning one of the Guaira falls snapped, hurtling forty tourists to their deaths in early 1982. If they were at all aware of the falls' imminent extinction, most Brazilians and Paraguayans seemed to feel that the hydroelectric riches of the new dam and its reservoir were ample compensation for one of the great ravages ever perpetrated on nature. The publicity releases churned out by the Itaipú engineers emphasized that Iguassú Falls 112 miles downstream were a far bigger tourist attraction and would remain undisturbed by the construction of Itaipú.

From the Brazilian side, I walked to the brink of the precipice where the ill-fated footbridge was once anchored in place. Terns and ducks circled over the endless roar of the cataracts, sometimes diving along the face of the cascading waters, disappearing and then miraculously reemerging from the billows of mist far below.

Guaira had been the focus of the earliest Spanish Jesuit missions in Paraguay, and the starting point of a stirring flight that some historians have compared to the biblical exodus. It was around Guaira in 1610 that the Jesuits created the model for their successful Indian settlements, wooing rival, nomadic tribes to a sedentary, communal, agricultural existence under priestly rule. By 1630, more than forty thousand Indians had congregated in eleven Jesuit towns, strung from Paraguay north and east into present-day Brazil. This expansion whetted the appetite of the *bandeirantes*, the mixed-blood Portuguese adventurers based in São Paulo, who viewed the missions as an easy source of disciplined Indian slave labor. A leading Brazilian historian, Alfredo Ellis Junior, estimated that in the sixteenth and seventeenth centuries alone these *bandeirantes* took as many as three hundred fifty thousand Indian prisoners, selling most of them as slaves to plantations north of São Paulo.

The incursions of the *bandeirantes* into the Guaira region increasingly terrorized the Jesuit missions and threatened to push the borders of the Spanish empire farther south into Paraguay. Finally, in 1631, as a large army of *bandeirantes* gathered for a climactic assault against the missions, Father Antonio Ruiz de Montoya, leader of the Jesuits in Guaira, decided that the settlements would have to be quickly abandoned.

Montoya assembled twelve thousand Guaraní Indians and a flotilla of three hundred longboats, and set out southward down the Paraná River. No sooner had the expedition begun than the *bandeirantes* arrived at the deserted villages and in a rage burned them down. Reaching the falls at Guaira, Montoya and his Indian wards disembarked. The priest gambled that some, perhaps most, of the empty boats could survive a passage down the cataracts. But all of the vessels splintered into fragments and sank under the battering, churning waters at the bottom of the falls. Montoya and his followers descended along the edge of the cataracts on foot, and walked through the dense forests for weeks, eluding the dreaded *bandeirantes* until they reached the comparative safety of other Jesuit missions.

Eventually, this Jesuit Moses and his successors established even more imposing settlements in Paraguay, northern Argentina and present-day Uruguay, with a population of more than a hundred thousand Indians and battle-toughened native troops who kept the *bandeirantes* at bay. Even after the expulsion of the Jesuits from the New World in 1767, the lost Paraguayan missions remained a source of constant fascination for European writers and philosophers. Voltaire used the Jesuit missions of Paraguay as the setting for one of the adventures that befell his peripatetic hero, Candide. Robert Southey, the nineteenth-century English Romantic writer, in his poem "A Tale of Paraguay," lauded the Jesuits for their zeal, although he described their missions as overly authoritarian. Perhaps the most detailed and sympathetic treatment accorded the Paraguayan Jesuits is found in an early-twentieth-century book, *A Vanished Arcadia*, by the Englishman R. B. Cunninghame Graham.

As well as agriculture and [ranch] life, the Jesuits had introduced amongst the Indians most of the arts and trades of Europe. They wove cotton largely; sometimes they made as much as eight thousand five hundred yards of cloth in a single town in the space of two or three months. In addition to weaving, they had tanneries, carpenters, shops, tailors, hat-makers, coopers, cordage-makers, boatbuilders, cartwrights, joiners, and almost every industry useful and necessary to life. They also made arms and powder, musical instruments, and had silversmiths, musicians, painters, turners, and printers to work their printing-presses: for many books were printed at the missions, and they produced manuscripts as finely executed as those made by the monks in European monasteries.

As I wandered through Guaira and around its tumultuous cataracts, there was not a trace of the once-flourishing missions. The only vague reminder was a lonely black-and-white Muscovy duck that floated calmly down the Paraná, picking up speed as it neared the deafening falls. I wondered whether it really was oblivious to the danger. Finally, not more than a few feet from the edge, just as it was about to be swallowed by the cauldron, the duck flicked its wings and soared to safety, avoiding the fate of Father Montoya's boats. I took a final long look at the spectacular falls. A broad, brilliant rainbow glowed in their misty spray, until a dark, rumbling cloud hid the sun. What a strange sensation it was knowing I would outlive this natural wonder.

I flew back to Itaipú to spend one last day there talking with a group of environmental experts who worked at the dam. They handed me thick volumes of studies they had undertaken over the past seven years on the impact of the 564-square-mile reservoir that Itaipú would create. They had planned two large wildlife refuges for animals that were supposed to be rescued during the three-week flooding period before the reservoir reached its final contours.

"The disappearance of the Guaira Falls could not possibly be avoided with a project this big," said Arnaldo Muller, the chief environmental engineer at Itaipú. "I consider myself a conservationist. But I could not honestly say that the falls are more important than Itaipú's electricity. We don't have the luxury of a choice."

It was certainly a classic dilemma between ecology and national requirements in a developing region. But somehow, I couldn't help recalling that a few years ago the construction of a large dam in the United States was suspended for many months because environ-

mentalists feared the project would endanger a nearly extinct species of small, blind fish dwelling in underwater caverns, unseen by human beings.

When I repeated the anecdote to engineers and workers at Itaipú, nobody believed me. It evidently sounded more incredible than anything that was happening here, at the end of South America's inner frontier lands, where Belaúnde's imaginary highway reached its ultimate destination.

17

eyond Itaipú, Belaúnde's mythical highway merges with the established road system that forks east to Brazil's bustling Atlantic industrial ports and south to the Argentine metropolis of Buenos Aires.

I took neither road. Instead, I decided to return to my starting point, to Lima, for a final rendezvous with Fernando Belaúnde Terry, president of Peru and architect of the imaginary frontier highway.

From the Brazilian side of the Itaipú Dam, I boarded the short flight back to Asunción, the Paraguayan capital. Then, in two giant hops, the jet from Asunción to La Paz and another plane connection to Lima reversed and compressed my transcontinental odyssey into five hours. The Chaco slid by like an unweeded backyard. The plains of Santa Cruz were a spongy darker green. The lush highlands of the Chapare hinted at the denser rain forests of the Amazon basin to the north. Then came the Bolivian Andes, brutish tan studded with regal purple and snow-white crowns. In Peru, the mountains were more of a patchwork: verdant where the jungles lapped over the smaller peaks, ocher turning to gray as the tropical tide receded on the western slopes.

Almost as soon as my plane touched down in Lima, I was joltingly reminded that the movement toward the frontier lands was still very much in its infancy. Here was the Spanish colonial city par excellence, its back turned resolutely on the continent's interior, its gaze fixed on the Pacific, the old route back to the European mother country.

After conquering the Incas and razing their most impressive structures in Cuzco, their Andean mountain stronghold, Francisco Pizarro had built his capital near the coast to serve as the fulcrum of a seaborne empire in the New World. He adhered in every detail to the rigorous specifications set down by the Spanish court. The main square, the Plaza de Armas, was bounded by the government palace, the cathedral, the *cabildo,* or municipal council, and a row of upper-class townhouses. And 450 years later, the city still evokes a feeling of relentless centralization. Political power, commerce, finance, industry, communications, population—all are concentrated in the capital. It is far less a gateway to the interior than a centrifugal magnet exerting an almost irresistible force on the periphery.

The roads that have been constructed in recent decades into the mountains and up to the fringe of the jungles have pulled many more people into Lima than they have drawn away. With almost six million inhabitants, greater Lima now has twelve times its population in 1940. Year after year, the hordes of migrants from the provinces have added successive peels of shantytowns around the old city core. The new *barriadas,* row upon row of cardboard-and-corrugated-tin hovels, stretch beyond the fertile fringes of the capital. Bereft of trees or even a blade of grass, the slums climb up gray-white hillsides of parched sand and stone beyond the reach of electricity and running water.

Lima was shrouded in its usual thick fog, the *garúa,* that promised a rain that would never come. With elbows-high reflexes, I worked my way from my downtown hotel through the teeming warren of streets toward the presidential palace on the Plaza de Armas a few blocks away. Almost every square foot of sidewalk was staked out by vendors hawking magazines, Indian tapestries and sweaters, fruits, vegetables, strips of charcoal-broiled meat, toys, razors, anything and everything. Glass-and-steel high rises were crammed like ill-fitting dentures between Spanish colonial-era townhouses with carved-wood balconies. Bedeviled by the pedestrian throngs who had been pushed by vendors off the sidewalks, the cars and overladen buses honked frenetically as they inched up ancient, narrow streets intended for horses and their carriages.

The shoving stopped only when the crowds and traffic disgorged into the broad Plaza de Armas. A few of the elderly caught their breaths on the stone benches. The curious and idle circled around troupes of mimes and actors rehearsing skits for a few pennies at each corner of the spacious square. A contingent of gold-helmeted, horseback Hussars silently changed the guard behind the front gates of the white-stoned presidential palace.

I walked into the cavernous building through a side entrance, past the massive metal-and-wood doors, and took a seat in the waiting room. The clicking of boot heels echoed through the marble hallway, and beyond, from the street, the tumult of pedestrians and vehicles was reduced to a distant, muffled roar. The waiting room was as lifeless as a museum. No tapestries softened the blue mosaic floor. The colonial-era furniture, hulking cabinets and chests of burnished oak carved with intricate, baroque whirls and twists, served only to fill the chamber's emptiness.

After fifteen minutes, a blue-uniformed Air Force officer escorted me to the audience with the president. Belaúnde rose from behind his large mahogany desk, which was spotlessly clean behind a battery of telephones. Facing each other, we sank into the soft, deep, leathery recesses of two easy chairs.

At almost seventy years of age, he had been rejuvenated by presidential power. A pronounced trembling of the hands which I had detected when we met years before was now gone. The squarish face had regained some of its angles, and the jawline had resurfaced from a double chin. The leonine mane, more white than brown, was gracefully swept back. A blue serge suit, tailored for a statesman, had replaced the softer, professorial tweeds.

"You have traveled all along my Highway of the Jungle?" he asked, somewhat taken aback. "There really is something out there, isn't there? I always said that the problem with Americans is that they are unemployed pioneers. You people have the frontier in your blood. But you have no place to go. All your territory has been settled and developed, and I suppose you're not about to jump into the Pacific searching for more frontiers."

I had looked forward to this encounter with Belaúnde as an august, climactic recapitulation of my frontier passage. I was prepared to play disciple to the prophet. But it turned out to be a rambling conversation, mostly a monologue by Belaúnde. When we had talked years before, he was a deposed head of state recently returned from exile and more anxious to reel out his frontier vision than to discuss politics. Now, the pressing burdens of government made it more difficult for him to focus on the distant wilderness. He was troubled by an economic recession and inflation that were threatening strikes and civil disturbances. In the Andean highlands and jungle fringes where his projected highway and road schemes were supposed to be built, bands of mysterious Maoist guerrillas were attacking isolated ranches, police posts and municipal offices.

"They will not keep me from traveling around the interior," said Belaúnde. "I still drop into the most remote villages by helicopter, unannounced, when least expected. I want to encourage people there to think that their isolation will someday end, that many others will someday join them on the frontier."

He pressed a button on the top of his desk. A white-uniformed military aide appeared at the door, and Belaúnde asked him to retrieve something. The aide returned, hidden except for his legs behind several huge, cardboard maps. Belaúnde took out a baton from a drawer and shined his desk lamp on the maps, held up by the silent aide standing like an easel.

They had all been drawn by Belaúnde, still more an architect than a politician or administrator at heart. There was a sketch for a new Peruvian frontier city deep in the Andean highlands. Behind it was a large rendition of South America on which the largest rivers had been linked by canals and artificial lakes so that the interior of the whole continent could be traveled by ship. And then there was the more familiar map of the imaginary thirty-five-hundred-mile highway, cutting through the continent's jungle highlands and rain forests and plains from northwest to southeast.

"I don't really know if my highway or the other projects will ever be built," he said. "In the end, they may not even be necessary. It was my intention to get South Americans to think about their frontier lands, to begin settling them and recovering the treasures they hold. And this is all happening even without a grand highway. You know, the conquest of South America by the Spaniards and Portuguese was one of the most extraordinary human events the world has ever witnessed. In the space of a few decades, this conquest carried Europeans and their seeds and livestock and implements and institutions everywhere on this great continent. And just as extraordinary, these seeds and institutions never took root in the interior. I have always believed that the failure to permanently settle the frontier lands has been one of the main causes for this continent's inability to realize its full potential. And now that this settlement is finally taking place, the very character of South America will have to change. I don't know what these changes will look like except in the broadest sense. After all, an architect can only design structures, not always build them or say who will inhabit them. But in the next two decades, the frontier drive into the interior will introduce a whole new set of factors in South America. There will be an expansion of agricultural and natural resources, more commerce and other contacts between neighboring countries. There will be a significant redistribution of population. In twenty years, it will be impossible to consider this continent without taking into account the wealth and forces unleashed by the new frontiers."

A secretary appeared to announce that the president was behind schedule and other visitors were waiting. Belaúnde walked me to the door and bid me farewell. I was left on my own to prognosticate the impact of the new drive into the frontiers.

My passage through these lands where the Iberian conquistadores once feverishly sought El Dorado convinced me that the assault now underway in the South American wilderness is more far-reaching and permanent than any previous effort. The sheer numbers of settlers and the variety of economic activities ensure that there will never be a return to the hollow frontiers of past centuries. The development of the continent's interior is no longer tied, as it once was, to a single commodity like rubber. Economic expansion is now linked to a multiplicity of products and enterprises—oil, hydroelectricity, cattle, cocoa, coffee, grains, minerals, wood, illicit drugs. Their quantity and variety will withstand the vicissitudes of the world market. Not even the global economic recession of recent years could staunch the growth of the frontier lands. The tide of settlers has continued unabated.

The conquest of these new frontiers has resisted formulas and molds and blueprints. At the northwest extreme of the vast territory traced by Belaúnde's mythical road, development has been dominated by American multinational corporations searching for oil. At the southeast end of the imaginary highway, a Brazilian government agency and its Paraguayan state counterpart have presided over the construction of the world's largest hydroelectric project. In the three thousand miles between these anchors, the continent's interior is being transformed by an assortment of businessmen, cattle barons, small farmers, peasants and drug traffickers.

The range of frontier experiences is so amorphous that it is useless to engage in ideological debates about whether the state or private initiative is better suited to carry out development. In Brazil, it was the military government that supervised the beginnings of the recent frontier drive. That ill-conceived effort, built around the Transamazon Highway through the northern Amazon jungles, quickly foundered. Its failure was less attributable to mismanagement than to the poor soils of the rain forests crossed by the highway. Large private enterprises in agriculture, forestry and livestock have been equally unable to overcome the natural deficiencies of those zones. Where settlement took hold most spectacularly in the Brazilian Amazon— in the more fertile lands of Rondônia—the pioneer movement was largely spontaneous. The hordes of colonists pouring into that western Amazon territory initially caught the Brazilian military authorities by surprise. But the Rondônia experience could easily have collapsed into violence and disarray if the government land colonization agency had not stepped in and imposed a measure of order between big property owners, homesteaders and squatters. A project on the scale of the Itaipú Dam would have been inconceivable without state supervision. Yet the cattle and cocaine barons of Bolivia have prospered in the absence of government intervention.

The discovery of new sources of wealth, the growth of commerce across previously ignored borders, the potential demographic shift away from congested urban and rural areas, each could benefit all of the South American nations as they expand into their frontier lands. But the windfalls and risks of frontier development will be unequally shared.

Brazil, by virtue of its huge territory and population, stands to gain the most. The Brazilian frontier drive is the culmination of a series of spectacular developments in that country since the beginning of this century. As Norman Gall, an American journalist, has pointed out, "a sustained demographic expansion is occurring [in Brazil] that is without precedent in human experience," raising the nation's population from only 17 million people in 1900 to 120 million in 1983. During this same time frame, Brazilian croplands have multiplied elevenfold to about 110 million acres, also one of the greatest rates of increase in the world. And, as Gall notes, "this cropland expansion was made possible by an enormous road-building effort in Brazil's undeveloped interior that multiplied the highway network tenfold since 1945."

Given this sort of momentum, Brazil is fast emerging as a truly continental power, not only in terms of territory but in economic and political influence on its neighboring countries. This influence is bound to grow if Brazil eventually finds road outlets to the Pacific Ocean through Peru and to the Caribbean through Venezuela, and if markets can be found for Brazilian frontier products in nations bordering its far-flung wilderness settlements.

The growth and success of Brazil's frontier efforts are helping to catalyze similar drives in neighboring countries. The transformation of eastern Paraguay's frontier lands is mainly the result of Brazilian money and manpower building Itaipú and the armies of Brazilian pioneers carving farmlands out of virgin forests. The profitability of cattle and agriculture in the northern and eastern Bolivian provinces is to a large extent predicated on Brazilian purchases.

Whether or not this massive rise in Brazilian influence across the continent's frontier lands will be a completely positive phenomenon remains to be seen. Up until the beginning of this century, Brazil had often used military force to expand its borders to its present territorial limits. In Paraguay, particularly, Brazil's dominating role seems bound to produce great tensions. Many Paraguayans are greatly concerned that they have been duped into signing an unequal treaty to divide the profits from the Itaipú Dam. Even more troubling is the overwhelminig position in numbers and wealth that Brazilian settlers have achieved in eastern Paraguay.

Elsewhere on the continent, the long legacy of border disputes could resurface as neighboring countries take steps to develop riches in their frontier lands. The brief war between Ecuador and Peru in early 1981 can be traced to the discovery of oil in a jungle region that has been contested by both nations for at least a century. Venezuela is currently pressing its claims over a huge chunk of territory in neighboring Guyana.

But I would prefer not to reduce South America's modern frontier drive to an accountant's ledger of assets and liabilities. My interest in the continent's interior began in childhood. It was a simple expression of schoolboy astonishment that such vast lands had failed to create a frontier mythology. Two decades later, I traveled through those enormous territories and discovered that a frontier spirit had finally awakened.

Statistics and geopolitical theories are not enough to measure this phenomenon. Far more revealing are the impressions gleaned from my notebooks and tapes as I flew back to New York from Lima a few days after meeting with Belaúnde. The tapes, especially, were a jumble because I had brought along too few and had to use them over and over again during the long journey through the South American wilderness. A cassette began with the drawl of an American oilman in Peru, picked up a conversation in Portuguese with a Rondônia pioneer and ended with a Paraguayan peasant mixing Guaraní and Spanish.

There was a merging of images and voices: "It bleeds and it bleeds," Antonio, the rubber tapper in Acre was saying as white latex oozed out of a tree he had slashed, "and it's the lifeblood of Brazil." "You can smell the fumes now, can't you?" Jaime asked as our boat puttered past the cocaine factories along the Ichilo River in eastern Bolivia. "So many people marching to the west, it seemed like the whole country was searching for land in Rondônia," Durvalina, the Brazilian pioneer woman, was telling me as she recalled the truck caravans lumbering toward the Amazon frontier.

They could not have been a more diverse legion. Among them were villains and minor heroes, people who would always be mired in poverty and a few who had stumbled upon unexpected wealth, benighted plodders and flamboyant adventurers, visionaries and simple survivors. But there were also strains that bound most of them together. At a crossroads in their lives, they had, either out of desperation or choice, abandoned civilization for the uncharted backlands. They were acutely conscious that they were pioneers on the margins of their societies, pitting themselves against the wilderness, recreating that most basic and ancient of human struggles. And this realization often gave them a surer sense of identity than I had detected in so many of their compatriots clinging to the old European colonial strongholds.

At times, the frontier seemed to me as barbaric and dehumanizing as Sarmiento, the great Argentine essayist of the last century, had asserted it was. More often, my thoughts drifted back to Turner, the American frontier ideologue. Not because the backlands of South America bear any resemblance to the democratic cauldron that he claimed to perceive in the Old West. On the contrary, the South American frontiers are no more democratic than the authoritarian governments that have presided over their development. Besides, Turner's democratic vision of the Old West—like the South American frontier lands almost a century later—was flawed by the Indian massacres and unequal struggles between big landlords and small settlers.

But I could find in South America plenty of parallels with Turner's notions of the frontier as a land of opportunity, as a social safety valve for discontents from the overcrowded cities and rural zones, as a potential driving force for renovation and mobility in troubled societies. And perhaps, just as Turner believed that the conquest of the West shattered Americans' perceptions of themselves as displaced Europeans, the physical integration of the frontier lands into the rest of South America will create a stronger nationalistic identity among many South Americans. Possibly they will no longer view themselves as dislocated Europeans, abandoned in an unshapen, inhospitable continent.

I emerged from the South American wilderness with a sensation of awe and discomfiture. I would not care to retrace my steps through these frontier lands. But it is a journey which many, many South Americans will make in the years ahead, until the void that extends over the vast interior of their continent is finally filled.

Bibliography

Bates, Henry W. *The Naturalist on the Rivers Amazon*. London: John Murray, 1892.

Belaúnde Terry, Fernando. *Peru's Own Conquest*. Lima: American Studies Press, 1965.

Bodard, Lucien. *Green Hell*. New York: Outerbridge & Dienstfrey, 1972.

Carvajal, Gaspar de. *The Discovery of the Amazon*. New York: American Geographical Society, 1934.

Cunha, Euclydes da. *Os Sertões*. Rio de Janeiro: P. de Azevedo, 1927.

———. *Á margem da historia*. Pôrto: Livr. Lello & Irmão, 1946.

Cunninghame Graham, R. B. *A Vanished Arcadia*. New York: Macmillan, 1901.

Danhof, Clarence H. *Change in Agriculture: The Northern United States, 1820–1870*. Cambridge: Harvard University Press, 1969.

Davis, Shelton H. *Victims of the Miracle: Development and the Indians of Brazil*. Cambridge, England: Cambridge University Press, 1977.

Denevan, William. *The Aboriginal Cultural Geography of the Llanos de Mojos of Bolivia*. Berkeley: University of California Press, 1966.

Díaz del Castillo, Bernál. *The Discovery and Conquest of Mexico*. New York: Farrar, Straus and Cudahy, 1956.

Duguid, Julian. *Green Hell*. London: The Century Co., 1931.

Fifer, J. Valerie. *Bolivia: Land, Location, and Politics Since 1825*. Cambridge: Cambridge University Press, 1972.

Freyre, Gilberto. *The Masters and the Slaves*. New York: Alfred A. Knopf, 1946.

Furneaux, Robin. *The Amazon: The Story of a Great River*. London: H. Hamilton, 1969.

Gall, Norman. "Letter from Rondonia," Parts I–V Hanover, New Hampshire: American Universities Field Staff, 1978.

Gates, Paul W. *The Farmer's Age: Agriculture, 1815–1860*. New York: Harper Torchbooks, 1968.

———. *Landlords and Tenants on the Prairie Frontier*. Ithaca, New York: Cornell University Press, 1972.

Goodland, R.J.A. and Irwin, H. S. *Amazon Jungle: Green Hell or Red Desert?* Amsterdam: Elsevier Scientific Publishing Co., 1975.

Gourou, Pierre. *The Tropical World.* London: Longmans, 1966.

Guevara, Ernesto. *El diario del Che en Bolivia.* Mexico: Siglo Veintiuno, 1972.

Guevara, José. *História de la conquista del Paraguay, Río de la Plata y Tucumán.* Buenos Aires, 1882.

Hagen, Victor W. von. *The Royal Road of the Incas.* London: Gordon & Cremonesi, 1976.

Hennessy, Alistair. *The Frontier in Latin American History.* Albuquerque: University of New Mexico Press, 1978.

Hudson, W. H. *Green Mansions.* New York: The Modern Library, 1920.

Katzman, Martin T. *Cities and Frontiers in Brazil: Regional Dimensions of Economic Development.* Cambridge: Harvard University Press, 1977.

Leonard, Irving A. *Books of the Brave.* New York: Gordon Press, 1964.

Lévi-Strauss, Claude. *Tristes Tropiques.* New York: Criterion Books, 1961.

Madariaga, Salvador de. *The Rise of the Spanish American Empire.* London: Hollis & Carter, 1947.

Mahar, Dennis J. *Frontier Development Policy in Brazil: A Study of Amazonia.* New York: Praeger, 1979.

Meggers, Betty Jane. *Amazonia: Man and Culture in a Counterfeit Paradise.* Chicago: Aldine, 1971.

Métraux, Alfred. *Les Incas.* Paris: Seuil, 1961.

Moog, Vianna. *Bandeirantes and Pioneers.* New York: George Braziller, 1964.

Mörner, Magnus, ed. *The Expulsion of the Jesuits from Latin America.* New York: Alfred A. Knopf, 1965.

Orbigny, Alcides d'. *Voyage à l'Amérique meridionale.* Paris, 1847.

Parry, J. H. *The Spanish Seaborne Empire.* New York: Alfred A. Knopf, 1966.

Pendle, George. *Paraguay: A Riverside Nation.* London: Royal Institute of International Affairs, 1954.

Rivera, José Eustasio. *La Vorágine.* New York: Putnam, 1935.

Rondon, Candido Mariano da Silva. *Lectures.* New York: Greenwood Press, 1969.

Roosevelt, Theodore. *Through the Brazilian Wilderness.* New York: C. Scribner's Sons, 1925.

Sarmiento, Domingo Faustino. *Facundo, o civilización y barbarie.* Buenos Aires: Sur, 1962.

Shannon, Fred A. *The Farmer's Last Frontier: Agriculture, 1860-1897.* New York: Farrar & Rinehart, 1945.

Shoumatoff, Alex. *The Rivers Amazon.* San Francisco: Sierra Club Books, 1978.

Skillings, R. F. and Tcheyan, N. O. *Economic Development Prospects of the Amazon Region of Brazil.* Washington, D.C.: Johns Hopkins, 1979.

Smith, Nigel J. H. *Rainforest Corridors: The Transamazon Colonization Scheme.* Berkeley: University of California Press, 1982.

Sternberg, Hilgard O'Reilly. *The Amazon River of Brazil.* Wiesbaden: Franz Steiner, 1975.

Taunay, Afonso D'Escragnolle. *História Geral das Bandeiras Paulistas.* São Paulo: Tipografia Ideal, 1936.

Tocqueville, Alexis de. *Democracy in America.* New York: Alfred A. Knopf, 1945.

Turner, Frederick Jackson. *The Significance of the Frontier in American History.* New York: Ungar, 1963.

Varese, Stefano. *La sal de los cerros.* Lima: Retablo de Papel Ediciones, 1973.

Véliz, Claudio. *The Centralist Tradition in Latin America.* Princeton, New Jersey: Princeton University Press, 1980.

Wagley, Charles. *Amazon Town: A Study of Man in the Tropics.* New York: Alfred A. Knopf, 1964.

———, ed. *Man in the Amazon.* Gainesville, Florida: University of Florida Press, 1974.

Wallace, Alfred Russel. *A Narrative of Travels on the Amazon and Rio Negro.* London: Reeve and Co., 1853.

Wolf, Howard and Ralph. *Rubber: A Story of Glory and Greed.* New York: Covici, Friede, 1936.

World Bank. "Paraguay: Regional Development in Eastern Paraguay." Washington, D.C., 1978.

———. "Brazil: Integrated Development of the Northwest Frontier." Washington, D.C., 1981.

Index

Rio de Janeiro, 40
Río de la Plata, 273
Rivera, José Eustasio, 73–74
Rodrigues, Roberval, 114–115
Rondon, Cândido Mariano da Silva,
    99–103, 141, 152, 167–168, 174
Rondônia, 101, 139–191
    American Old West compared to,
        172–177, 179, 185
    economic development of, 173–174,
        177–180
    government regulations in,
        145–152, 158–160, 164–167, 174,
        185, 187–188, 194, 299
    Indian relations in, 144–145, 150,
        157–158, 167–168
    land disputes in, 142, 148–152,
        157–160, 167–170, 174, 188–189
    land rush in, 139–145, 154–155,
        160–161, 164–166, 188, 301
    pioneer life in, 155–157, 159–164,
        186–187
    soil conditions in, 141, 179
    squatters in, 166–170, 178, 188–
        189
    transportation in, 141–143, 161,
        166, 171, 180, 186, 189–190,
        194
    see also Amazonia; Brazil
Roosevelt, Theodore, 96, 99
Rosa (prostitute), 68–69, 73, 77
Rosas, Juan Manuel, 36, 248
rubber industry, 16–18, 29–30, 86–96,
    103–105, 108–112, 116–129,
    132–133, 203–204
    decline of, 17, 30, 90, 98, 104–105,
        108–110, 121–126, 129, 133, 204
    financing of, 30, 88, 93–94, 105
    labor for, 86–90, 93–95, 100,
        104–105, 108, 110–112, 118–124,
        127–129
    land ownership and, 110–112,
        117–118, 122–124, 126–127
    technical aspects of, 30, 91, 95,
        103–104, 119–120, 123–124, 127
    transportation in, 17, 30, 96,
        108–111

wealth generated by, 17–18, 30,
    87–88, 93, 95, 128

Sala, Gabriel, 87
Salomón, Colonel Norberto, 242
San Juan ranch, 210–213, 215–219,
    222–226
    see also Beni
Santa Cruz, 245–258
    anti-cocaine movement in, 252–
        255
    as cocaine center, 233, 248–255
    independence movement in,
        253–254
    La Paz vs., 245–248, 253–254
    money exchange in, 252–253
    as power center, 247–248
Santana, Edvaldo, 164–165, 167, 172,
    178
São Paulo, 40
Sarmiento, Domingo, 36–38, 247–248,
    301
Schenstrom, Carlos, 206, 209–219,
    223–227
Schenstrom, Irene, 212–213, 223–224
Schmid, Jorge, 285–287
Shannon, Fred A., 173–176, 179
Siles Zuazo, Hernán, 243
Silva, Durvalina da, 152, 160, 301
Silva, Jesuino da, 152–161
Solano López, Francisco, 264–265
Southey, Robert, 291
Spain, 25, 29, 31, 34, 201–202, 247,
    283, 295
State Department, U.S., 243–244,
    255–256
Steve (DEA agent), 229, 245, 255
stingrays, 220–221
Strategic Telegraph Line, 96, 99–100,
    103, 141
Stroessner, Alfredo, 267–269, 270,
    272–274, 283–284, 287
Suárez, Nicolás, 203–205, 209, 228, 233
Suárez, Renato Roca, 238–239
Suárez, Roberto, 205, 209, 228–230,
    233–241, 244, 257
    political influence of, 241